P9-EEE-553

Yamaha YFM350 ATV Owners Workshop Manual

by Alan Ahlstrand and John H Haynes

Member of the Guild of Motoring Writers

Models covered:

Yamaha YFM350ER 2-wheel drive. 348 cc. 1987 thru 1995

Yamaha YFM350FW (Big Bear) 4-wheel drive. 348 cc.
1987 thru 1997

Yamaha YFM350U (Big Bear 2x4 and Big Bear 2WD)
2-wheel drive. 348 cc. 1996 thru 1999

Yamaha YFM350FWB (Big Bear 4x4 and Big Bear 4WD)
4-wheel drive. 348 cc. 1997 thru 1999

(11C1 - 2126)

ABCDE
FGHIJ
KLMNO
PQRS

Haynes Publishing
Sparkford Nr Yeovil
Somerset BA22 7JJ England

Haynes North America, Inc
861 Lawrence Drive
Newbury Park
California 91320 USA

Acknowledgments
Our thanks to Grand Prix Yamaha/Kawasaki/Suzuki, Santa Clara, California, for providing the facilities used for these photographs; to Brian Kinney, service manager, for arranging the facilities and fitting the mechanical work into his shop's busy schedule; and to Dave Jewell, service technician, for doing the mechanical work and providing valuable technical information.

A book in the Haynes Owners Workshop Manual Series

Printed in the U.S.A.

ISBN 1 56392 414 5

Library of Congress Card Number 00-110808

British Library Cataloguing in Publication Data
A catalogue record for this book is available from the British Library

---

We take great pride in the accuracy of information given in this manual, but vehicle manufacturers make alterations and design changes during the production run of a particular vehicle of which they do not inform us. No liability can be accepted by the authors or publishers for loss, damage or injury caused by any errors in, or omissions from, the information given.

Contents

Yamaha YFM350FW (Big Bear) - 1992 model

About this manual

Its purpose

The purpose of this manual is to help you get the best value from your vehicle. It can do so in several ways. It can help you decide what work must be done, even if you choose to have it done by a dealer service department or a repair shop; it provides information and procedures for routine maintenance and servicing; and it offers diagnostic and repair procedures to follow when trouble occurs.

We hope you use the manual to tackle the work yourself. For many simpler jobs, doing it yourself may be quicker than arranging an appointment to get the vehicle into a shop and making the trips to leave it and pick it up. More importantly, a lot of money can be saved by avoiding the expense the shop must pass on to you to cover its labor and overhead costs. An added benefit is the sense of satisfaction and accomplishment that you feel after doing the job yourself.

Using the manual

The manual is divided into Chapters. Each Chapter is divided into numbered Sections, which are headed in bold type between horizontal lines. Each Section consists of consecutively numbered paragraphs.

At the beginning of each numbered Section you will be referred to any illustrations which apply to the procedures in that Section. The reference numbers used in illustration captions pinpoint the pertinent Section and the Step within that Section. That is, illustration 3.2 means the illustration refers to Section 3 and Step (or paragraph) 2 within that Section.

Procedures, once described in the text, are not normally repeated. When it's necessary to refer to another Chapter, the reference will be given as Chapter and Section number. Cross references given without use of the word "Chapter" apply to Sections and/or paragraphs in the same Chapter. For example, "see Section 8" means in the same Chapter.

References to the left or right side of the vehicle assume you are sitting on the seat, facing forward.

All-terrain vehicle manufacturers continually make changes to specifications and recommendations, and these, when notified, are incorporated into our manuals at the earliest opportunity.

Even though we have prepared this manual with extreme care, neither the publisher nor the author can accept responsibility for any errors in, or omissions from, the information given.

NOTE

A **Note** provides information necessary to properly complete a procedure or information which will make the procedure easier to understand.

CAUTION

A **Caution** provides a special procedure or special steps which must be taken while completing the procedure where the Caution is found. Not heeding a Caution can result in damage to the assembly being worked on.

WARNING

A **Warning** provides a special procedure or special steps which must be taken while completing the procedure where the Warning is found. Not heeding a Warning can result in personal injury.

Introduction to the Yamaha YFM350

The Yamaha YFM350 series are highly successful and popular all-terrain vehicles.

Four basic models are covered in this manual:

YFM350ER (old style 2WD)
YFM350U (new style 2WD)
YFM350FW (old style 4WD)
YFM350FWB (new style 4WD)

The YFM350FH Hunter Edition model is a version of the YFM350FWB. The only differences are cosmetic (camouflage bodywork and rack bag and black brush guards).

The names "Big Bear" and "Big Bear 4 X 4" have been used on both the YFM350FW and YFM350FWB. The name "Big Bear 2 X 4" is used for the YFM350U. The YFM350ER did not use the name "Big Bear." Because this may cause confusion about which model is which – compounded by the fact that both the old-style and new-style 4WD models were sold during the 1997 model year – procedures in this manual are identified by model number. If you aren't sure which model you have, look at the model label on the vehicle's frame, generally located under the seat (not the vehicle identification number, which is stamped on a lower frame rail).

The engine on all models is an air-cooled single with an overhead camshaft.

Fuel is delivered to the cylinder by a single Mikuni carburetor.

The front suspension on 2WD models uses a coil spring/shock absorber unit and a single control arm on each side of the vehicle. 4WD models use upper and lower control arms on each side of the vehicle, with a coil spring/shock absorber unit attached to each upper control arm.

The rear suspension on all models uses a single shock absorber and coil spring.

1987 through 1998 models use a sealed drum brake at each front wheel. On YFM350ER models, the front brakes are actuated mechanically; on all others, they're actuated hydraulically. 1999 models use a hydraulically disc brake at each front wheel. 1987 through 1995 models use a single mechanically actuated disc brake at the rear. 1996 and later models use a single mechanically actuated drum brake at the rear.

Shaft final drive is used at the rear of all models covered in this manual. On YFM350FW models, power is transmitted to the front wheels by an external transfer case, front driveshaft, front differential and driveaxles to the front wheel hubs. On YFM350FWB models, there's no external transfer case. Instead, the middle driven gear shaft (located inside the engine crankcase) operates the front driveshaft, which in turn powers the front differential, driveaxles and wheel hubs.

Identification numbers

The frame serial number is stamped into the left side of the frame. The engine number is stamped into the right side of the crankcase. Both of these numbers should be recorded and kept in a safe place so they can be furnished to law enforcement officials in the event of a theft.

The frame serial number, engine serial number and carburetor identification number should also be kept in a handy place (such as with your driver's license) so they are always available when purchasing or ordering parts for your machine.

The models covered by this manual are as follows:
YFM350ER, 1987 through 1995
YFM350FW (Big Bear and Big Bear SE), 1987 through 1997
YFM350U (Big Bear 2 X 4 and Big Bear 2WD), 1996 through 1999
YFM350FWB (Big Bear 4 X 4 and Big Bear 4WD), 1997 through 1999

Identifying model years

The procedures in this manual identify the machines by model year. The model year is included in a decal on the frame, but in case the decal is missing or obscured, the following table identifies the initial frame number of each model year.

Year	Initial frame number or model code
1987	
YFM350ER	1YW-000101
YFM350FW	2HR-000101
1988	
YFM350ER	2VA-000101
YFM350FW	2HR-050101
1989	
YFM350ER	3HP-000101
YFM350FW	3HN-000101
1990	
YFM350ER	3HP-024101
YFM350FW	3HN-023101
1991	
YFM350ER	Not available
YFM350FW	3HN-048101
1992	
YFM350ER	3HP-049101
YFM350FW	3HN-079101
1993	
YFM350ER	3HP-059101
YFM350FW	3HN-107101

Year	Initial frame number or model code
1994	
YFM350ER	3HP-070101
YFM350FW	3HN-149101
1995	
YFM350ER	3HP-080101
YFM350FW	3HN-175101
1996	
YFM350U	Not available
YFM350FW	3HN-209101
1997	
YFM350U	4UH4
YFM350FW	3HNX
YFM350FWB	4WU1
1998	
YFM350U	4UH7
YFM350FWB (except California)	4WU6
YFM350FWB (California)	4WU5
1999	
YFM350U (except California)	5FE1
YFM350U (California)	5FE2
YFM350FW (except California)	5FT1
YFM350FW (California)	5FT2
YFM350FW Hunting (except California)	5FT6
YFM350FW Hunting (California)	5FT7

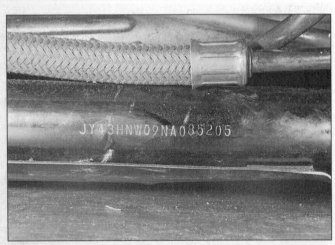

The frame serial number is located on the left side of the frame

The engine serial number is located on the right side of the crankcase

Buying parts

Once you have found all the identification numbers, record them for reference when buying parts. Since the manufacturers change specifications, parts and vendors (companies that manufacture various components on the machine), providing the ID numbers is the only way to be reasonably sure that you are buying the correct parts.

Whenever possible, take the worn part to the dealer so direct comparison with the new component can be made. Along the trail from the manufacturer to the parts shelf, there are numerous places that the part can end up with the wrong number or be listed incorrectly.

The two places to purchase new parts for your vehicle - the accessory store and the franchised dealer - differ in the type of parts they carry. While dealers can obtain virtually every part for your vehicle, the accessory dealer is usually limited to normal high wear items such as shock absorbers, tune-up parts, various engine gaskets, cables, chains, brake parts, etc. Rarely will an accessory outlet have major suspension components, cylinders, transmission gears, or cases.

Used parts can be obtained for roughly half the price of new ones, but you can't always be sure of what you're getting. Once again, take your worn part to the wrecking yard (breaker) for direct comparison.

Whether buying new, used or rebuilt parts, the best course is to deal directly with someone who specializes in parts for your particular make.

General specifications

Wheelbase
YFM350ER .... 1185 mm (46.6 inches)
YFM350FW .... 1210 mm (47.6 inches)
YFM350U
    1996 through 1998 models................ 1210 mm (47.6 inches)
    1999 models .... 1236 mm (48.7 inches)
YFM350FWB .... 1236 mm (48.7 inches)

Overall length
YFM350ER .... 1860 mm(723.2 inches)
YFM350FW
    1987 through 1993 models................ 1885 mm (74.6 inches)
    1994 and later models .... 1915 mm (75.4 inches)
YFM350U
    1996 through 1998 models................ 1915 mm (75.4 inches)
    1999 models .... 1945 mm (76.6 inches)
YFM350FWB .... 1945 mm (76.6 inches)

Overall height
YFM350ER .... 1030 mm (40.6 inches)
YFM350FW
    1987 through 1993 models................ 1110 mm (43.7 inches)
    1994 and later models .... 1130 mm (44.5 inches)
YFM350U
    1996 through 1998 models................ 1130 mm (44.5 inches)
    1999 models .... 1165 mm (45.9 inches)
YFM350FWB .... 1165 mm (45.9 inches)

Seat height
YFM350ER .... 750 mm (29.5 inches)

YFM350FW
    1987 through 1993 models................ 830 mm (32.7 inches)
    1994 and later models .... 850 mm (33.5 inches)
YFM350U
    1996 through 1998 models................ 850 mm (33.5 inches)
    1999 models .... 835 mm (32.9 inches)
YFM350FWB .... 835 mm (32.9 inches)

Ground clearance
YFM350ER .... 135 mm (5.3 inches)
YFM350FW .... 180 mm (7.1 inches)
YFM350U
    1996 through 1998 models................ 180 mm (7.1 inches)
    1999 models .... 245 mm (9.65 inches)
YFM350FWB .... 245 mm (133.9 inches)

Weight with oil and full fuel tank
YFM350ER
    1987 through 1989 models................ 237 kg (522 lbs)
    1990 and later models .... 244 kg (538 lbs)
YFM350FW
    1987 through 1993 US models.......... 262 kg (578 lbs)
    1987 through 1993 Canadian models 265 kg (584 lbs)
    1994 and later models .... 269 kg (593 lbs)
YFM350U
    1996 through 1998 models................ 261 kg (575 lbs)
    1999 models .... 245 mm (545 lbs)
YFM350FWB
    1997 and 1998 models..................... 259 kg (571 lbs)
    1999 models .... 257 kg (567 lbs)

Maintenance techniques, tools and working facilities

Basic maintenance techniques

There are a number of techniques involved in maintenance and repair that will be referred to throughout this manual. Application of these techniques will enable the amateur mechanic to be more efficient, better organized and capable of performing the various tasks properly, which will ensure that the repair job is thorough and complete.

Fastening systems

Fasteners, basically, are nuts, bolts and screws used to hold two or more parts together. There are a few things to keep in mind when working with fasteners. Almost all of them use a locking device of some type (either a lock washer, locknut, locking tab or thread adhesive). All threaded fasteners should be clean, straight, have undamaged threads and undamaged corners on the hex head where the wrench fits. Develop the habit of replacing all damaged nuts and bolts with new ones.

Rusted nuts and bolts should be treated with a penetrating oil to ease removal and prevent breakage. Some mechanics use turpentine in a spout type oil can, which works quite well. After applying the rust penetrant, let it "work" for a few minutes before trying to loosen the nut or bolt. Badly rusted fasteners may have to be chiseled off or removed with a special nut breaker, available at tool stores.

If a bolt or stud breaks off in an assembly, it can be drilled out and removed with a special tool called an E-Z out (or screw extractor). Most dealer service departments and vehicle repair shops can perform this task, as well as others (such as the repair of threaded holes that have been stripped out).

Flat washers and lock washers, when removed from an assembly, should always be replaced exactly as removed. Replace any damaged washers with new ones. Always use a flat washer between a lock washer and any soft metal surface (such as aluminum), thin sheet metal or plastic. Special locknuts can only be used once or twice before they lose their locking ability and must be replaced.

Tightening sequences and procedures

When threaded fasteners are tightened, they are often tightened to a specific torque value (torque is basically a twisting force). Over-tightening the fastener can weaken it and cause it to break, while under-tightening can cause it to eventually come loose. Each bolt, depending on the material it's made of, the diameter of its shank and the material it is threaded into, has a specific torque value, which is noted in the Specifications. Be sure to follow the torque recommendations closely.

Fasteners laid out in a pattern (i.e. cylinder head bolts, engine case bolts, etc.) must be loosened or tightened in a sequence to avoid warping the component. Initially, the bolts/nuts should go on finger tight only. Next, they should be tightened one full turn each, in a criss-cross or diagonal pattern. After each one has been tightened one full turn, return to the first one tightened and tighten them all one half turn, following the same pattern. Finally, tighten each of them one quarter turn at a time until each fastener has been tightened to the proper torque. To loosen and remove the fasteners the procedure would be reversed.

Disassembly sequence

Component disassembly should be done with care and purpose to help ensure that the parts go back together properly during reassembly. Always keep track of the sequence in which parts are removed. Take note of special characteristics or marks on parts that can be installed more than one way (such as a grooved thrust washer on a shaft). It's a good idea to lay the disassembled parts out on a clean surface in the order that they were removed. It may also be helpful to make sketches or take instant photos of components before removal.

When removing fasteners from a component, keep track of their locations. Sometimes threading a bolt back in a part, or putting the washers and nut back on a stud, can prevent mixups later. If nuts and bolts can't be returned to their original locations, they should be kept in a compartmented box or a series of small boxes. A cupcake or muffin tin is ideal for this purpose, since each cavity can hold the bolts and nuts from a particular area (i.e. engine case bolts, valve cover bolts, engine mount bolts, etc.). A pan of this type is especially helpful when working on assemblies with very small parts (such as the carburetors and the valve train). The cavities can be marked with paint or tape to identify the contents.

Whenever wiring looms, harnesses or connectors are separated, it's a good idea to identify the two halves with numbered pieces of masking tape so they can be easily reconnected.

Gasket sealing surfaces

Throughout any vehicle, gaskets are used to seal the mating surfaces between components and keep lubricants, fluids, vacuum or pressure contained in an assembly.

Many times these gaskets are coated with a liquid or paste type gasket sealing compound before assembly. Age, heat and pressure can sometimes cause the two parts to stick together so tightly that they are very difficult to separate. In most cases, the part can be loosened by striking it with a soft-faced hammer near the mating surfaces. A regular hammer can be used if a block of wood is placed between the hammer and the part. Do not hammer on cast parts or parts that could be easily damaged. With any particularly stubborn part, always recheck to make sure that every fastener has been removed.

Avoid using a screwdriver or bar to pry apart components, as they can easily mar the gasket sealing surfaces of the parts (which must remain smooth). If prying is absolutely necessary, use a piece of wood, but keep in mind that extra clean-up will be necessary if the wood splinters.

After the parts are separated, the old gasket must be carefully scraped off and the gasket surfaces cleaned. Stubborn gasket material can be soaked with a gasket remover (available in aerosol cans) to soften it so it can be easily scraped off. A scraper can be fashioned from a piece of copper tubing by flattening and sharpening one end. Copper is recommended because it is usually softer than the surfaces to be scraped, which reduces the chance of gouging the part. Some gaskets can be removed with a wire brush, but regardless of the method used, the mating surfaces must be left clean and smooth. If for some reason the gasket surface is gouged, then a gasket sealer thick enough to fill scratches will have to be used during reassembly of the components. For most applications, a non-drying (or semi-drying) gasket sealer is best.

Hose removal tips

Hose removal precautions closely parallel gasket removal precautions. Avoid scratching or gouging the surface that the hose mates against or the connection may leak. Because of various chemical reactions, the rubber in hoses can bond itself to the metal spigot that the hose fits over. To remove a hose, first loosen the hose clamps that secure it to the spigot. Then, with slip joint pliers, grab the hose at the clamp and rotate it around the spigot. Work it back and forth until it is completely free, then pull it off (silicone or other lubricants will ease removal if they can be applied between the hose and the outside of the spigot). Apply the same lubricant to the inside of the hose and the outside of the spigot to simplify installation.

Spark plug gap adjusting tool

Feeler gauge set

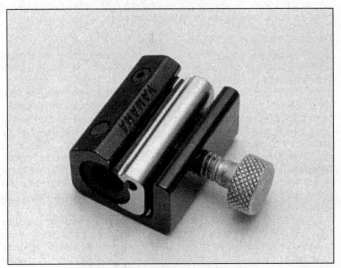

Control cable pressure luber

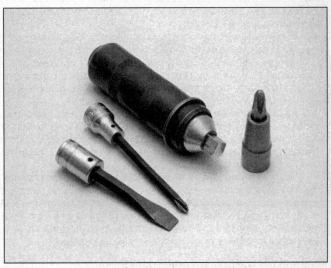

Hand impact screwdriver and bits

If a hose clamp is broken or damaged, do not reuse it. Also, do not reuse hoses that are cracked, split or torn.

Tools

A selection of good tools is a basic requirement for anyone who plans to maintain and repair a vehicle. For the owner who has few tools, if any, the initial investment might seem high, but when compared to the spiraling costs of routine maintenance and repair, it is a wise one.

To help the owner decide which tools are needed to perform the tasks detailed in this manual, the following tool lists are offered: Maintenance and minor repair, Repair and overhaul and Special. The newcomer to practical mechanics should start off with the Maintenance and minor repair tool kit, which is adequate for the simpler jobs. Then, as confidence and experience grow, the owner can tackle more difficult tasks, buying additional tools as they are needed. Eventually the basic kit will be built into the Repair and overhaul tool set. Over a period of time, the experienced do-it-yourselfer will assemble a tool set complete enough for most repair and overhaul procedures and will add tools from the Special category when it is felt that the expense is justified by the frequency of use.

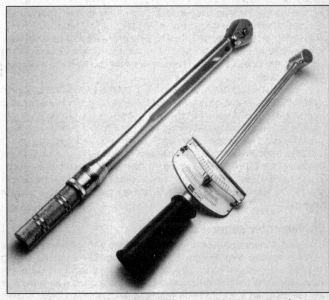

Torque wrenches (left, click type; right, beam type)

Snap-ring pliers (top - external; bottom - internal)

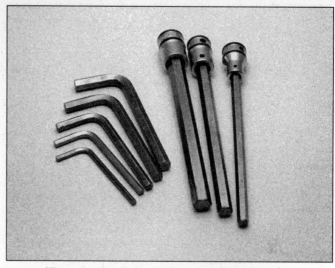

Allen wrenches (left), and Allen head sockets (right)

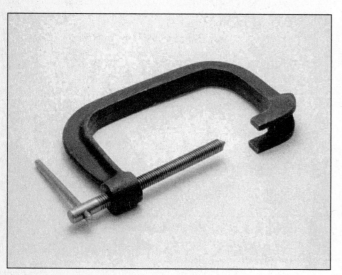

Valve spring compressor

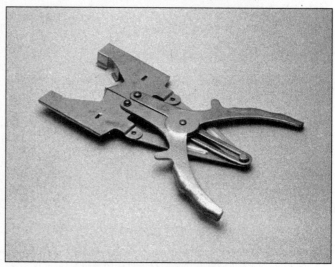

Piston ring removal/installation tool

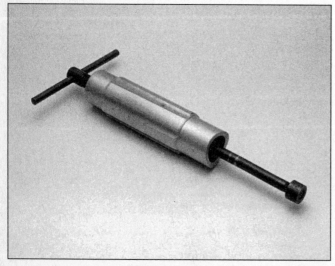

Piston pin puller

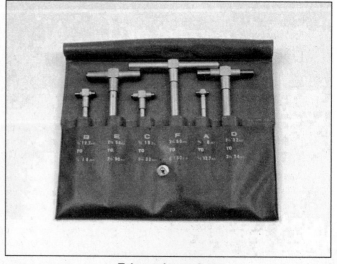

Telescoping gauges

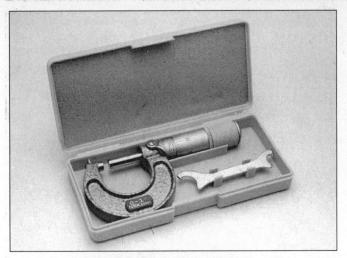

0-to-1 inch micrometer

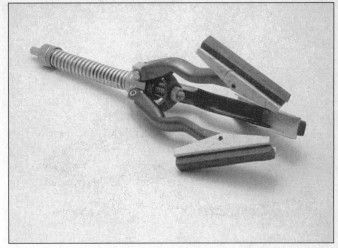

Cylinder surfacing hone

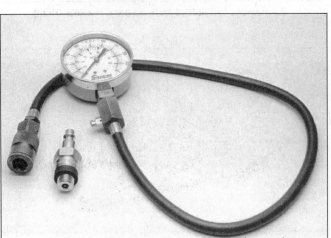

Cylinder compression gauge

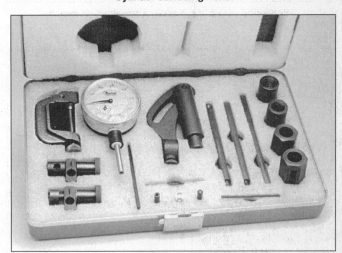

Dial indicator set

Maintenance and minor repair tool kit

The tools in this list should be considered the minimum required for performance of routine maintenance, servicing and minor repair work. We recommend the purchase of combination wrenches (box end and open end combined in one wrench); while more expensive than open-ended ones, they offer the advantages of both types of wrench.

Combination wrench set (6 mm to 22 mm)
Adjustable wrench - 8 in
Spark plug socket (with rubber insert)
Spark plug gap adjusting tool
Feeler gauge set
Standard screwdriver (5/16 in x 6 in)
Phillips screwdriver (No. 2 x 6 in)
Allen (hex) wrench set (4 mm to 12 mm)
Combination (slip-joint) pliers - 6 in
Hacksaw and assortment of blades
Tire pressure gauge
Control cable pressure luber
Grease gun
Oil can
Fine emery cloth
Wire brush
Hand impact screwdriver and bits
Funnel (medium size)
Safety goggles
Drain pan
Work light with extension cord

Repair and overhaul tool set

These tools are essential for anyone who plans to perform major repairs and are intended to supplement those in the Maintenance and minor repair tool kit. Included is a comprehensive set of sockets which, though expensive, are invaluable because of their versatility (especially when various extensions and drives are available). We recommend the 3/8 inch drive over the 1/2 inch drive for general vehicle maintenance and repair (ideally, the mechanic would have a 3/8 inch drive set and a 1/2 inch drive set).

Alternator rotor puller tool
Socket set(s)
Reversible ratchet
Extension - 6 in
Universal joint
Torque wrench (same size drive as sockets)
Ball peen hammer - 8 oz
Soft-faced hammer (plastic/rubber)
Standard screwdriver (1/4 in x 6 in)
Standard screwdriver (stubby - 5/16 in)
Phillips screwdriver (No. 3 x 8 in)
Phillips screwdriver (stubby - No. 2)
Pliers - locking
Pliers - lineman's
Pliers - needle nose
Pliers - snap-ring (internal and external)
Cold chisel - 1/2 in
Scriber

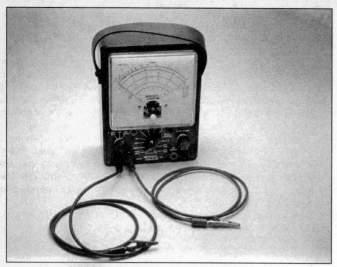

Multimeter (volt/ohm/ammeter)

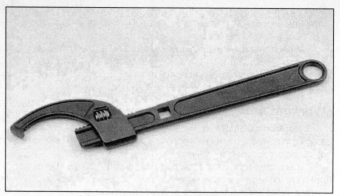

Adjustable spanner

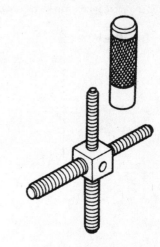

Alternator rotor puller

Scraper (made from flattened copper tubing)
Center punch
Pin punches (1/16, 1/8, 3/16 in)
Steel rule/straightedge - 12 in
Pin-type spanner wrench
A selection of files
Wire brush (large)

Note: *Another tool which is often useful is an electric drill with a chuck capacity of 3/8 inch (and a set of good quality drill bits).*

Special tools

The tools in this list include those which are not used regularly, are expensive to buy, or which need to be used in accordance with their manufacturer's instructions. Unless these tools will be used frequently, it is not very economical to purchase many of them. A consideration would be to split the cost and use between yourself and a friend or friends (i.e. members of a vehicle club).

This list primarily contains tools and instruments widely available to the public, as well as some special tools produced by the vehicle manufacturer for distribution to dealer service departments. As a result, references to the manufacturer's special tools are occasionally included in the text of this manual. Generally, an alternative method of doing the job without the special tool is offered. However, sometimes there is no alternative to their use. Where this is the case, and the tool can't be purchased or borrowed, the work should be turned over to the dealer service department or a vehicle repair shop.

Valve spring compressor
Piston ring removal and installation tool
Piston pin puller
Telescoping gauges
Micrometer(s) and/or dial/Vernier calipers
Cylinder surfacing hone
Cylinder compression gauge
Dial indicator set
Multimeter
Adjustable spanner
Manometer or vacuum gauge set
Small air compressor with blow gun and tire chuck

Buying tools

For the do-it-yourselfer who is just starting to get involved in vehicle maintenance and repair, there are a number of options available when purchasing tools. If maintenance and minor repair is the extent of the work to be done, the purchase of individual tools is satisfactory. If, on the other hand, extensive work is planned, it would be a good idea to purchase a modest tool set from one of the large retail chain stores. A set can usually be bought at a substantial savings over the individual tool prices (and they often come with a tool box). As additional tools are needed, add-on sets, individual tools and a larger tool box can be purchased to expand the tool selection. Building a tool set gradually allows the cost of the tools to be spread over a longer period of time and gives the mechanic the freedom to choose only those tools that will actually be used.

Tool stores and vehicle dealers will often be the only source of some of the special tools that are needed, but regardless of where tools are bought, try to avoid cheap ones (especially when buying screwdrivers and sockets) because they won't last very long. There are plenty of tools around at reasonable prices, but always aim to purchase items which meet the relevant national safety standards. The expense involved in replacing cheap tools will eventually be greater than the initial cost of quality tools.

It is obviously not possible to cover the subject of tools fully here. For those who wish to learn more about tools and their use, there is a book entitled *Vehicle Workshop Practice Manual* (Book no. 1454) available from the publishers of this manual. It also provides an introduction to basic workshop practice which will be of interest to a home mechanic working on any type of vehicle.

Care and maintenance of tools

Good tools are expensive, so it makes sense to treat them with respect. Keep them clean and in usable condition and store them properly when not in use. Always wipe off any dirt, grease or metal chips before putting them away. Never leave tools lying around in the work area.

Some tools, such as screwdrivers, pliers, wrenches and sockets, can be hung on a panel mounted on the garage or workshop wall, while others should be kept in a tool box or tray. Measuring instruments, gauges, meters, etc. must be carefully stored where they can't be damaged by weather or impact from other tools.

When tools are used with care and stored properly, they will last a very long time. Even with the best of care, tools will wear out if used frequently. When a tool is damaged or worn out, replace it; subsequent jobs will be safer and more enjoyable if you do.

Working facilities

Not to be overlooked when discussing tools is the workshop. If anything more than routine maintenance is to be carried out, some sort of suitable work area is essential.

It is understood, and appreciated, that many home mechanics do not have a good workshop or garage available and end up removing an engine or doing major repairs outside (it is recommended, however, that the overhaul or repair be completed under the cover of a roof).

A clean, flat workbench or table of comfortable working height is an absolute necessity. The workbench should be equipped with a vise that has a jaw opening of at least four inches.

As mentioned previously, some clean, dry storage space is also required for tools, as well as the lubricants, fluids, cleaning solvents, etc. which soon become necessary.

Sometimes waste oil and fluids, drained from the engine or cooling system during normal maintenance or repairs, present a disposal problem. To avoid pouring them on the ground or into a sewage system, simply pour the used fluids into large containers, seal them with caps and take them to an authorized disposal site or service station. Plastic jugs are ideal for this purpose.

Always keep a supply of old newspapers and clean rags available. Old towels are excellent for mopping up spills. Many mechanics use rolls of paper towels for most work because they are readily available and disposable. To help keep the area under the vehicle clean, a large cardboard box can be cut open and flattened to protect the garage or shop floor.

Whenever working over a painted surface (such as the fuel tank) cover it with an old blanket or bedspread to protect the finish.

Safety first!

Professional mechanics are trained in safe working procedures. However enthusiastic you may be about getting on with the job at hand, take the time to ensure that your safety is not put at risk. A moment's lack of attention can result in an accident, as can failure to observe simple precautions.

There will always be new ways of having accidents, and the following is not a comprehensive list of all dangers; it is intended rather to make you aware of the risks and to encourage a safe approach to all work you carry out on your bike.

Essential DOs and DON'Ts

DON'T start the engine without first ascertaining that the transmission is in neutral.

DON'T attempt to drain oil until you are sure it has cooled sufficiently to avoid scalding you.

DON'T grasp any part of the engine or exhaust system without first ascertaining that it is cool enough not to burn you.

DON'T allow brake fluid to contact the machine's paint work or plastic components.

DON'T siphon toxic liquids such as fuel, hydraulic fluid or antifreeze by mouth, or allow them to remain on your skin.

DON'T inhale dust - it may be injurious to health (see *Asbestos* heading).

DON'T allow any spilled oil or grease to remain on the floor - wipe it up right away, before someone slips on it.

DON'T use ill fitting wrenches or other tools which may slip and cause injury.

DON'T attempt to lift a heavy component which may be beyond your capability - get assistance.

DON'T rush to finish a job or take unverified short cuts.

DON'T allow children or animals in or around an unattended vehicle.

DON'T inflate a tire to a pressure above the recommended maximum. Apart from over stressing the carcase and wheel rim, in extreme cases the tire may blow off forcibly. ATV tires, which are designed to operate at very low air pressures, may rupture if overinflated.

DO ensure that the machine is supported securely at all times. This is especially important when the machine is blocked up to aid wheel or suspension removal.

DO take care when attempting to loosen a stubborn nut or bolt. It is generally better to pull on a wrench, rather than push, so that if you slip, you fall away from the machine rather than onto it.

DO wear eye protection when using power tools such as drill, sander, bench grinder etc.

DO use a barrier cream on your hands prior to undertaking dirty jobs - it will protect your skin from infection as well as making the dirt easier to remove afterwards; but make sure your hands aren't left slippery. Note that long-term contact with used engine oil can be a health hazard.

DO keep loose clothing (cuffs, ties etc. and long hair) well out of the way of moving mechanical parts.

DO remove rings, wristwatch etc., before working on the vehicle - especially the electrical system.

DO keep your work area tidy - it is only too easy to fall over articles left lying around.

DO exercise caution when compressing springs for removal or installation. Ensure that the tension is applied and released in a controlled manner, using suitable tools which preclude the possibility of the spring escaping violently.

DO ensure that any lifting tackle used has a safe working load rating adequate for the job.

DO get someone to check periodically that all is well, when working alone on the vehicle.

DO carry out work in a logical sequence and check that everything is correctly assembled and tightened afterwards.

DO remember that your vehicle's safety affects that of yourself and others. If in doubt on any point, get professional advice.

IF, in spite of following these precautions, you are unfortunate enough to injure yourself, seek medical attention as soon as possible.

Asbestos

Certain friction, insulating, sealing and other products - such as brake pads, clutch linings, gaskets, etc. - may contain asbestos. *Extreme care must be taken to avoid inhalation of dust from such products since it is hazardous to health*. If in doubt, assume that they *do* contain asbestos.

Fire

Remember at all times that gasoline (petrol) is highly flammable. Never smoke or have any kind of naked flame around, when working on the vehicle. But the risk does not end there - a spark caused by an electrical short-circuit, by two metal surfaces contacting each other, by careless use of tools, or even by static electricity built up in your body under certain conditions, can ignite gasoline (petrol) vapor, which in a confined space is highly explosive. Never use gasoline (petrol) as a cleaning solvent. Use an approved safety solvent.

Always disconnect the battery ground (earth) terminal before working on any part of the fuel or electrical system, and never risk spilling fuel on to a hot engine or exhaust.

It is recommended that a fire extinguisher of a type suitable for fuel and electrical fires is kept handy in the garage or workplace at all times. Never try to extinguish a fuel or electrical fire with water.

Fumes

Certain fumes are highly toxic and can quickly cause unconsciousness and even death if inhaled to any extent. Gasoline (petrol) vapor comes into this category, as do the vapors from certain solvents such as trichloroethylene. Any draining or pouring of such volatile fluids should be done in a well ventilated area.

When using cleaning fluids and solvents, read the instructions carefully. Never use materials from unmarked containers - they may give off poisonous vapors.

Never run the engine of a motor vehicle in an enclosed space such as a garage. Exhaust fumes contain carbon monoxide which is extremely poisonous; if you need to run the engine, always do so in the open air or at least have the rear of the vehicle outside the workplace.

The battery

Never cause a spark, or allow a bare light bulb near the vehicle's battery. It will normally be giving off a certain amount of hydrogen gas, which is highly explosive.

Always disconnect the battery ground (earth) terminal before working on the fuel or electrical systems (except where noted).

Do not charge the battery at an excessive rate or the battery may burst.

Take care when cleaning or carrying the battery. The acid electrolyte, even when diluted, is very corrosive and should not be allowed to contact the eyes or skin. Always wear rubber gloves and goggles or a face shield. If you ever need to prepare electrolyte yourself, always add the acid slowly to the water; never add the water to the acid.

Electricity

When using an electric power tool, inspection light etc., always ensure that the appliance is correctly connected to its plug and that, where necessary, it is properly grounded (earthed). Do not use such appliances in damp conditions and, again, beware of creating a spark or applying excessive heat in the vicinity of fuel or fuel vapor. Also ensure that the appliances meet national safety standards.

A severe electric shock can result from touching certain parts of the electrical system, such as the spark plug wires (HT leads), when the engine is running or being cranked, particularly if components are damp or the insulation is defective. Where an electronic ignition system is used, the secondary (HT) voltage is much higher and could prove fatal.

ATV chemicals and lubricants

A number of chemicals and lubricants are available for use in vehicle maintenance and repair. They include a wide variety of products ranging from cleaning solvents and degreasers to lubricants and protective sprays for rubber, plastic and vinyl.

Contact point/spark plug cleaner is a solvent used to clean oily film and dirt from points, grime from electrical connectors and oil deposits from spark plugs. It is oil free and leaves no residue. It can also be used to remove gum and varnish from carburetor jets and other orifices.

Carburetor cleaner is similar to contact point/spark plug cleaner but it usually has a stronger solvent and may leave a slight oily residue. It is not recommended for cleaning electrical components or connections.

Brake system cleaner is used to remove grease or brake fluid from brake system components (where clean surfaces are absolutely necessary and petroleum-based solvents cannot be used); it also leaves no residue.

Silicone-based lubricants are used to protect rubber parts such as hoses and grommets, and are used as lubricants for hinges and locks.

Multi-purpose grease is an all purpose lubricant used wherever grease is more practical than a liquid lubricant such as oil. Some multi-purpose grease is colored white and specially formulated to be more resistant to water than ordinary grease.

Gear oil (sometimes called gear lube) is a specially designed oil used in transmissions and final drive units, as well as other areas where high friction, high temperature lubrication is required. It is available in a number of viscosities (weights) for various applications.

Motor oil, of course, is the lubricant specially formulated for use in the engine. It normally contains a wide variety of additives to prevent corrosion and reduce foaming and wear. Motor oil comes in various weights (viscosity ratings) of from 5 to 80. The recommended weight of the oil depends on the seasonal temperature and the demands on the engine. Light oil is used in cold climates and under light load conditions; heavy oil is used in hot climates and where high loads are encountered. Multi-viscosity oils are designed to have characteristics of both light and heavy oils and are available in a number of weights from 5W-20 to 20W-50. On these machines, the same oil supply is shared by the engine and transmission.

Gas (petrol) additives perform several functions, depending on their chemical makeup. They usually contain solvents that help dissolve gum and varnish that build up on carburetor and intake parts. They also serve to break down carbon deposits that form on the inside surfaces of the combustion chambers. Some additives contain upper cylinder lubricants for valves and piston rings.

Brake fluid is a specially formulated hydraulic fluid that can withstand the heat and pressure encountered in brake systems. Care must be taken that this fluid does not come in contact with painted surfaces or plastics. An opened container should always be resealed to prevent contamination by water or dirt.

Chain lubricants are formulated especially for use on the final drive chains of vehicles so equipped (all models covered in this manual are equipped with shaft drive). A good chain lube should adhere well and have good penetrating qualities to be effective as a lubricant inside the chain and on the side plates, pins and rollers. Most chain lubes are either the foaming type or quick drying type and are usually marketed as sprays.

Degreasers are heavy duty solvents used to remove grease and grime that may accumulate on engine and frame components. They can be sprayed or brushed on and, depending on the type, are rinsed with either water or solvent.

Solvents are used alone or in combination with degreasers to clean parts and assemblies during repair and overhaul. The home mechanic should use only solvents that are non-flammable and that do not produce irritating fumes.

Gasket sealing compounds may be used in conjunction with gaskets, to improve their sealing capabilities, or alone, to seal metal-to-metal joints. Many gasket sealers can withstand extreme heat, some are impervious to gasoline and lubricants, while others are capable of filling and sealing large cavities. Depending on the intended use, gasket sealers either dry hard or stay relatively soft and pliable. They are usually applied by hand, with a brush, or are sprayed on the gasket sealing surfaces.

Thread cement is an adhesive locking compound that prevents threaded fasteners from loosening because of vibration. It is available in a variety of types for different applications.

Moisture dispersants are usually sprays that can be used to dry out electrical components such as the fuse block and wiring connectors. Some types can also be used as treatment for rubber and as a lubricant for hinges, cables and locks.

Waxes and polishes are used to help protect painted and plated surfaces from the weather. Different types of paint may require the use of different types of wax polish. Some polishes utilize a chemical or abrasive cleaner to help remove the top layer of oxidized (dull) paint on older vehicles. In recent years, many non-wax polishes (that contain a wide variety of chemicals such as polymers and silicones) have been introduced. These non-wax polishes are usually easier to apply and last longer than conventional waxes and polishes.

Troubleshooting

Contents

Engine doesn't start or is difficult to start

1   Starter motor does not rotate

1   Engine kill switch Off.
2   Fuse blown. Check fuse (Chapter 8).
3   Battery voltage low. Check and recharge battery (Chapter 8).
4   Starter motor defective. Make sure the wiring to the starter is secure. Test starter relay (Chapter 8). If the relay is good, then the fault is in the wiring or motor.
5   Starter relay faulty. Check it according to the procedure in Chapter 8.
6   Starter switch not contacting. The contacts could be wet, corroded or dirty. Disassemble and clean the switch (Chapter 8).
7   Wiring open or shorted. Check all wiring connections and harnesses to make sure that they are dry, tight and not corroded. Also check for broken or frayed wires that can cause a short to ground (see *Wiring Diagrams*, Chapter 9).
8   Ignition (main) switch defective. Check the switch according to the procedure in Chapter 8. Replace the switch with a new one if it is defective.
9   Engine kill switch defective. Check for wet, dirty or corroded contacts. Clean or replace the switch as necessary (Chapter 8).
10   Starting circuit cut-off relay, neutral relay, neutral switch, reverse switch or front brake switch defective. Check the switches according to the procedure in Chapter 8. Replace the switch with a new one if it is defective.

2   Starter motor rotates but engine does not turn over

1   Starter motor clutch defective. Inspect and repair or replace (Chapter 8).
2   Damaged starter idle or wheel gears. Inspect and replace the damaged parts (Chapter 8).

3   Starter works but engine won't turn over (seized)

Seized engine caused by one or more internally damaged components. Failure due to wear, abuse or lack of lubrication. Damage can include seized valves, valve lifters, camshaft, piston, crankshaft, connecting rod bearings, or transmission gears or bearings. Refer to Chapter 2 for engine disassembly.

4   No fuel flow

1   No fuel in tank.
2   Tank cap air vent obstructed. Usually caused by dirt or water. Remove it and clean the cap vent hole.
3   Clogged strainer in fuel tap. Remove and clean the strainer (Chapter 1).
4   Fuel line clogged. Pull the fuel line loose and carefully blow through it.
5   Inlet needle valve clogged. A very bad batch of fuel with an unusual additive may have been used, or some other foreign material has entered the tank. Many times after a machine has been stored for many months without running, the fuel turns to a varnish-like liquid and forms deposits on the inlet needle valve and jets. The carburetor should be removed and overhauled if draining the float chamber doesn't solve the problem.

5   Engine flooded

1   Float level too high. Check as described in Chapter 3 and replace the float if necessary.
2   Inlet needle valve worn or stuck open. A piece of dirt, rust or other debris can cause the inlet needle to seat improperly, causing excess fuel to be admitted to the float bowl. In this case, the float chamber should be cleaned and the needle and seat inspected. If the needle and seat are worn, then the leaking will persist and the parts should be replaced with new ones (Chapter 3).
3   Starting technique incorrect. Under normal circumstances (i.e., if all the carburetor functions are sound) the machine should start with little or no throttle. When the engine is cold, the choke should be operated and the engine started without opening the throttle. When the engine is at operating temperature, only a very slight amount of throttle should be necessary. If the engine is flooded, turn the fuel tap off and hold the throttle open while cranking the engine. This will allow additional air to reach the cylinder. Remember to turn the fuel tap back on after the engine starts.

6   No spark or weak spark

1   Ignition switch Off.
2   Engine kill switch turned to the Off position.
3   Battery voltage low. Check and recharge battery as necessary (Chapter 8).
4   Spark plug dirty, defective or worn out. Locate reason for fouled plug using spark plug condition chart and follow the plug maintenance procedures in Chapter 1.
5   Spark plug cap or secondary (HT) wiring faulty. Check condition. Replace either or both components if cracks or deterioration are evident (Chapter 4).
6   Spark plug cap not making good contact. Make sure that the plug cap fits snugly over the plug end.
7   CDI magneto defective. Check the unit, referring to Chapter 4 for details.
8   CDI unit defective. Check the unit, referring to Chapter 4 for details.
9   Ignition coil defective. Check the coil, referring to Chapter 4.
10   Ignition or kill switch shorted. This is usually caused by water, corrosion, damage or excessive wear. The kill switch can be disassembled and cleaned with electrical contact cleaner. If cleaning does not help, replace the switches (Chapter 8).
11   Wiring shorted or broken between:
   a) *Ignition switch and engine kill switch (or blown fuse)*
   b) *CDI unit and engine kill switch*
   c) *CDI and ignition coil*
   d) *Ignition coil and plug*
   e) *CDI unit and CDI magneto*
   Make sure that all wiring connections are clean, dry and tight. Look for chafed and broken wires (Chapters 4 and 8).

7   Compression low

1   Spark plug loose. Remove the plug and inspect the threads. Reinstall and tighten to the specified torque (Chapter 1).
2   Cylinder head not sufficiently tightened down. If the cylinder head is suspected of being loose, then there's a chance that the gasket or head is damaged if the problem has persisted for any length of time. The head nuts and bolts should be tightened to the proper torque in the correct sequence (Chapter 2).
3   Improper valve clearance. This means that the valve is not closing completely and compression pressure is leaking past the valve. Check and adjust the valve clearances (Chapter 1).
4   Cylinder and/or piston worn. Excessive wear will cause compression pressure to leak past the rings. This is usually accompanied by worn rings as well. A top end overhaul is necessary (Chapter 2).
5   Piston rings worn, weak, broken, or sticking. Broken or sticking

piston rings usually indicate a lubrication or carburetion problem that causes excess carbon deposits or seizures to form on the pistons and rings. Top end overhaul is necessary (Chapter 2).

6   Piston ring-to-groove clearance excessive. This is caused by excessive wear of the piston ring lands. Piston replacement is necessary (Chapter 2).

7   Cylinder head gasket damaged. If the head is allowed to become loose, or if excessive carbon build-up on a piston crown and combustion chamber causes extremely high compression, the head gasket may leak. Retorquing the head is not always sufficient to restore the seal, so gasket replacement is necessary (Chapter 2).

8   Cylinder head warped. This is caused by overheating or improperly tightened head nuts and bolts. Machine shop resurfacing or head replacement is necessary (Chapter 2).

9   Valve spring broken or weak. Caused by component failure or wear; the spring(s) must be replaced (Chapter 2).

10   Valve not seating properly. This is caused by a bent valve (from over-revving or improper valve adjustment), burned valve or seat (improper carburetion) or an accumulation of carbon deposits on the seat (from carburetion or lubrication problems). The valves must be cleaned and/or replaced and the seats serviced if possible (Chapter 2).

8   Stalls after starting

1   Improper choke action. Make sure the choke knob or lever is getting a full stroke and staying in the out position.

2   Ignition malfunction. See Chapter 4.

3   Carburetor malfunction. See Chapter 3.

4   Fuel contaminated. The fuel can be contaminated with either dirt or water, or can change chemically if the machine is allowed to sit for several months or more. Drain the tank and float bowl and refill with fresh fuel (Chapter 3).

5   Intake air leak. Check for loose carburetor-to-intake joint connections or loose carburetor top (Chapter 3).

6   Engine idle speed incorrect. Turn throttle stop screw until the engine idles at the specified rpm (Chapter 1).

9   Rough idle

1   Ignition malfunction. See Chapter 4.

2   Idle speed incorrect. See Chapter 1.

3   Carburetor malfunction. See Chapter 3.

4   Idle fuel/air mixture incorrect. See Chapter 3.

5   Fuel contaminated. The fuel can be contaminated with either dirt or water, or can change chemically if the machine is allowed to sit for several months or more. Drain the tank and float bowl (Chapter 3).

6   Intake air leak. Check for loose carburetor-to-intake joint connections, loose or missing vacuum gauge access port cap or hose, or loose carburetor top (Chapter 3).

7   Air cleaner clogged. Service or replace air cleaner element (Chapter 1).

Poor running at low speed

10   Spark weak

1   Battery voltage low. Check and recharge battery (Chapter 8).

2   Spark plug fouled, defective or worn out. Refer to Chapter 1 for spark plug maintenance.

3   Spark plug cap or secondary (HT) wiring defective. Refer to Chapters 1 and 4 for details on the ignition system.

4   Spark plug cap not making contact.

5   Incorrect spark plug. Wrong type, heat range or cap configuration. Check and install correct plug listed in Chapter 1. A cold plug or

one with a recessed firing electrode will not operate at low speeds without fouling.

6   CDI unit defective. See Chapter 4.

7   CDI magneto defective. See Chapter 4.

8   Ignition coil defective. See Chapter 4.

11   Fuel/air mixture incorrect

1   Pilot screw out of adjustment (Chapter 3).

2   Pilot jet or air passage clogged. Remove and overhaul the carburetor (Chapter 3).

3   Air bleed holes clogged. Remove carburetor and blow out all passages (Chapter 3).

4   Air cleaner clogged, poorly sealed or missing.

5   Air cleaner-to-carburetor boot poorly sealed. Look for cracks, holes or loose clamps and replace or repair defective parts.

6   Float level too high or too low. Check and replace the float if necessary (Chapter 3).

7   Fuel tank air vent obstructed. Make sure that the air vent passage in the filler cap is open.

8   Carburetor intake joint loose. Check for cracks, breaks, tears or loose clamps or bolts. Repair or replace the rubber boot and its O-ring.

12   Compression low

1   Spark plug loose. Remove the plug and inspect the threads. Reinstall and tighten to the specified torque (Chapter 1).

2   Cylinder head not sufficiently tightened down. If the cylinder head is suspected of being loose, then there's a chance that the gasket and head are damaged if the problem has persisted for any length of time. The head nuts and bolts should be tightened to the proper torque in the correct sequence (Chapter 2).

3   Improper valve clearance. This means that the valve is not closing completely and compression pressure is leaking past the valve. Check and adjust the valve clearances (Chapter 1).

4   Cylinder and/or piston worn. Excessive wear will cause compression pressure to leak past the rings. This is usually accompanied by worn rings as well. A top end overhaul is necessary (Chapter 2).

5   Piston rings worn, weak, broken, or sticking. Broken or sticking piston rings usually indicate a lubrication or carburetion problem that causes excess carbon deposits or seizures to form on the pistons and rings. Top end overhaul is necessary (Chapter 2).

6   Piston ring-to-groove clearance excessive. This is caused by excessive wear of the piston ring lands. Piston replacement is necessary (Chapter 2).

7   Cylinder head gasket damaged. If the head is allowed to become loose, or if excessive carbon build-up on the piston crown and combustion chamber causes extremely high compression, the head gasket may leak. Retorquing the head is not always sufficient to restore the seal, so gasket replacement is necessary (Chapter 2).

8   Cylinder head warped. This is caused by overheating or improperly tightened head nuts and bolts. Machine shop resurfacing or head replacement is necessary (Chapter 2).

9   Valve spring broken or weak. Caused by component failure or wear; the spring(s) must be replaced (Chapter 2).

10   Valve not seating properly. This is caused by a bent valve (from over-revving or improper valve adjustment), burned valve or seat (improper carburetion) or an accumulation of carbon deposits on the seat (from carburetion, lubrication problems). The valves must be cleaned and/or replaced and the seats serviced if possible (Chapter 2).

13   Poor acceleration

1   Carburetor leaking or dirty. Overhaul the carburetor (Chapter 3).

2 Timing not advancing. The CDI magneto or the CDI unit may be defective. If so, they must be replaced with new ones, as they can't be repaired.

3 Engine oil viscosity too high. Using a heavier oil than that recommended in Chapter 1 can damage the oil pump or lubrication system and cause drag on the engine.

4 Brakes dragging. Usually caused by debris which has entered the brake piston sealing boots (4WD front brakes), corroded wheel cylinders (4WD front brakes), sticking brake cam (2WD front brakes and all rear brakes), or from a warped drum, warped disc or bent axle. Repair as necessary (Chapter 6).

Poor running or no power at high speed

14 Firing incorrect

1 Air cleaner restricted. Clean or replace element (Chapter 1).

2 Spark plug fouled, defective or worn out. See Chapter 1 for spark plug maintenance.

3 Spark plug cap or secondary (HT) wiring defective. See Chapters 1 and 4 for details of the ignition system.

4 Spark plug cap not in good contact. See Chapter 4.

5 Incorrect spark plug. Wrong type, heat range or cap configuration. Check and install correct plugs listed in Chapter 1. A cold plug or one with a recessed firing electrode will not operate at low speeds without fouling.

6 CDI unit or CDI magneto defective. See Chapter 4.

7 Ignition coil defective. See Chapter 4.

15 Fuel/air mixture incorrect

1 Pilot screw out of adjustment. See Chapter 3 for adjustment procedures.

2 Main jet clogged. Dirt, water or other contaminants can clog the main jets. Clean the fuel tap strainer and in-tank strainer, the float bowl area, and the jets and carburetor orifices (Chapter 3).

3 Main jet wrong size. The standard jetting is for sea level atmospheric pressure and oxygen content. See Chapter 3 for high altitude adjustments.

4 Throttle shaft-to-carburetor body clearance excessive. Refer to Chapter 3 for inspection and part replacement procedures.

5 Air bleed holes clogged. Remove and overhaul carburetor (Chapter 3).

6 Air cleaner clogged, poorly sealed, or missing.

7 Air cleaner-to-carburetor boot poorly sealed. Look for cracks, holes or loose clamps, and replace or repair defective parts.

8 Float level too high or too low. Check float level and replace the float if necessary (Chapter 3).

9 Fuel tank air vent obstructed. Make sure the air vent passage in the filler cap is open.

10 Carburetor intake joint loose. Check for cracks, breaks, tears or loose clamps or bolts. Repair or replace the rubber boots (Chapter 3).

11 Fuel tap clogged. Remove the tap and clean it (Chapter 1).

12 Fuel line clogged. Pull the fuel line loose and carefully blow through it.

16 Compression low

1 Spark plug loose. Remove the plug and inspect the threads. Reinstall and tighten to the specified torque (Chapter 1).

2 Cylinder head not sufficiently tightened down. If the cylinder head is suspected of being loose, then there's a chance that the gasket and head are damaged if the problem has persisted for any length of time. The head nuts and bolts should be tightened to the proper torque in the correct sequence (Chapter 2).

3 Improper valve clearance. This means that the valve is not closing completely and compression pressure is leaking past the valve. Check and adjust the valve clearances (Chapter 1).

4 Cylinder and/or piston worn. Excessive wear will cause compression pressure to leak past the rings. This is usually accompanied by worn rings as well. A top end overhaul is necessary (Chapter 2).

5 Piston rings worn, weak, broken, or sticking. Broken or sticking piston rings usually indicate a lubrication or carburetion problem that causes excess carbon deposits or seizures to form on the pistons and rings. Top end overhaul is necessary (Chapter 2).

6 Piston ring-to-groove clearance excessive. This is caused by excessive wear of the piston ring lands. Piston replacement is necessary (Chapter 2).

7 Cylinder head gasket damaged. If a head is allowed to become loose, or if excessive carbon build-up on the piston crown and combustion chamber causes extremely high compression, the head gasket may leak. Retorquing the head is not always sufficient to restore the seal, so gasket replacement is necessary (Chapter 2).

8 Cylinder head warped. This is caused by overheating or improperly tightened head nuts and bolts. Machine shop resurfacing or head replacement is necessary (Chapter 2).

9 Valve spring broken or weak. Caused by component failure or wear; the spring(s) must be replaced (Chapter 2).

10 Valve not seating properly. This is caused by a bent valve (from over-revving or improper valve adjustment), burned valve or seat (improper carburetion) or an accumulation of carbon deposits on the seat (from carburetion or lubrication problems). The valves must be cleaned and/or replaced and the seats serviced if possible (Chapter 2).

17 Knocking or pinging

1 Carbon build-up in combustion chamber. Use of a fuel additive that will dissolve the adhesive bonding the carbon particles to the crown and chamber is the easiest way to remove the build-up. Otherwise, the cylinder head will have to be removed and decarbonized (Chapter 2).

2 Incorrect or poor quality fuel. Old or improper grades of fuel can cause detonation. This causes the piston to rattle, thus the knocking or pinging sound. Drain old fuel and always use the recommended fuel grade.

3 Spark plug heat range incorrect. Uncontrolled detonation indicates the plug heat range is too hot. The plug in effect becomes a glow plug, raising cylinder temperatures. Install the proper heat range plug (Chapter 1).

4 Improper air/fuel mixture. This will cause the cylinder to run hot, which leads to detonation. Clogged jets or an air leak can cause this imbalance. See Chapter 3.

18 Miscellaneous causes

1 Throttle valve doesn't open fully. Adjust the cable slack (Chapter 1).

2 Clutch slipping. May be caused by improper adjustment or loose or worn clutch components. Refer to Chapter 1 for adjustment or Chapter 2 for clutch overhaul procedures.

3 Timing not advancing.

4 Engine oil viscosity too high. Using a heavier oil than the one recommended in Chapter 1 can damage the oil pump or lubrication system and cause drag on the engine.

5 Brakes dragging. Usually caused by debris which has entered the brake piston sealing boot, or from a warped drum (front brakes), warped disc (rear brakes) or bent axle. Repair as necessary.

Overheating

19 Engine overheats

1   Engine oil level low. Check and add oil (Chapter 1).
2   Wrong type of oil. If you're not sure what type of oil is in the engine, drain it and fill with the correct type (Chapter 1).
3   Air leak at carburetor intake joint. Check and tighten or replace as necessary (Chapter 3).
4   Fuel level low. Check and adjust if necessary (Chapter 3).
5   Worn oil pump or clogged oil passages. Replace pump or clean passages as necessary.
6   Clogged external oil line. Remove and check for foreign material (see Chapter 2).
7   Carbon build-up in combustion chambers. Use of a fuel additive that will dissolve the adhesive bonding the carbon particles to the piston crown and chambers is the easiest way to remove the build-up. Otherwise, the cylinder head will have to be removed and decarbonized (Chapter 2).
8   Operation in high ambient temperatures.

20 Firing incorrect

1   Spark plug fouled, defective or worn out. See Chapter 1 for spark plug maintenance.
2   Incorrect spark plug (see Chapter 1).
3   Faulty ignition coil(s) (Chapter 4).

21 Fuel/air mixture incorrect

1   Pilot screw out of adjustment (Chapter 3).
2   Main jet clogged. Dirt, water and other contaminants can clog the main jet. Clean the fuel tap strainer, the float bowl area and the jets and carburetor orifices (Chapter 3).
3   Main jet wrong size. The standard jetting is for sea level atmospheric pressure and oxygen content.
4   Air cleaner poorly sealed or missing.
5   Air cleaner-to-carburetor boot poorly sealed. Look for cracks, holes or loose clamps and replace or repair.
6   Fuel level too low. Check fuel level and float level and adjust or replace the float if necessary (Chapter 3).
7   Fuel tank air vent obstructed. Make sure that the air vent passage in the filler cap is open.
8   Carburetor intake manifold loose. Check for cracks or loose clamps or bolts. Check the carburetor-to-manifold gasket and the manifold-to-cylinder head O-ring Chapter 3).

22 Compression too high

1   Carbon build-up in combustion chamber. Use of a fuel additive that will dissolve the adhesive bonding the carbon particles to the piston crown and chamber is the easiest way to remove the build-up. Otherwise, the cylinder head will have to be removed and decarbonized (Chapter 2).
2   Improperly machined head surface or installation of incorrect gasket during engine assembly.

23 Engine load excessive

1   Clutch slipping. Can be caused by damaged, loose or worn clutch components. Refer to Chapter 2 for overhaul procedures.
2   Engine oil level too high. The addition of too much oil will cause pressurization of the crankcase and inefficient engine operation. Check

Specifications and drain to proper level (Chapter 1).
3   Engine oil viscosity too high. Using a heavier oil than the one recommended in Chapter 1 can damage the oil pump or lubrication system as well as cause drag on the engine.
4   Brakes dragging. Usually caused by debris which has entered the brake piston sealing boots (4WD front brakes), corroded wheel cylinders (4WD front brakes), sticking brake cam (2WD front or all rear brakes) or from a warped drum, warped disc or bent axle. Repair as necessary (Chapter 6).

24 Lubrication inadequate

1   Engine oil level too low. Friction caused by intermittent lack of lubrication or from oil that is overworked can cause overheating. The oil provides a definite cooling function in the engine. Check the oil level (Chapter 1).
2   Poor quality engine oil or incorrect viscosity or type. Oil is rated not only according to viscosity but also according to type. Some oils are not rated high enough for use in this engine. Check the Specifications section and change to the correct oil (Chapter 1).
3   Camshaft or journals worn. Excessive wear causing drop in oil pressure. Replace cam or cylinder head. Abnormal wear could be caused by oil starvation at high rpm from low oil level or improper viscosity or type of oil (Chapter 1).
4   Crankshaft and/or bearings worn. Same problems as paragraph 3. Check and replace crankshaft assembly if necessary (Chapter 2).

25 Miscellaneous causes

Modification to exhaust system. Most aftermarket exhaust systems cause the engine to run leaner, which makes it run hotter. When installing an aftermarket exhaust system, always rejet the carburetor.

Clutch problems

26 Clutch slipping

1   Secondary clutch friction plates worn or warped. Overhaul the secondary clutch assembly (Chapter 2).
2   Secondary clutch metal plates worn or warped (Chapter 2).
3   Secondary clutch spring(s) broken or weak. Old or heat-damaged spring(s) (from slipping clutch) should be replaced with new ones (Chapter 2).
4   Secondary clutch release mechanism defective. Replace any defective parts (Chapter 2).
5   Secondary clutch boss or housing unevenly worn. This causes improper engagement of the plates. Replace the damaged or worn parts (Chapter 2).
6   Primary (centrifugal) clutch weight linings or drum worn (Chapter 2).

27 Clutch not disengaging completely

1   Secondary clutch improperly adjusted (see Chapter 1).
2   Secondary clutch plates warped or damaged. This will cause clutch drag, which in turn will cause the machine to creep. Overhaul the clutch assembly (Chapter 2).
3   Sagged or broken secondary clutch spring(s). Check and replace the spring(s) (Chapter 2).
4   Engine oil deteriorated. Old, thin, worn out oil will not provide proper lubrication for the discs, causing the secondary clutch to drag. Replace the oil and filter (Chapter 1).
5   Engine oil viscosity too high. Using a thicker oil than recommended in Chapter 1 can cause the secondary clutch plates to

stick together, putting a drag on the engine. Change to the correct viscosity oil (Chapter 1).

6 Secondary clutch housing seized on shaft. Lack of lubrication, severe wear or damage can cause the housing to seize on the shaft. Overhaul of the clutch, and perhaps transmission, may be necessary to repair the damage (Chapter 2).

7 Secondary clutch release mechanism defective. Worn or damaged release mechanism parts can stick and fail to apply force to the pressure plate. Overhaul the release mechanism (Chapter 2).

8 Loose secondary clutch center nut. Causes housing and center misalignment putting a drag on the engine. Engagement adjustment continually varies. Overhaul the clutch assembly (Chapter 2).

9 Weak or broken primary clutch springs (Chapter 2).

Gear shifting problems

28 Doesn't go into gear or lever doesn't return

1 Clutch not disengaging. See Section 27.

2 Shift fork(s) bent or seized. May be caused by lack of lubrication. Overhaul the transmission (Chapter 2).

3 Gear(s) stuck on shaft. Most often caused by a lack of lubrication or excessive wear in transmission bearings and bushings. Overhaul the transmission (Chapter 2).

4 Shift drum binding. Caused by lubrication failure or excessive wear. Replace the drum and bearing (Chapter 2).

5 Shift lever return spring weak or broken (Chapter 2).

6 Shift lever broken. Splines stripped out of lever or shaft, caused by allowing the lever to get loose. Replace necessary parts (Chapter 2).

7 Shift mechanism pawl broken or worn. Full engagement and rotary movement of shift drum results. Replace shaft assembly (Chapter 2).

8 Pawl spring broken. Allows pawl to float, causing sporadic shift operation. Replace spring (Chapter 2).

29 Jumps out of gear

1 Shift fork(s) worn. Overhaul the transmission (Chapter 2).

2 Gear groove(s) worn. Overhaul the transmission (Chapter 2).

3 Gear dogs or dog slots worn or damaged. The gears should be inspected and replaced. No attempt should be made to service the worn parts.

30 Overshifts

1 Pawl spring weak or broken (Chapter 2).

2 Shift cam stopper lever not functioning (Chapter 2).

Abnormal engine noise

31 Knocking or pinging

1 Carbon build-up in combustion chamber. Use of a fuel additive that will dissolve the adhesive bonding the carbon particles to the piston crown and chamber is the easiest way to remove the build-up. Otherwise, the cylinder head will have to be removed and decarbonized (Chapter 2).

2 Incorrect or poor quality fuel. Old or improper fuel can cause detonation. This causes the pistons to rattle, thus the knocking or pinging sound. Drain the old fuel (Chapter 3) and always use the recommended grade fuel (Chapter 1).

3 Spark plug heat range incorrect. Uncontrolled detonation indicates that the plug heat range is too hot. The plug in effect becomes a glow plug, raising cylinder temperatures. Install the proper heat range plug (Chapter 1).

4 Improper air/fuel mixture. This will cause the cylinder to run hot and lead to detonation. Clogged jets or an air leak can cause this imbalance. See Chapter 3.

32 Piston slap or rattling

1 Cylinder-to-piston clearance excessive. Caused by improper assembly. Inspect and overhaul top end parts (Chapter 2).

2 Connecting rod bent. Caused by over-revving, trying to start a badly flooded engine or from ingesting a foreign object into the combustion chamber. Replace the damaged parts (Chapter 2).

3 Piston pin or piston pin bore worn or seized from wear or lack of lubrication. Replace damaged parts (Chapter 2).

4 Piston ring(s) worn, broken or sticking. Overhaul the top end (Chapter 2).

5 Piston seizure damage. Usually from lack of lubrication or overheating. Replace the pistons and bore the cylinder, as necessary (Chapter 2).

6 Connecting rod upper or lower end clearance excessive. Caused by excessive wear or lack of lubrication. Replace worn parts.

33 Valve noise

1 Incorrect valve clearances. Adjust the clearances by referring to Chapter 1.

2 Valve spring broken or weak. Check and replace weak valve springs (Chapter 2).

3 Camshaft or cylinder head worn or damaged. Lack of lubrication at high rpm is usually the cause of damage. Insufficient oil or failure to change the oil at the recommended intervals are the chief causes.

34 Other noise

1 Cylinder head gasket leaking.

2 Exhaust pipe leaking at cylinder head connection. Caused by improper fit of pipe, damaged gasket or loose exhaust flange. All exhaust fasteners should be tightened evenly and carefully. Failure to do this will lead to a leak.

3 Crankshaft runout excessive. Caused by a bent crankshaft (from over-revving) or damage from an upper cylinder component failure.

4 Engine mounting bolts or nuts loose. Tighten all engine mounting bolts and nuts to the specified torque (Chapter 2).

5 Crankshaft bearings worn (Chapter 2).

6 Camshaft chain tensioner defective. Replace according to the procedure in Chapter 2.

7 Camshaft chain, sprockets or guides worn (Chapter 2).

Abnormal driveline noise

35 Clutch noise

1 Secondary clutch housing/friction plate clearance excessive (Chapter 2).

2 Loose or damaged secondary clutch pressure plate and/or bolts (Chapter 2).

3 Broken primary clutch springs (Chapter 2).

36 Transmission noise

1   Bearings worn. Also includes the possibility that the shafts are worn. Overhaul the transmission (Chapter 2).
2   Gears worn or chipped (Chapter 2).
3   Metal chips jammed in gear teeth. Probably pieces from a broken gear or shift mechanism that were picked up by the gears. This will cause early bearing failure (Chapter 2).
4   Engine oil level too low. Causes a howl from transmission. Also affects engine power and clutch operation (Chapter 1).

37 Transfer case noise

1   Bearings worn. Also includes the possibility that the shafts are worn. Have the transfer case overhauled (Chapter 6).
2   Gears worn or chipped (Chapter 6).
3   Metal chips jammed in gear teeth. This will cause early bearing failure (Chapter 6).
4   Engine oil level too low. Causes a howl from transmission. Also affects engine power and clutch operation (Chapter 1).

38 Final drive noise

1   Final drive oil level low (Chapter 1).
2   Final drive gear lash out of adjustment. Checking and adjustment require special tools and skills and should be done by a Yamaha dealer.
3   Final drive gears damaged or worn. Overhaul requires special tools and skills and should be done by a Yamaha dealer.

Abnormal chassis noise

39 Suspension noise

1   Spring weak or broken. Makes a clicking or scraping sound.
2   Steering shaft bearings worn or damaged. Clicks when braking. Check and replace as necessary (Chapter 5).
3   Shock absorber fluid level incorrect. Indicates a leak caused by defective seal. Shock will be covered with oil. Replace shock (Chapter 5).
4   Defective shock absorber with internal damage. This is in the body of the shock and can't be remedied. The shock must be replaced with a new one (Chapter 5).
5   Bent or damaged shock body. Replace the shock with a new one (Chapter 5).

40 Driveaxle noise (4WD models)

1   Worn or damaged outer joint. Makes clicking noise in turns. Check for cut or damaged seals and repair as necessary (see Chapter 5).
2   Worn or damaged inner joint. Makes knock or clunk when accelerating after coasting. Check for cut or damaged seals and repair as necessary (see Chapter 5).

41 Brake noise

1   Brake linings worn or contaminated. Can cause scraping or

squealing. Replace the shoes (front) or pads (rear) (Chapter 6).
2   Brake linings warped or worn unevenly. Can cause chattering. Replace the linings (Chapter 6).
3   Brake drum out of round or disc warped. Can cause chattering. Replace brake drum or disc (Chapter 6).
7   Loose or worn knuckle or rear axle bearings. Check and replace as needed (Chapter 5).

Oil temperature indicator light comes on

42 Engine lubrication system

1   High oil temperature due to operation in high ambient temperatures. Shut the engine off and let it cool.
2   Engine oil level low. Inspect for leak or other problem causing low oil level and add recommended oil (Chapters 1 and 2).

43 Electrical system

1   Oil temperature sensor defective. Check the sensor according to the procedure in Chapter 8. Replace it if it's defective.
2   Oil temperature indicator light circuit defective. Check for pinched, shorted, disconnected or damaged wiring (Chapter 8).
3   Oil temperature thermistor defective. Check according to the procedure in Chapter 8. Replace it if it's defective.

Excessive exhaust smoke

44 White smoke

1   Piston oil ring worn. The ring may be broken or damaged, causing oil from the crankcase to be pulled past the piston into the combustion chamber. Replace the rings with new ones (Chapter 2).
2   Cylinders worn, cracked, or scored. Caused by overheating or oil starvation. If worn or scored, the cylinders will have to be rebored and new pistons installed. If cracked, the cylinder block will have to be replaced (see Chapter 2).
3   Valve oil seal damaged or worn. Replace oil seals with new ones (Chapter 2).
4   Valve guide worn. Perform a complete valve job (Chapter 2).
5   Engine oil level too high, which causes the oil to be forced past the rings. Drain oil to the proper level (Chapter 1).
6   Head gasket broken between oil return and cylinder. Causes oil to be pulled into the combustion chamber. Replace the head gasket and check the head for warpage (Chapter 2).
7   Abnormal crankcase pressurization, which forces oil past the rings. Clogged breather or hoses usually the cause (Chapter 2).

45 Black smoke

1   Air cleaner clogged. Clean or replace the element (Chapter 1).
2   Main jet too large or loose. Compare the jet size to the Specifications (Chapter 3).
3   Choke stuck, causing fuel to be pulled through choke circuit (Chapter 3).
4   Fuel level too high. Check the fuel level and float level and adjust if necessary (Chapter 3).
5   Inlet needle held off needle seat. Clean the float chamber and fuel line and replace the needle and seat if necessary (Chapter 3).

46 Brown smoke

1   Main jet too small or clogged. Lean condition caused by wrong size main jet or by a restricted orifice. Clean float chamber and jets and compare jet size to Specifications (Chapter 3).
2   Fuel flow insufficient. Fuel inlet needle valve stuck closed due to chemical reaction with old fuel. Float level incorrect; check and replace float if necessary. Restricted fuel line. Clean line and float chamber.
3   Carburetor intake tube loose (Chapter 3).
4   Air cleaner poorly sealed or not installed (Chapter 1).

Poor handling or stability

47 Handlebar hard to turn

1   Steering shaft nut too tight (Chapter 5).
2   Lower bearing or upper bushing damaged. Roughness can be felt as the bars are turned from side-to-side. Replace bearing and bushing (Chapter 5).
3   Steering shaft bearing lubrication inadequate. Causes are grease getting hard from age or being washed out by high pressure car washes. Remove steering shaft and replace bearing (Chapter 5).
4   Steering shaft bent. Caused by a collision, hitting a pothole or by rolling the machine. Replace damaged part. Don't try to straighten the steering shaft (Chapter 5).
5   Front tire air pressure too low (Chapter 1).

48 Handlebar shakes or vibrates excessively

1   Tires worn or out of balance (Chapter 1 or 6).
2   Swingarm bearings worn. Replace worn bearings by referring to Chapter 6.
3   Wheel rim(s) warped or damaged. Inspect wheels (Chapter 6).
4   Wheel bearings worn. Worn front or rear wheel bearings can cause poor tracking. Worn front bearings will cause wobble (Chapter 6).
5   Wheel hubs installed incorrectly (Chapter 5 or Chapter 6).
6   Handlebar clamp bolts or bracket nuts loose (Chapter 5).
7   Steering shaft nut or bolts loose. Tighten them to the specified torque (Chapter 5).
8   Motor mount bolts loose. Will cause excessive vibration with increased engine rpm (Chapter 2).

49 Handlebar pulls to one side

1   Uneven tire pressures (Chapter 1).
2   Frame bent. Definitely suspect this if the machine has been rolled. May or may not be accompanied by cracking near the bend. Replace the frame (Chapter 5).
3   Wheel out of alignment. Caused by incorrect toe-in adjustment (Chapter 1) or bent tie-rod (Chapter 5).
4   Swingarm bent or twisted. Caused by age (metal fatigue) or impact damage. Replace the swingarm (Chapter 5).
5   Steering shaft bent. Caused by impact damage or by rolling the vehicle. Replace the steering stem (Chapter 5).

50 Poor shock absorbing qualities

1   Too hard:
a)   Shock internal damage.
b)   Tire pressure too high (Chapters 1 and 6).

2   Too soft:
a)   Shock oil insufficient and/or leaking (Chapter 5).
d)   Fork springs weak or broken (Chapter 5).

Braking problems

51 Front brakes are spongy, don't hold

1   Air in brake line (4WD). Caused by inattention to master cylinder fluid level or by leakage. Locate problem and bleed brakes (Chapter 6).
2   Linings worn (Chapters 1 and 6).
3   Brake fluid leak (4WD). See paragraph 1.
4   Contaminated linings. Caused by contamination with oil, grease, brake fluid, etc. Clean or replace linings. Clean drum thoroughly with brake cleaner (Chapter 6).
5   Brake fluid deteriorated (4WD). Fluid is old or contaminated. Drain system, replenish with new fluid and bleed the system (Chapter 6).
6   Master cylinder internal parts worn or damaged causing fluid to bypass (4WD) (Chapter 6).
7   Master cylinder bore scratched by foreign material or broken spring (4WD). Repair or replace master cylinder (Chapter 6).
8   Drum warped. Replace drum (Chapter 6).

52 Brake lever or pedal pulsates

1   Axle bent. Replace axle (Chapter 5).
2   Wheel warped or otherwise damaged (Chapter 6).
3   Hub or axle bearings damaged or worn (Chapter 6).
4   Brake drum out of round (front) or disc warped (rear). Replace brake drum or disc (Chapter 6).

53 Brakes drag

1   Master cylinder piston seized (4WD). Caused by wear or damage to piston or cylinder bore (Chapter 6).
2   Lever balky or stuck. Check pivot and lubricate (Chapter 6).
3   Wheel cylinder piston seized in bore (4WD). Caused by wear or ingestion of dirt past deteriorated seal (Chapter 6).
4   Front brake shoes or rear brake pads damaged. Lining material separated from shoes or pads. Usually caused by faulty manufacturing process or from contact with chemicals. Replace shoes or pads (Chapter 6).
5   Shoes or pads improperly installed (Chapter 6).
6   Rear brake pedal or lever free play insufficient (Chapter 1).
7   Front brake springs weak (2WD). Replace brake springs (Chapter 6).

Electrical problems

54 Battery dead or weak

1   Battery faulty. Caused by sulfated plates which are shorted through sedimentation or low electrolyte level. Also, broken battery terminal making only occasional contact (Chapter 8).
2   Battery cables making poor contact (Chapter 8).
3   Load excessive. Caused by addition of high wattage lights or other electrical accessories.
4   Ignition switch defective. Switch either grounds/earths internally

or fails to shut off system. Replace the switch (Chapter 8).

5   Regulator/rectifier defective (Chapter 8).

6   Stator coil open or shorted (Chapter 8).

7   Wiring faulty. Wiring grounded or connections loose in ignition, charging or lighting circuits (Chapter 8).

55 Battery overcharged

1   Regulator/rectifier defective. Overcharging is noticed when battery gets excessively warm or boils over (Chapter 8).

2   Battery defective. Replace battery with a new one (Chapter 8).

3   Battery amperage too low, wrong type or size. Install manufacturer's specified amp-hour battery to handle charging load (Chapter 8).

Chapter 1
Tune-up and routine maintenance

Contents

Specifications

Engine

Compression pressure (at sea level)
Standard	850 kPa (121 psi)
Maximum	900 kPa (128 psi)
Minimum	800 kPa (114 psi)

Spark plug
Type
YFM350ER, YFM350FW .... NGK D8EA or ND X24ES-U
YFM350U, YFM350FWB
US models .... NGK D8EA or ND X24ES-U
Canadian models .... NGK DR8EA
Gap .... 0.6 to 0.7 mm (0.024 to 0.028 in)
Engine idle speed
YFM350ER
1987 .... 1450 to 1550 rpm
1988-on .... 1350 to 1450 rpm
YFM350FW .... 1350 to 1450 rpm
YFM350U
1996 through 1998 models .... 1350 to 1450 rpm
1999 models .... 1450 to 1550 rpm
YFM350FWB .... 1450 to 1550 rpm
Valve clearance (COLD engine)
Intake .... 0.06 to 0.10 mm (0.002 to 0.004 inch)
Exhaust .... 0.16 to 0.20 mm (0.006 to 0.008 inch)
Battery specific gravity .... 1.280 at 20-degrees C (68-degrees F)

Miscellaneous

Front brake shoe lining thickness (drum brakes)
    New .... 4 mm (5/32 inch)
    Limit
        YFM350ER models .... 2 mm (5/64 inch)
        YFM350FW, YFM350U, YFM350FWB models .... 1 mm (3/64 inch)
Front brake pad lining thickness (disc brakes)
    New .... 4.5 mm (3/16 inch)
    Limit .... 1 mm (3/64 inch)
Rear brake pad lining thickness (disc brake)
    New .... 8 mm (5/16 inch)
    Limit .... 2 mm (5/64 inch)
Rear brake shoe lining thickness (drum brake)
    New .... 4 mm (5/32 inch)
    Limit
        YFM350FW, YFM350FWB .... 2 mm (5/64 inch)
        YFM350U .... 1 mm (3/64 inch)
Front brake lever freeplay
    YFM350ER (at pivot)
        1987 through 1989 .... 5 to 8 mm (13/64 to 5/16 inch)
        1990 on .... 3 to 5 mm (1/8 to 13/64 inch)
    YFM350FW (at lever tip)
        1987 through 1993 .... 3 to 5 mm (1/8 to 13/64 inch)
        1994 on .... 4 to 8 mm (5/32 to 5/16 inch)
    YFM350U, YFM350FWB (at lever tip)
        1996 through 1998 models .... 2 to 5 mm (5/64 to 13/64 inch)
        1999 models .... Not applicable
Rear brake pedal freeplay .... 20 to 30 mm (51/64 to 1-13/64 inch)
Rear brake pedal height .... 5 mm (13/64 inch) below top of footpeg
Rear brake lever freeplay
    YFM350ER (at lever pivot) .... 10 mm (25/64 inch) minimum
    YFM350FW (at lever pivot)
        1987 through 1996 .... 4 to 5 mm (5/32 to 13/64 inch)
        1997 .... 4 to 8 mm (5/32 to 5/16 inch)
    YFM350U, YFM350FWB .... 4 to 8 mm (5/32 to 5/16 inch)
Rear brake pin and slot gap .... 0 to 1 mm (0 to 3/64 inch)
Throttle lever freeplay .... 3 to 5 mm (1/8 to 13/64 inch)
Choke freeplay .... Not adjustable
Speed limiter screw standard length .... 12 mm (15/32 inch)
Minimum tire tread depth .... 3 mm (1/8 inch)
Tire pressures (cold)
    1987 and 1988 (YFM350ER and YFM350FW, front and rear tires)
        Standard .... 2.8 psi
        Maximum .... 3.2 psi
        Minimum .... 2.4 psi
    1989 and later YFM350ER models
        Front tires
            Standard .... 4.2 psi
            Maximum .... 4.6 psi
            Minimum .... 3.8 psi
        Rear tires
            Standard .... 2.8 psi
            Maximum .... 3.2 psi
            Minimum .... 2.4 psi
    1989 through 1993 YFM350FW models (front and rear tires)
        Standard .... 2.9 psi
        Maximum .... 3.3 psi
        Minimum .... 2.5 psi
    1994 and later YFM350FW models
        Front tires
            Standard .... 2.9 psi
            Maximum .... 3.3 psi
            Minimum .... 2.5 psi
        Rear tires
            Standard .... 3.6 psi
            Maximum .... 4.0 psi
            Minimum .... 3.2 psi

YFM350U models (front and rear tires)

    1996 through 1998 .... 2.5 to 3.3 psi

    1999 .... 3.2 to 4.0 psi

YFM350FWB models (front and rear)

    1997 and 1998 .... 3.1 to 4.0 psi

    1999 .... 3.2 to 4.0 psi

Front wheel toe-in

    YFM350ER models .... 0 to 10 mm (0 to 25/64 inch)

    YFM350FW models .... 5 to 15 mm (13/64 to 19/32 inch)

    YFM350U models .... 5 to 15 mm (13/64 to 19/32 inch)

    YFM350FWB models .... 0 to 10 mm (0 to 25/64 inch)

Torque specifications

Oil drain plug .... 32 Nm (23 ft-lbs)

Oil filter cover bolts .... 10 Nm (84 in-lbs) (1)

Oil gallery plug .... 7 Nm (60 in-lbs)

Clutch adjusting screw locknut .... 15 Nm (132 in-lbs)

Valve adjuster cover bolts

    YFM350ER, YFM350FW, 1996 through 1998 YFM350U .... 10 Nm (84 in-lbs)

    YFM350FWB and 1999 YFM350U models .... 18 Nm (156 in-lbs)

Valve adjusting screw locknuts .... 20 Nm (168 in-lbs)

Spark plug

    YFM350ER, YFM350FW, 1996 through 1998 YFM350U .... 17.5 Nm (210 in-lbs)

    YFM350FWB and 1999 YFM350U models .... 18 Nm (156 in-lbs)

Front differential filler plug .... 12 Nm (144 in-lbs)

Front differential drain plug(s)

    YFM350FW

        Front plug .... 23 Nm (17 ft-lbs)

        Rear plug .... 15 Nm (132 in-lbs)

    YFM350FWB .... 12 Nm (105 in-lbs)

Final drive unit filler and drain plugs .... 23 Nm (17 ft-lbs)

Transfer case filler plug .... 23 Nm (17 ft-lbs)

Transfer case drain plug .... 20 Nm (168 in-lbs)

Tie-rod locknuts .... 30 Nm (22 ft-lbs)

Recommended lubricants and fluids

Engine/transmission oil

    Type .... API grade SE, SF or SG multigrade oil

    Viscosity

        32-degrees F (0-degrees C) or above 20W40

        10-degrees F (-10-degrees C) or above 10W30

        32-degrees F(0-degrees C) or below 5W30

    Capacity

    YFM350ER

        After oil/filter change .... 2.5 liters (2.6 US qt, 2.2 Imp qt)

        After engine overhaul .... 3.2 liters (3.2 liters (3.4 US qt, 2.8 Imp qt)

    YFM350FW (including transfer case) (2)

        After oil/filter change .... 2.8 liters (2.6 US qt, 2.2. Imp qt)

        After engine overhaul .... 3.7 liters (3.9 US qt, 3.3 Imp qt)

    YFM350U

        1996 through 1998

            After oil/filter change .... 2.8 liters (3.0 US qt, 2.5 Imp qt)

            After engine overhaul .... 3.2 liters (3.4 US qt, 2.8 Imp qt)

        1999

            After oil/filter change .... 3.0 liters (3.2 US qt, 2.6 Imp qt)

            After engine overhaul .... 3.5 liters (3.7 US qt, 3.1 Imp qt)

    YFM350FWB

        After oil/filter change .... 3.0 liters (3.2 US qt, 2.6 Imp qt)

        After engine overhaul .... 3.5 liters (3.7 US qt, 3.1 Imp qt)

Differential oil

    Type .... Hypoid gear oil

    Viscosity .... SAE 80

    Capacity

    YFM350ER

        Oil change .... 90 cc (3.0 US fl oz)

        After overhaul .... 100 cc (3.4 US fl oz)

    YFM350FW (rear differential)

        Oil change .... 90 cc (3.0 US fl oz)

        After overhaul .... 100 cc (3.4 US fl oz)

1

Recommended lubricants and fluids (continued)

Differential oil
    Capacity
        YFM350FW (front differential)

Oil change	190 cc (6.4 US fl oz)
After overhaul	200 cc (6.8 US fl oz)

        YFM350U, YFM350FWB (rear differential)

Oil change	190 cc (6.4 US fl oz)
After overhaul	250 cc (8.5 US fl oz)

        YFM350FWB (rear differential)

Oil change	180 cc (6.0 US fl oz)
After overhaul	200 cc (6.8 US fl oz)
Brake fluid..	DOT 3 or DOT 4

Miscellaneous

Wheel bearings...	Medium weight, lithium-based multi-purpose grease (NLGI no. 3)
Swingarm pivot...	Medium weight, lithium-based multi-purpose grease (NLGI no. 3)
Cables and lever pivots	Chain and cable lubricant or 10W30 motor oil
Brake pedal/shift pedal/throttle lever pivots..............................	Chain and cable lubricant or 10W30 motor oil

(1)   On YFM350ER and YFM350FW models, apply non-hardening gasket sealant to the bolt threads. On 1996 through 1998 YFM350U models, apply non-permanent thread locking agent to the upper bolt only.

(2)   Of this total, add 300 cc (10.2 US fl oz) to the transfer case plug on the left side of the transfer case. Add the rest through the crankcase filler plug.

1 Yamaha YFM350 Routine maintenance intervals

Note: *The pre-ride inspection outlined in the owner's manual covers checks and maintenance that should be carried out on a daily basis. It's condensed and included here to remind you of its importance. Always perform the pre-ride inspection at every maintenance interval (in addition to the procedures listed). The intervals listed below are the shortest intervals recommended by the manufacturer for each particular operation during the model years covered in this manual. Your owner's manual may have different intervals for your model.*

Daily or before riding

Check the engine oil level (including transfer case oil on 4WD models)

Check the fuel level and inspect for leaks

Check the operation of both brakes - check the front brake fluid level and look for leakage (4WD models); check the front brake lever (2WD models), rear brake pedal and lever (all models) for correct freeplay

Check the tires for damage, the presence of foreign objects and correct air pressure

Check the rear final drive (and front differential on 4WD models) for visible oil leaks

Check the throttle for smooth operation and correct freeplay

Make sure the steering operates smoothly

Check for proper operation of the headlight, tail light, brake light (if equipped) and indicator lights

Make sure the engine kill switch works properly

Check the driveaxle boots for damage or deterioration (4WD models)

Check the air cleaner drain tube and clean it if necessary

Check all fasteners, including wheel nuts and axle nuts, for tightness

Check the underbody for mud or debris that could start a fire or interfere with vehicle operation

Make sure any cargo is properly loaded and securely fastened

Every 20 to 40 operating hours

Clean the air filter element (1)
Clean the air cleaner housing drain tube (2)

Every 6 months

Perform all of the daily checks plus:

Check and adjust the valve clearances

Check the cleanliness of the fuel system and the condition of the fuel line

Clean the fuel tap strainer screen

Check/adjust the idle speed

Check/adjust the throttle lever freeplay

Check choke operation

Change the engine oil and oil filter; clean the oil strainer

Inspect the suspension

Clean and gap the spark plug

Check/adjust the drive select system freeplay

Check the skid plates for looseness or damage

Adjust the clutch

Check the exhaust system for leaks and check fastener tightness

Inspect the wheels and tires

Check the wheel bearings for looseness or damage

Inspect the steering system and steering shaft bearing

Lubricate the steering knuckle shafts, suspension arm pivots and steering shaft bearing (2WD models)

Once a year

Check the brake shoes for wear
Change the final drive oil and front differential oil
Check the driveaxle boots (4WD models)

Every two years

Overhaul the brake master and wheel cylinders (4WD models)

Every four years

Replace the brake fluid hoses (4WD models) (2)

(1) More often in dusty or wet conditions.
(2) Or whenever cracks or damage are visible.

1

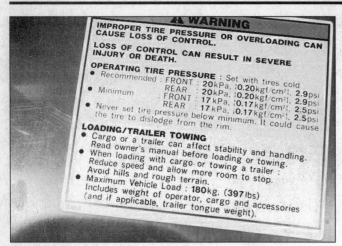

2.1a Decals on the vehicle include maintenance information such as tire pressures . . .

2.1b . . . and safety information

2 Introduction to tune-up and routine maintenance

Refer to illustrations 2.1a and 2.1b

This Chapter covers in detail the checks and procedures necessary for the tune-up and routine maintenance of your vehicle. Section 1 includes the routine maintenance schedule, which is designed to keep the machine in proper running condition and prevent possible problems. The remaining Sections contain detailed procedures for carrying out the items listed on the maintenance schedule, as well as additional maintenance information designed to increase reliability. Maintenance information is also printed on decals, which are mounted in various locations on the vehicle **(see illustrations)**. Where information on the decals differs from that presented in this Chapter, use the decal information.

Since routine maintenance plays such an important role in the safe and efficient operation of your vehicle, it is presented here as a comprehensive check list. For the rider who does all his own maintenance, these lists outline the procedures and checks that should be done on a routine basis.

Deciding where to start or plug into the routine maintenance schedule depends on several factors. If you have a vehicle whose warranty has recently expired, and if it has been maintained according to the warranty standards, you may want to pick-up routine maintenance as it coincides with the next mileage or calendar interval. If you have owned the machine for some time but have never performed any maintenance on it, then you may want to start at the nearest interval and include some additional procedures to ensure that nothing important is overlooked. If you have just had a major engine overhaul, then you may

want to start the maintenance routine from the beginning. If you have a used machine and have no knowledge of its history or maintenance record, you may desire to combine all the checks into one large service initially and then settle into the maintenance schedule prescribed.

The Sections which actually outline the inspection and maintenance procedures are written as step-by-step comprehensive guides to the actual performance of the work. They explain in detail each of the routine inspections and maintenance procedures on the check list. References to additional information in applicable Chapters is also included and should not be overlooked.

Before beginning any actual maintenance or repair, the machine should be cleaned thoroughly, especially around the oil filter housing, spark plug, cylinder head covers, side covers, carburetor, etc. Cleaning will help ensure that dirt does not contaminate the engine and will allow you to detect wear and damage that could otherwise easily go unnoticed.

3 Fluid levels - check

Engine/transfer case oil

Refer to illustrations 3.4a and 3.4b

1   The engine and transfer case on YFM350FW models share a common oil supply, which is checked through the crankcase filler plug/dipstick. No other models have a separate transfer case.

2   Support the vehicle in a level position, then start the engine and allow it to reach normal operating temperature. **Caution:** *Do not run the engine in an enclosed space such as a garage or shop.*

3.4a Unscrew the oil filler cap . . .

3.4b . . . and pull out the dipstick; the engine oil level must be between the upper and lower marks on the dipstick

3.8 The brake fluid level must be above the Lower mark on the reservoir; remove the cover screws (arrows) to add fluid

3.16a On 4WD models, unscrew the filler plug (arrow) to check front differential oil level

3.16b On all models, unscrew the filler plug (arrow) to check rear differential oil level

3   Stop the engine and allow the machine to sit undisturbed in a level position for about five minutes.

4   With the engine off, unscrew the dipstick from the right side of the crankcase **(see illustration)**. Pull it out, wipe it off with a clean rag, and reinsert it (let the dipstick rest on the threads; don't screw it back in). Pull the dipstick out and check the oil level on the dipstick scale. The oil level should be between the upper and lower level marks on the scale **(see illustration)**.

5   If the level is below the Minimum mark, add oil through the dipstick hole. Add enough oil of the recommended grade and type to bring the level up to the Maximum mark. Do not overfill.

Brake fluid (hydraulic brakes)

Refer to illustration 3.8

6   In order to ensure the proper operation of the hydraulic front brakes (if equipped), the fluid lever in the master cylinder reservoir must be properly maintained.

7   With the vehicle supported in a level position, turn the handlebars until the top of the front brake master cylinder is as level as possible.

8   The fluid level is visible through the master cylinder reservoir. Make sure that the fluid level is above the Lower mark on the reservoir **(see illustration)**.

9   If the level is low, the fluid must be replenished. Before removing the master cylinder cap, place rags beneath the reservoir (to protect the paint from brake fluid spills) and remove all dust and dirt from the area around the cap.

10   Remove the cover screws, then lift off the cover, rubber diaphragm and float (if equipped). **Note:** *Don't operate the brake lever with the cover removed.*

11   Add new, clean brake fluid of the recommended type to bring the level above the Lower mark. Don't mix different brands of brake fluid in the reservoir, as they may not be compatible. Also, don't mix different specifications (DOT 3 with DOT 4).

12   Reinstall the float (if equipped), rubber diaphragm and cover. Tighten the cover screws securely, but don't overtighten and strip the threads.

13   Wipe any spilled fluid off the reservoir body.

14   If the brake fluid level was low, inspect the front or rear brake system for leaks.

Differential oil

Refer to illustrations 3.16a and 3.16b

15   Park the vehicle on a level surface.

16   Remove the differential filler cap **(see illustrations)**. Feel the oil level inside the differential; it should be up to the bottom of the filler threads.

17   Add oil if necessary of the type recommended in this Chapter's Specifications.

18   Reinstall the filler cap and tighten securely.

4.3 Battery electrolyte should be between the horizontal lines on the battery; disconnect the negative cable and remove the battery cover bolt (right arrows), then slide the retainer to the right to remove it

1

4   Battery electrolyte level/specific gravity - check

Refer to illustrations 4.3, 4.7, 4.13a and 4.13b

Warning: *Be extremely careful when handling or working around the battery. The electrolyte is very caustic and an explosive gas (hydrogen) is given off when the battery is charging.*

1   This procedure applies to batteries that have removable filler caps, which can be removed to add water to the battery. If the original equipment battery has been replaced by a sealed maintenance-free battery, the electrolyte can't be topped up.

2   If you're working on a 2WD model, remove the rear rack and fender (see Chapter 7).

3   The electrolyte level is visible through the translucent battery case - it should be between the Upper and Lower level marks **(see illustration)**.

4   Disconnect the negative cable and remove the battery retainer bolt **(see illustration 4.3)**. Slide the retainer to the right, lift the battery cover and disconnect the positive cable. **Warning:** *Always disconnect the negative cable first and reconnect it last to avoid sparks which could cause a battery explosion.*

5   If the electrolyte is low, remove the cell caps and fill each cell to the upper level mark with distilled water. Do not use tap water (except in an emergency) and do not overfill. The cell holes are quite small, so it may help to use a plastic squeeze bottle with a small spout to add the water. If the level is within the marks on the case, additional water is not necessary.

6   Next, check the specific gravity of the electrolyte in each cell with

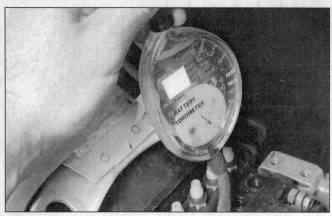

4.7 Check the specific gravity with a hydrometer

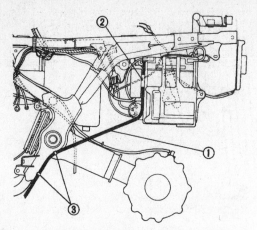

4.13a Be sure to route the battery vent tube correctly (this is a typical 2WD model) . . .

1 Vent tube   3 Clips
2 Bracket

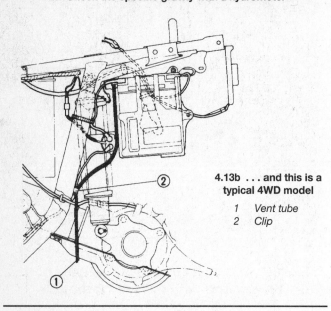

4.13b . . . and this is a typical 4WD model

1   Vent tube
2   Clip

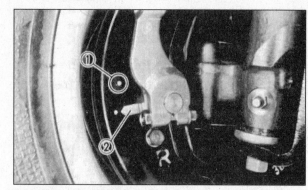

5.7 If the pointer (2) aligns with the mark (1) when the front brakes are applied, it's time to replace the front brake shoes

a small hydrometer made especially for motorcycle batteries. These are available from most dealer parts departments or motorcycle accessory stores.

7   Remove the caps, draw some electrolyte from the first cell into the hydrometer **(see illustration)**, then note the specific gravity. Compare the reading to the value listed in this Chapter's Specifications. **Note:** *Add 0.004 points to the reading for every 10-degrees F above 68-degrees F (20-degrees C) - subtract 0.004 points from the reading for every 10-degrees below 68-degrees F (20-degrees C).*

8   Return the electrolyte to the appropriate cell and repeat the check for the remaining cells. When the check is complete, rinse the hydrometer thoroughly with clean water.

9   If the specific gravity of the electrolyte in each cell is as specified, the battery is in good condition and is apparently being charged by the machine's charging system.

10   If the specific gravity is low, the battery is not fully charged. This may be due to corroded battery terminals, a dirty battery case, a malfunctioning charging system, or loose or corroded wiring connections. On the other hand, it may be that the battery is worn out, especially if the machine is old, or that infrequent use of the machine prevents normal charging from taking place.

11   Be sure to correct any problems and charge the battery if necessary. Refer to Chapter 8 for additional battery maintenance and charging procedures.

12   Install the battery cell caps, tightening them securely. Reconnect the cables to the battery, attaching the positive cable first and the negative cable last. Make sure to install the insulating boots over the terminals.

13   Install all components removed for access and route the battery vent tube correctly **(see illustrations)**. Be very careful not to pinch or otherwise restrict the tube, as the battery may build up enough internal pressure during normal charging system operation to explode.

14   If the vehicle will be stored for an extended time, fully charge the battery, then disconnect the negative cable before storage.

5   Brake system - general check

1   A routine general check of the brakes will ensure that any problems are discovered and remedied before the rider's safety is jeopardized.

2   Check the brake levers and pedal for loose connections, excessive play, bends, and other damage. Replace any damaged parts with new ones (see Chapter 8).

3   Make sure all brake fasteners are tight. Check the brake for wear as described below.

4   If you're working on a 4WD model, make sure the fluid level in the reservoir is correct (see Section 3). Look for leaks at the hose connections and check for cracks in the hoses. If the lever is spongy, bleed the brakes as described in Chapter 6.

5   Make sure the brake light (if equipped) operates when the front brake lever is depressed. The front brake light switch is not adjustable. If it fails to operate properly, replace it with a new one (see Chapter 8).

6   Operate the rear brake lever and pedal. If operation is rough or sticky, refer to Section 12 and lubricate the cables.

Front drum brakes

Refer to illustrations 5.7, 5.8a and 5.8b

7   If you're working on a YFM350ER model, apply the front brake (or

5.8a Remove the adjusting hole plug (arrow) from the brake drum

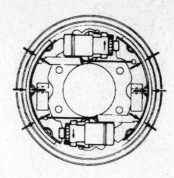

5.8b Measure the thickness of the brake lining material (arrows)

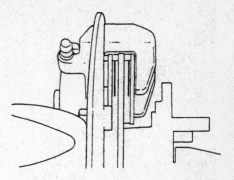

5.11 Replace the front brake pads if they're worn to or near the indicator lines

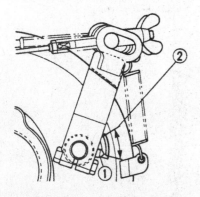

5.12 If the pointer (1) is at the wear limit (2), replace the brake shoes

6.1 Measure the freeplay of the 2WD front brake lever at the lever tip (a); loosen the pivot lockwheel (2) and turn the adjuster (1) to adjust freeplay

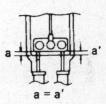

6.2a The gaps in the cable joint should be equal . . .

have an assistant do it) and look at the wear indicators (see illustration). If the pointer is at the wear limit line, refer to Chapter 6 and replace the front brake shoes.

8   Remove the adjusting hole plug from the brake drum (see illustration). Look through the hole to inspect the thickness of the lining material on the brake shoes (use a flashlight if necessary) (see illustration). If it's worn to near the limit listed in this Chapter's Specifications, refer to Chapter 6 and replace the brake shoes.

Rear disc brake

9   Look at the adjusting bolt on the rear brake (see Section 6). If the adjusting bolt is near the locknut with the rear brake properly adjusted, refer to Chapter 6 and replace the brake pads.

Front disc brakes

Refer to illustration 5.11

10   Raise the front of the vehicle and support it securely on jackstands. Remove the front wheels.

11   Look at the friction material on the brake pads (see illustration). If it's worn to or almost to the wear indicator lines, replace the pads (see Chapter 6). Replace all four pads, even if only one is worn.

Rear drum brake

Refer to illustration 5.12

12   A rear drum brake is used on 1996 and later models. To check the linings for wear, have an assistant hold down the pedal while you look at the wear indicator on the brake drum (see illustration). If the pointer is at the limit line (and the brakes are properly adjusted), replace the brake shoes (see Chapter 6).

6   Brake lever and pedal freeplay - check and adjustment

Front brake lever (drum brakes only)

YFM350ER models

Refer to illustrations 6.1, 6.2a and 6.2b

1   Loosen the locknut at the handlebar adjuster and turn the adjuster all the way in to get maximum cable slack (see illustration).

2   Follow the cable to the equalizer and make sure the joint is horizontal (see illustration). If not, locate the cable adjusters at the front wheels (see illustration). Turn them as needed to place the

6.2b . . . if not, turn the adjuster (1) at each front brake until they are

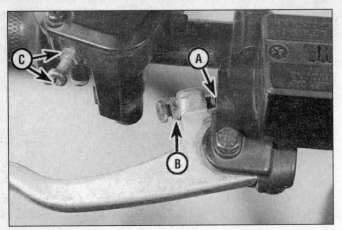

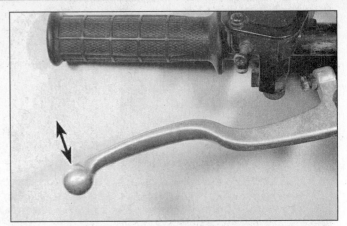

6.5a Squeeze the front brake lever until the adjusting screw just contacts the master cylinder piston . . .

   A   *Contact point of adjusting screw and master cylinder piston*
   B   *Adjusting screw locknut*
   C   *Speed limiter screw and locknut*

6.5b . . . at this point, measure how far the outer tip of the brake lever has traveled

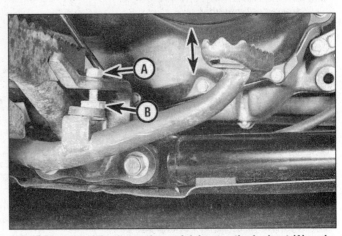

6.7 There's an adjuster on each wheel cylinder (later model shown, early model similar); turn the adjusters out, in the direction of the arrow cast on each wheel cylinder, to expand the shoes against the drum (brake drum removed for clarity)

   A   Adjusters   *B   Arrows*

6.11 Measure freeplay at the pedal; loosen the locknut (A) and turn the adjuster (B) to adjust it

equalizer joint in a horizontal position.

3   Jack up the front end of the vehicle and support it securely. Spin the front wheels by hand and make sure the brakes have a slight drag. If they don't, turn the adjusters at the wheel until they do, making sure the equalizer joint remains horizontal. Remove the jackstands and lower the vehicle.

4   Turn the cable adjuster at the handlebar until lever freeplay (measured at the pivot) is the amount listed in this Chapter's Specifications, then tighten the locknut.

YFM350FW, YFM350U and YFM350FWB models

Refer to illustrations 6.5a, 6.5b and 6.7

5   Operate the front brake lever and note the amount of play from rest until just before the adjuster touches the master cylinder piston **(see illustration)**. Measure play at the outer end of the lever **(see illustration)**. If it's not within the range listed in this Chapter's Specifications, loosen the locknut, turn the adjusting screw to obtain the correct freeplay, then tighten the locknut.

6   Jack up the front end of the vehicle and support it securely. Spin the front wheels by hand (you'll probably need an assistant to do this) and pull the front brake lever. Note the amount of travel required to lock

the wheels (measured at the tip of the lever). If it's not within the range listed in this Chapter's Specifications, adjust the front wheel cylinders.

7   To adjust the brakes, remove the adjusting hole plug **(see illustration 5.8a)**. There's an adjuster wheel at each wheel cylinder, located at the sides of the brake panel **(see illustration)**.

8   Insert a screwdriver through the adjusting hole and turn the adjuster wheel out (away from the center of the wheel) until the tire can't be turned by hand, then back it off three notches. Spin the tire by hand to make sure the brake lining isn't dragging on the drum; if it is, back off the adjuster just enough so the dragging stops. Then align the hole with the second adjuster wheel and repeat the adjustment.

9   Push the adjusting hole cap securely into its hole with a screwdriver.

10   Repeat the adjustment on the other front wheel, then remove the jackstands and lower the vehicle.

Rear disc brake

Refer to illustrations 6.11, 6.13, 6.14, 6.15 and 6.19

11   Check freeplay at the brake pedal **(see illustration)**. If it's not within the range listed in this Chapter's Specifications, loosen the locknut, turn the pedal adjuster to set correct freeplay and tighten the locknut.

12   After adjustment, operate the brake pedal two or three times.

13   Loosen the cable adjuster at the left handlebar all the way (to give maximum cable slack) **(see illustration)**.

14   Loosen the cable adjuster wing nuts at the rear wheel all the way **(see illustration)**.

15   Loosen the adjusting bolt locknut and back off the bolt **(see illustration)**. Tighten the lever cable adjuster (not the pedal rod/cable

6.13 Loosen the lockwheel (right arrow) and turn the adjuster (left arrow) to adjust freeplay of the rear brake lever

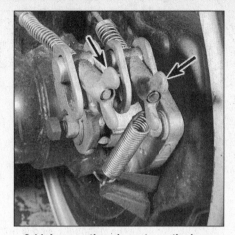

6.14 Loosen the wingnuts on the lever cable (right arrow) and pedal cable (left arrow)

6.15 Loosen the locknut and turn the adjusting bolt (A) to align the pointer with the cast indicator mark (B); if the adjusting bolt is almost to the locknut after adjustment, it's time to replace the rear brake pads

6.19 Adjust the gap (arrow) between the cable pin and its slot by turning the pedal cable wingnut

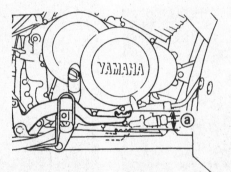

6.23 Set pedal height (a) by loosening the locknut and turning the adjuster

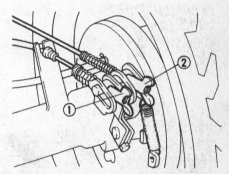

6.25 On rear drum brakes, the cable adjuster (1) is farthest from the wheel and the rod adjuster (2) is closest to it

adjuster) until the pointer lines up with the index mark on the caliper.

16   Carefully tighten the adjusting bolt until you feel resistance, then back it out 1/4 turn. Hold the adjusting bolt with a wrench and tighten the locknut with another wrench. **Note:** *If the adjusting bolt is close to the locknut after adjustment, it's time for new brake pads.*

17   If you're working on a 2WD model, securely block both front wheels so the vehicle can't roll. Jack up the rear and support it securely on jackstands. If you're working on a 4WD model, jack up both ends and support the vehicle securely.

18   Spin the rear wheels by hand to make sure the brake doesn't drag. If it does, repeat the adjustment.

19   Turn the pedal rod/cable adjuster to set the gap between the cable pin and the slot it rides in to the value listed in this Chapter's Specifications **(see illustration).**

20   Recheck to make sure the brake doesn't drag and repeat the adjustment as necessary.

21   Recheck pedal freeplay and adjust as necessary (Step 11). If you have to adjust it, recheck the gap between the pedal cable pin and its slot **(see illustration 6.19).**

22   At the handlebar, turn the cable adjuster to obtain the lever freeplay listed in this Chapter's Specifications **(see illustration 6.13).** Tighten the locknut.

Rear drum brake

Refer to illustrations 6.23, 6.25 and 6.27

23   If you're working on a 2wd model, check pedal height below the floorboard **(see illustration).** If it's not within the range listed in this Chapter's Specifications, loosen the locknut, turn the adjuster to set

the correct pedal height, then tighten the locknut **(see illustration 6.11).**

24   Press the brake pedal two or three times.

25   Loosen the wing nut on the brake cable (not the rod) all the way **(see illustration).**

26   Check freeplay at the brake pedal. If it's not within the range listed in this Chapter's Specifications, adjust it by turning the wingnut on the brake rod **(see illustration 6.25).**

27   Loosen the brake lever adjuster at the handlebar all the way **(see illustration 6.13).** Then turn the wingnut on the brake cable to set the gap between the cable pin and the slot it rides in to the value listed in this Chapter's Specifications **(see illustration).**

28   Finally, use the brake lever adjuster at the handlebar to set lever

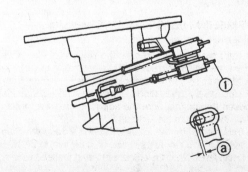

6.27 Set the gap (a) to specifications by turning the adjusting wing nut (1)

7.4 Check tire pressure with a gauge that will read accurately at the low pressures used in ATV tires

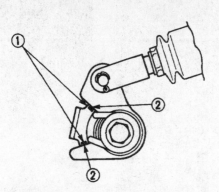

8.2 The match marks (1) should align with the edges of the outer lever (2) . . .

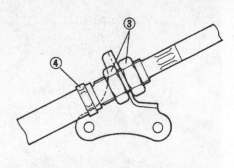

8.3 . . . if they don't, loosen the locknuts (3) and turn the cable adjuster (4)

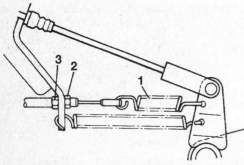

8.4a The spring attached to no. 2 cable should be just pulled tight, but not stretched, so there's no slack in the cable (on early models the spring is attached to the brake pedal below the brake rod) . . .

1	Spring	3	Cable adjusting nut
2	Cable locknut		

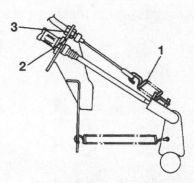

8.4b . . . and on later models it's attached to the pedal above the brake rod

1	Spring	3	Cable adjusting nut
2	Cable locknut		

freeplay (measured at the pivot gap) to the value listed in this Chapter's Specifications, then tighten the locknut.

29   After adjustment is complete, jack up up both ends of the vehicle and support it securely on jackstands. Turn the rear wheels by hand and make sure the brakes don't drag. If they do, repeat the adjustment.

7   Tires/wheels - general check

Refer to illustration 7.4

1   Routine tire and wheel checks should be made with the realization that your safety depends to a great extent on their condition.

2   Check the tires carefully for cuts, tears, embedded nails or other sharp objects and excessive wear. Operation of the vehicle with excessively worn tires is extremely hazardous, as traction and handling are directly affected. Measure the tread depth at the center of the tire and replace worn tires with new ones when the tread depth is less than that listed in this Chapter's Specifications.

3   Repair or replace punctured tires as soon as damage is noted. Do not try to patch a torn tire, as wheel balance and tire reliability may be impaired.

4   Check the tire pressures when the tires are cold and keep them properly inflated (**see illustration**). Proper air pressure will increase tire life and provide maximum stability and ride comfort. Keep in mind that low tire pressures may cause the tire to slip on the rim or come off, while high tire pressures will cause abnormal tread wear and unsafe handling.

5   The steel wheels used on this machine are virtually maintenance free, but they should be kept clean and checked periodically for cracks, bending and rust. Never attempt to repair damaged wheels; they must be replaced with new ones.

6   Check the valve stem locknuts to make sure they're tight. Also, make sure the valve stem cap is in place and tight. If it is missing, install a new one made of metal or hard plastic.

8   Shift linkage – check and adjustment

Caution: *Be sure the machine is at a complete stop with the throttle closed before making adjustments or transmission damage could occur.*

YFM350ER models

Refer to illustrations 8.2, 8.3, 8.4a and 8.4b

1   Press in the button on the side of the lever and move the lever to Low. Make sure the button returns to its out position.

2   If the match marks on the inner lever align with the edges of the outer lever, no adjustment is needed (**see illustration**). If they don't align, adjust the cable as described below.

3   Loosen the locknuts at the right side of the engine (**see illustration**). Turn the cable adjuster to align the match marks, then tighten the locknuts securely.

4   Inspect the spring attached to no. 2 cable (**see illustrations**). The spring should be pulled just tight enough to remove all slack, but not stretched. If not, loosen the locknut, turn the adjuster to achieve the correct amount of spring tension and tighten the locknut.

8.6a The spring (A) on later 4WD models is attached to the top of the brake pedal . . .

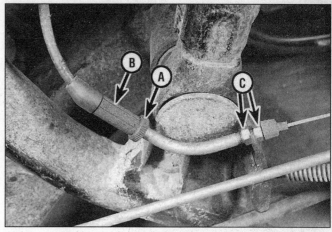

8.6b . . . make initial adjustments by loosening the lockwheel (A) and turning the adjuster (B); if further adjustment is necessary, loosen the cable locknuts (C) and reposition the cable

8.8a Remove the cotter pin and washer (arrow) and pull the clevis pin out of the cable and lever . . .

8.8b . . . if the holes in the pin and lever don't align perfectly, loosen the locknuts and reposition the cable until they do

YFM350FW models

Refer to illustrations 8.6a, 8.6b, 8.8a and 8.8b

5   Press in the button on the side of the lever and move the lever to Low. Make sure the button returns to its out position.

6   Inspect the spring attached to no. 2 cable **(see illustration 8.4a or the accompanying illustration)**. The spring should be pulled just tight enough to remove all slack, but not stretched. If not, loosen the locknut, turn the adjuster to achieve the correct amount of spring tension and tighten the locknut. If the adjuster doesn't provide the correct setting, loosen the locknuts on the cable bracket, reposition the cable as necessary and tighten the locknuts **(see illustrations)**.

7   Make sure the select lever can be shifted into Reverse only when the brake pedal is pressed. If Reverse can be selected when the pedal is not pressed (or when it's pressed only slightly and the rear brake is not actually operating), check the adjustment of the brake pedal and recheck the no. 2 cable adjustment.

8   Remove the cotter pin, washer and clevis pin from the end of no. 1 cable **(see illustration)**. The clevis pin holes in the cable and lever should align exactly. If they don't, loosen the locknuts on the cable **(see illustration)**, reposition the cable until the holes align exactly, then tighten the locknuts.

9   Slip the clevis pin through the holes. It should go easily. If it does, pull it back out, lubricate it lightly with silicone grease and reinstall it.

10   Secure the clevis pin with the washer and a new cotter pin.

11   Pull back the ends of the cable boot and lubricate the exposed areas of the cable with grease.

1996 through 1998 YFM350U models

Refer to illustrations 8.13, 8.14, 8.15, 8.17 and 8.18

12   The linkage includes a safety lockout that prevents the transmission from being shifted into Reverse unless the rear brake is engaged. Since the rear brake pedal must be pressed before the transmission can be shifted into Reverse, adjust the rear brakes before adjusting the shift linkage (see Section 6).

13   Make sure the vehicle is stopped and the throttle lever is in the

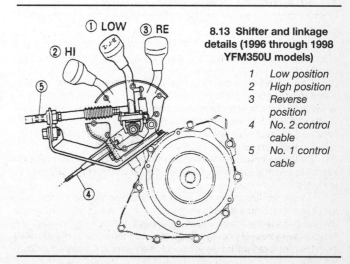

8.13 Shifter and linkage details (1996 through 1998 YFM350U models)

1   Low position
2   High position
3   Reverse position
4   No. 2 control cable
5   No. 1 control cable

① LOW   ③ RE
② HI

1

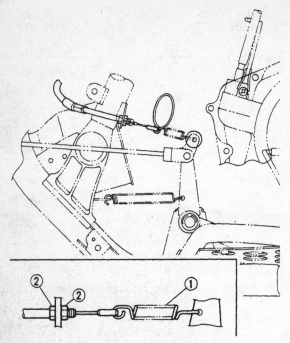

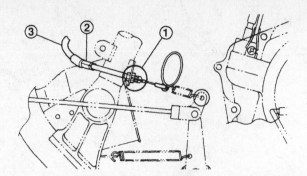

8.15 With the locknuts (2) tightened, adjust the control cable (3) with the adjuster (4)

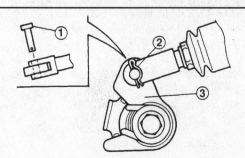

8.14 No. 2 control cable details (1996 through 1998 YFM350U models)

| 1 | Spring | 2 | Locknuts |

8.17 No. 1 control cable details (1996 through 1998 YFM350U models)

| 1 | Clevis pin | 2 | Clip | 3 | Shift arm |

closed position. Place the select lever in Low **(see illustration)**.

14   Check the adjustment of the no. 2 control cable **(see illustration)**. There should be no slack in the return spring, and there should be no freeplay in the cable. If necessary, reposition the cable locknuts to adjust it.

15   Try to shift into Reverse while pressing the brake pedal. With the rear brake not engaged (pedal pressed less than 1 to 1-1/4 inch), it should not be possible to shift into Reverse. With the rear brake engaged (pedal pressed 1 to 1-1/4-inch or more), it should be possible to shift into Reverse.

a) *If the select lever and brake pedal work as described, go on to Step 9.*

b) *If the select lever and brake pedal don't work as described, adjust the no. 2 control cable using the cable adjuster* **(see illustration)**.

16   Once the brake pedal and elect lever are working properly together, check to make sure the cable locknuts are tight.

17   Place the select lever in Low. Locate the end of the no. 1 control cable and remove its clip and clevis pin **(see illustration)**.

18   Check to see whether the clevis pin holes in the cable and shift arm are perfectly aligned. If they aren't, loosen the cable locknuts **(see**

illustration), then use the locknuts to reposition the cable until the holes align perfectly. Apply a light coat of silicone grease to the clevis pin, slip it through the holes and secure it with the clip.

19   Tighten the cable locknuts, making sure not to disturb the alignment of the clevis pin holes in the cable and shift arm.

20   Slide the dust boot along the control cable to expose one end of the cable, then lubricate it with silicone grease. Lubricate the other end of the cable in the same way.

1999 YFM350U and all YFM350FWB models

Refer to illustrations 8.21a, 8.21b, 8.22 and 8.23

21   Measure the length from the reverse control cable bracket to the center of the shift arm pin **(see illustration)**. If it's not within the range listed in this Chapter's Specifications, loosen the locknuts and reposition the cable, then tighten the locknuts **(see illustration)**.

22   There should be no slack in the reverse control cable. If there is, loosen the cable adjuster locknut, turn the adjuster to eliminate the

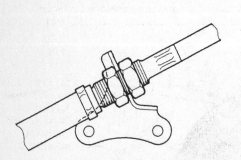

8.18 No. 1 control cable locknuts (1996 through 1998 YFM350U models)

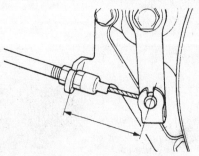

8.21a Measure the cable end length and adjust it if necessary . . .

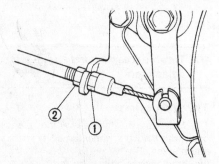

8.21b . . . by loosening the locknut (1) and turning the adjuster (2) . . .

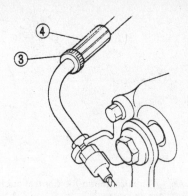

8.22 . . . eliminate cable slack by loosening the locknut (3) and turning the adjuster (4)

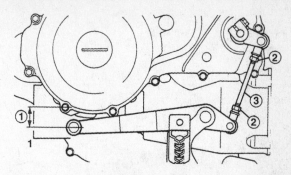

8.23 If pedal height (1) is incorrect, loosen the locknuts (2) and turn the shift pedal rod (3)

9.2 Loosen the locknut, then hold it with a wrench while you turn the adjusting screw

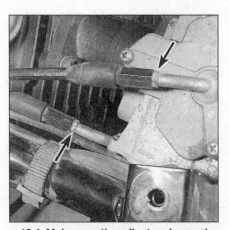

10.4 Make sure the adjusters (arrows) at the carburetor ends of the cables aren't loose

10.5 Loosen the lockwheel (right arrow) and turn the adjuster (left arrow) to adjust throttle freeplay

slack, then tighten the locknut (see illustration).
23   Measure the dimension from the shift pedal to the lower forward engine cover bolt (see illustration). If it's not within the range listed in this Chapter's Specifications, loosen the locknuts and turn the shift pedal rod to change the pedal height, then tighten the locknuts.

---

9   Clutch - check and freeplay adjustment

Refer to illustration 9.2
1   The clutch release mechanism on these models disengages the secondary clutch automatically when the shift lever is operated, so there is no clutch lever. If shifting gears becomes difficult, the clutch may be in need of adjustment.
2   Loosen the locknut on the right side of the engine. Carefully turn the adjusting screw counterclockwise (anti-clockwise) until you feel resistance, then turn it back in 1/8 turn while holding the locknut with a wrench (see illustration). Hold the screw in this position and tighten the locknut to the torque listed in this Chapter's Specifications.

---

10   Throttle freeplay and speed limiter - check and adjustment

Throttle check

1   Make sure the throttle lever moves easily from fully closed to fully open with the front wheel turned at various angles. The grip should return automatically from fully open to fully closed when released. If the throttle sticks, check the throttle cable for cracks or kinks in the housings. Also, make sure the inner cable is clean and well-lubricated.
2   Check for a small amount of freeplay at the lever and compare the freeplay to the value listed in this Chapter's Specifications.

Throttle adjustment

YFM350ER and YFM350FW models

Refer to illustrations 10.4 and 10.5
3   Before making adjustments, check and adjust idle speed (see Section 20).
4   Check the adjusters on the carburetor end of the throttle cables to make sure they're tightened securely (see illustration).
5   Freeplay adjustments can be made at the throttle lever end of the accelerator cable. Loosen the lockwheel on the cable (see illustration) and turn the adjuster until the desired freeplay is obtained, then retighten the lockwheel.

YFM350U and YFM350FWB models

Refer to illustration 10.7
6   Before making adjustments, check and adjust idle speed (see Section 20).
7   Make the initial adjustment at the carburetor end of the cable (see

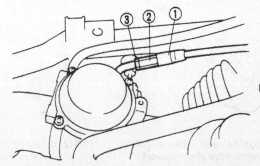

10.7 Pull back the boot (1), loosen the locknut (2) and turn the adjuster (3)

11.1 Slide the choke knob back and forth and check for smooth operation

A   *Choke knob*   B   *Fuel line*

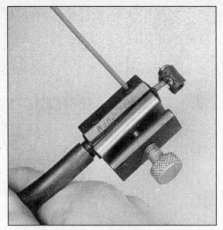

12.3 Lubricating a cable with a pressure lube adapter (make sure the tool seats around the inner cable)

13.6a Unscrew the oil drain plug and remove the O-ring, spring and strainer

illustration). Slide back the rubber boot, loosen the adjuster locknut and turn the adjuster. Once correct freeplay is obtained, tighten the locknut.

8   If correct freeplay can't be obtained at the carburetor end of the cable, make the adjustment at the handlebar end as described in Step 5.

Speed limiter adjustment

9   The speed limiter can be used to restrict maximum throttle opening **(see illustration 6.5a)**. Turning the screw all the way in reduces the maximum throttle opening; turning it out to the maximum length listed in this Chapter's Specifications allows maximum throttle opening.

10   To make adjustments, loosen the locknut, turn the screw in or out as necessary and tighten the locknut. Screw length is measured from the underside of the screw head to the throttle housing. Never turn the screw out farther than the maximum specified length.

11   Choke - operation check

Refer to illustration 11.1

1   Operate the choke knob or lever while you feel for smooth operation **(see illustration)**.

2   If the knob doesn't move smoothly, refer to Chapter 3 and remove the choke mechanism for inspection.

12   Lubrication - general

Refer to illustration 12.3

1   Since the controls, cables and various other components of a vehicle are exposed to the elements, they should be lubricated periodically to ensure safe and trouble-free operation.

2   The throttle and brake levers and brake pedal, should be lubricated frequently. In order for the lubricant to be applied where it will do the most good, the component should be disassembled. However, if chain and cable lubricant is being used, it can be applied to the pivot joint gaps and will usually work its way into the areas where friction occurs. If motor oil or light grease is being used, apply it sparingly as it may attract dirt (which could cause the controls to bind or wear at an accelerated rate). **Note:** *One of the best lubricants for the control lever pivots is a dry-film lubricant (available from many sources by different names).*

3   The throttle, brake and shift select cables should be removed and treated with a commercially available cable lubricant which is specially formulated for use on ATV control cables. Small adapters for pressure

lubricating the cables with spray can lubricants are available and ensure that the cable is lubricated along its entire length **(see illustration)**. When attaching the cable to the lever, be sure to lubricate the barrel-shaped fitting at the end with multi-purpose grease.

4   To lubricate the cables, disconnect them at the lower end, then lubricate the cable with a pressure lube adapter **(see illustration 12.3)**. See Section 8 (drive select cables), Chapter 3 (throttle cable) or Chapter 6 (brake cables).

5   Refer to Chapter 5 for the following lubrication procedures:
   a) *Swingarm bearing and dust seals*
   b) *Front driveaxle splines (4WD models)*
   c) *Rear driveshaft coupling spline*
   d) *Rear axle shaft splines*

6   Refer to Chapter 6 for brake pedal removal procedures.

13   Engine/transfer case oil/filter and differential oil - change

Engine/transfer case oil/filter

Refer to illustrations 13.6a, 13.6b, 13.7, 13.9a through 13.9e, 13.10, 13.11, 13.15a and 13.15b

1   The transfer case on YFM350FW models shares a common oil supply with the engine, but has a separate drain plug. All of the other models covered in this manual have only a single drain plug for the crankcase.

2   Consistent routine oil and filter changes are the single most important maintenance procedure you can perform on a vehicle. The oil not only lubricates the internal parts of the engine, transmission, clutch and 4WD transfer case, but it also acts as a coolant, a cleaner, a sealant, and a protectant. Because of these demands, the oil takes a terrific amount of abuse and should be replaced often with new oil of the recommended grade and type. Saving a little money on the difference in cost between a good oil and a cheap oil won't pay off if the engine is damaged.

3   Before changing the oil and filter, warm up the engine so the oil will drain easily. Be careful when draining the oil, as the exhaust pipe, the engine and the oil itself can cause severe burns.

4   Park the vehicle over a clean drain pan.

5   Remove the dipstick/oil filler cap to vent the crankcase and act as a reminder that there is no oil in the engine.

6   Next, remove the drain plug from the engine **(see illustrations)** and allow the oil to drain into the pan. The O-ring, spring and strainer will probably fall out as the plug is removed, so be careful not to lose them.

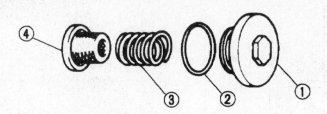

13.6b Engine oil drain plug details

1	Drain plug	3	Spring
2	O-ring	4	Strainer

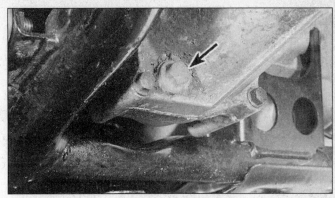

13.7 The transfer case drain plug (YFM350FW models only) is at the lower rear of the case (arrow)

13.9a Remove the filter outer cover bolts (arrows) and lift off the cover; the bolt on the left has a thinner head then the others

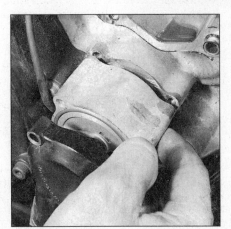

13.9b Pull off the inner cover and its O-rings . . .

13.9c . . . the open end of the inner cover faces the engine . . .

YFM350ER and YFM350FW models

7   As the oil is draining, remove the transfer case drain plug (YFM350FW models only) **(see illustration)**.

8   Remove the shift pedal (see Chapter 7).

9   Remove the oil filter cover bolts, then remove the outer cover, inner cover with O-rings and filter element **(see illustrations)**. If additional maintenance is planned for this time period, check or service another component while the oil is allowed to drain completely.

13.9d . . . and so does the open end of the filter element; be sure to install them facing the proper direction

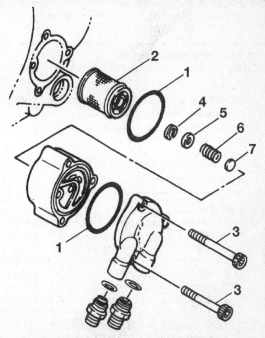

13.9e Oil filter details

1	O-rings	3	Cover bolts	6	Spring
2	Filter element	4	Snap-ring	7	Plug
		5	Washer		

13.10 If the snap-ring is loose, remove it and install a new one

13.11 Make sure the oil passage in the filter housing (arrow) is clear

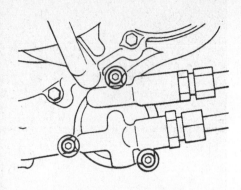

13.15a Oil filter cover bolts (YFM350FWB and 1999 YFM350U)

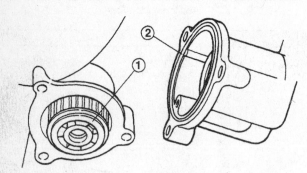

13.15b Remove the cover, pull out the filter (1) and remove the O-ring (2)

13.20 Loosen the oil gallery plug (arrow) slightly; oil should seep from the plug within one minute of idling the engine

10   Check the inside of the inner cover to make sure the snap-ring, washer, spring and plug are securely in position **(see illustration)**.

11   Wipe any remaining oil out of the filter housing area of the crankcase and make sure the oil passage is clear **(see illustration)**. Clean the oil strainer with solvent and let it dry completely.

12   Check the condition of the drain plug threads and the O-rings.

13   Install the filter element **(see illustrations 13.9c and 13.9d)**. **Caution:** *The filter must be installed facing the correct direction or oil starvation may cause severe engine damage.*

14   Install new O-rings on the inner filter cover **(see illustrations 13.9b and 13.9c)**. Install the covers. Apply gasket sealant to the threads of the outer cover bolts, install them and tighten them to the torque listed in this Chapter's Specifications.

YFM350U and YFM350FWB models

15   Remove the filter cover bolts **(see illustration)**. Take the filter cover off the engine. Note carefully which end of the filter faces outward and take it out of the engine **(see illustration)**.

16   Clean the filter housing and check its oil passage as described in Step 11 above.

17   Install the new filter in the engine, making sure it faces the correct direction. Install a new O-ring on the cover, then install it on the engine. Coat the filter housing bolts with gasket sealant and tighten them to the torque listed in this Chapter's Specifications.

All models

18   Install the oil strainer, spring and engine drain plug, using a new O-ring if the old one is worn or damaged. Tighten the plug to the torque listed in this Chapter's Specifications. Avoid overtightening, as damage to the engine case will result.

19   If you're working on a YFM350FW model, install the transfer case drain plug with a new sealing washer and tighten it to the torque listed in this Chapter's Specifications.

20   Before refilling the engine, check the old oil carefully. If the oil was drained into a clean pan, small pieces of metal or other material can be easily detected. If the oil is very metallic colored, then the engine is experiencing wear from break-in (new engine) or from insufficient lubrication. If there are flakes or chips of metal in the oil, then something is drastically wrong internally and the engine will have to be disassembled for inspection and repair.

21   If there are pieces of fiber-like material in the oil, the secondary clutch is experiencing excessive wear and should be checked.

22   If the inspection of the oil turns up nothing unusual, refill the crankcase and transfer case (YFM350FW) to the proper level with the recommended oil and install the dipstick/filler cap. Start the engine and let it run for two or three minutes. Shut it off, wait a few minutes, then check the oil level. If necessary, add more oil to bring the level up to the upper level mark on the dipstick. Check around the drain plug(s) and filter cover for leaks.

23   Loosen the oil gallery plug on the cylinder head slightly **(see illustration)**. Start the engine and let it idle. Oil should seep from the plug within one minute. If not, oil is not flowing properly. Shut the engine off and find out the problem before running it further.

24   The old oil drained from the engine cannot be reused in its present state and should be disposed of. Check with your local refuse disposal company, disposal facility or environmental agency to see whether they will accept the oil for recycling. Don't pour used oil into drains or onto the ground. After the oil has cooled, it can be drained into a suitable container (capped plastic jugs, topped bottles, milk cartons, etc.) for transport to one of these disposal sites.

13.26a The two drain plugs for the front differential (arrows) are accessible through the skid plate

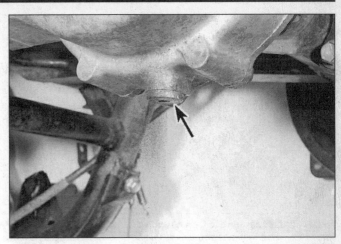

13.26b Unscrew the rear differential drain plug (arrow) and let the oil drain into a pan

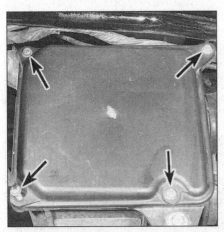

14.2 Remove the cover screws (arrows)

14.3 Detach the filter element from the housing and lift out the element and core

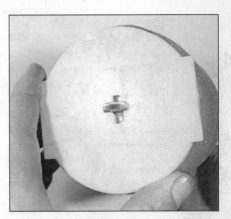

14.4a Turn the cover so the tab aligns with the slot and remove it; on assembly, make sure the tab aligns with the two arrows molded in the cover

Differential oil

Refer to illustrations 13.26a and 13.26b

25   Place a drain pan beneath the differential being drained.

26   Remove the oil filler plug, then the drain bolt and sealing washer **(see illustrations 3.16a, 3.16b and the accompanying illustrations)**. There are two drain plugs for the front differential. Let the oil drain for several minutes, until it stops dripping.

27   Clean the drain bolt and sealing washer. If the sealing washer is in good condition, it can be reused; otherwise, replace it.

28   Install the drain bolt and tighten it to the torque listed in this Chapter's Specifications.

29   Add oil of the type and amount listed in this Chapter's Specifications, then install the filler plug and tighten it to the torque listed in this Chapter's Specifications.

30   Refer to Step 21 to dispose of the drained oil.

14   Air cleaner - filter element and drain tube cleaning

Element cleaning

Refer to illustrations 14.2, 14.3, 14.4a and 14.4b

1   Remove the seat (see Chapter 7).

2   Remove the screws that secure the filter cover and lift it off **(see illustration)**.

3   Detach the element from the case and lift it out **(see illustration)**.

4   Compress the cap, rotate it 1/4 turn to align the slot with the tab

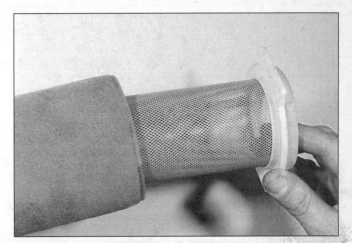

14.4b Separate the foam element from the metal core

and take the cap off **(see illustration)**. Pull the foam element off the metal core **(see illustration)**.

5   Clean the element and core in a high flash point solvent, squeeze the solvent out of the foam and let the core and element dry completely.

6   Soak the foam element in the amount and type of foam filter oil listed in this Chapter's Specifications, then squeeze it firmly to remove the excess oil. Don't wring it out or the foam may be damaged. The

14.10 Open the clip and pull the drain tube (arrow) off its fitting; if it's full of clean oil, like this one, the element may have been oversaturated

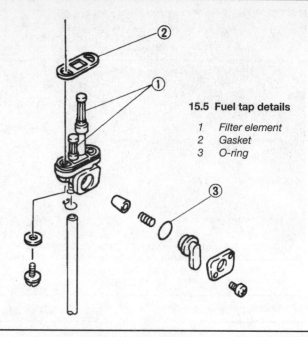

15.5 Fuel tap details

1   Filter element
2   Gasket
3   O-ring

element should be wet through with oil, but no oil should drip from it.

7   Place the element on the core.

8   Install the cap and rotate it 1/4 turn to lock it in position **(see illustration 14.4a)**.

9   Install the element in the case so its squared-off ends align with the slots in the case.

Drain tube cleaning

Refer to illustration 14.10

10   Check the drain tube for accumulated water and oil **(see illustration)**. If oil or water has built up in the tube, squeeze its clamp, remove it from the air cleaner housing and clean it out. Install the drain tube on the housing and secure it with the clamp. **Note:** *A drain tube that's full indicates the need to clean the filter element and the inside of the case.*

15   Fuel system - check and filter cleaning

Refer to illustrations 15.5 and 15.9

Warning: *Gasoline (petrol) is extremely flammable, so take extra precautions when you work on any part of the fuel system. Don't smoke or allow open flames or bare light bulbs near the work area, and don't work in a garage where a natural gas-type appliance (such as a water heater or clothes dryer) with a pilot light is present. Since gasoline is carcinogenic, wear latex gloves when there's a possibility of being exposed to fuel, and, if you spill any fuel on your skin, rinse it off immediately with soap and water. Mop up any spills immediately and do not store fuel-soaked rags where they could ignite. When you perform any kind of work on the fuel system, wear safety glasses and have a fire extinguisher suitable for a class B type fire (flammable liquids) on hand.*

1   Check the carburetor, fuel tank, the fuel tap and the line for leaks and evidence of damage **(see illustration 11.1)**.

2   If carburetor gaskets are leaking, the carburetor should be disassembled and rebuilt by referring to Chapter 3.

3   If the fuel tap is leaking, tightening the screws may help. If leakage persists, the tap should be disassembled and repaired or replaced with a new one.

4   If the fuel line is cracked or otherwise deteriorated, replace it with a new one.

5   Place the fuel tap lever in the Off position. Place a wrench on the hex at the bottom of the fuel tap and remove the cup, strainer and O-ring **(see illustration)**.

6   Clean the strainer with solvent and let it dry.

7   Installation is the reverse of the removal steps, with the following additions:

a) *Use a new gasket.*

b) *Hand-tighten the screws firmly, but don't overtighten or the gasket will be squashed, resulting in fuel leaks.*

8   After installation, run the engine and check for fuel leaks.

9   If the vehicle will be stored for a month or more, remove and drain the fuel tank. Also loosen the float chamber drain screw and drain the fuel from the carburetor **(see illustration)**.

16   Exhaust system - inspection

1   Periodically check the exhaust system for leaks and loose fasteners. If tightening the holder nuts at the cylinder head fails to stop any leaks, replace the gasket with a new one (a procedure which requires removal of the system).

2   The exhaust pipe flange nuts at the cylinder head are especially prone to loosening, which could cause damage to the head. Check them frequently and keep them tight.

15.9 If the vehicle will be stored more than a month, loosen the float chamber drain screw and drain the fuel through the drain hose

A   Float chamber drain screw
B   Throttle stop screw

17.2 Unscrew the plug with a spark plug socket

17 Spark plug - replacement

Refer to illustrations 17.2, 17.6a and 17.6b

1   This vehicle is equipped with a spark plug that has an 18 mm wrench hex.

2   Twist the spark plug cap to break it free from the plug, then pull it off. If available, use compressed air to blow any accumulated debris from around the spark plug. Remove the plug **(see illustration)**.

3   Inspect the electrodes for wear. Both the center and side electrodes should have square edges and the side electrode should be of uniform thickness. Look for excessive deposits and evidence of a cracked or chipped insulator around the center electrode. Compare your spark plug to the color spark plug reading chart on the inside of the back cover. Check the threads, the washer and the ceramic insulator body for cracks and other damage.

4   If the electrodes are not excessively worn, and if the deposits can be easily removed with a wire brush, the plug can be regapped and reused (if no cracks or chips are visible in the insulator). If in doubt concerning the condition of the plug, replace it with a new one, as the expense is minimal.

5   Cleaning the spark plug by sandblasting is permitted, provided you clean the plug with a high flash-point solvent afterwards.

6   Before installing a new plug, make sure it is the correct type and heat range. Check the gap between the electrodes, as it is not preset. For best results, use a wire-type gauge rather than a flat gauge to check the gap **(see illustration)**. If the gap must be adjusted, bend the side electrode only and be very careful not to chip or crack the insulator nose **(see illustration)**. Make sure the washer is in place before installing the plug.

7   Since the cylinder head is made of aluminum, which is soft and easily damaged, thread the plug into the head by hand. Slip a short length of hose over the end of the plug to use as a tool to thread it into place. The hose will grip the plug well enough to turn it, but will start to slip if the plug begins to cross-thread in the hole - this will prevent damaged threads and the accompanying repair costs.

8   Once the plug is finger tight, the job can be finished with a socket. If a torque wrench is available, tighten the spark plug to the torque listed in this Chapter's Specifications. If you do not have a torque wrench, tighten the plug finger tight (until the washer bottoms on the cylinder head) then use a spark plug socket to tighten it an additional 1/4 turn. Regardless of the method used, do not overtighten it.

9   Reconnect the spark plug cap.

18 Cylinder compression - check

Refer to illustration 18.5

1   Among other things, poor engine performance may be caused by leaking valves, incorrect valve clearances, a leaking head gasket, or a worn piston, rings and/or cylinder wall. A cylinder compression check will help pinpoint these conditions and can also indicate the presence of excessive carbon deposits in the cylinder head.

2   The only tools required are a compression gauge and a spark plug wrench. Depending on the outcome of the initial test, a squirt-type oil can may also be needed.

3   Check valve clearances and adjust if necessary (see Section 19). Start the engine and allow it to reach normal operating temperature, then remove the spark plug (see Section 17, if necessary). Work carefully - don't strip the spark plug hole threads and don't burn your hands.

4   Disable the ignition by disconnecting the primary (low tension) wires from the coil (see Chapter 4). Be sure to mark the locations of the wires before detaching them.

5   Install the compression gauge in the spark plug hole **(see illustration)**. Hold or block the throttle wide open.

6   Crank the engine over a minimum of four or five revolutions (or until the gauge reading stops increasing) and observe the initial

1

17.6a Spark plug manufacturers recommend using a wire type gauge when checking the gap - if the wire doesn't slide between the electrodes with a slight drag, adjustment is required

17.6b To change the gap, bend the side electrode only, as indicated by the arrows, and be very careful not to crack or chip the ceramic insulator surrounding the center electrode

18.5 A compression gauge with a threaded fitting for the spark plug hole is preferred over the type that requires hand pressure to maintain the seal

19.7a Remove the Allen bolts (arrows) and lift the adjusting hole cover off; the exhaust side (shown) has three bolts and the intake side cover has two . . .

19.7b . . . replace the cover O-ring if its condition is in doubt; the ridge inside the cover goes upward on installation

19.8 Remove the timing hole plug

19.9 Align the notch in the crankcase cover with the TDC line on the alternator rotor inside the hole - the TDC line has a T next to it (right arrow); the line next to the F mark (left arrow) is the advance timing mark, used to check ignition timing (cover removed for clarity)

movement of the compression gauge needle as well as the final total gauge reading. Compare the results to the value listed in this Chapter's Specifications.

7   If the compression built up quickly and evenly to the specified amount, you can assume the engine upper end is in reasonably good mechanical condition. Worn or sticking piston rings and a worn cylinder will produce very little initial movement of the gauge needle, but compression will tend to build up gradually as the engine spins over. Valve and valve seat leakage, or head gasket leakage, is indicated by low initial compression which does not tend to build up.

8   To further confirm your findings, add a small amount of engine oil to the cylinder by inserting the nozzle of a squirt-type oil can through the spark plug hole. The oil will tend to seal the piston rings if they are leaking.

9   If the compression increases significantly after the addition of the oil, the piston rings and/or cylinder are definitely worn. If the compression does not increase, the pressure is leaking past the valves or the head gasket. Leakage past the valves may be due to insufficient valve clearances, burned, warped or cracked valves or valve seats or valves that are hanging up in the guides.

10   If compression readings are considerably higher than specified, the combustion chamber is probably coated with excessive carbon deposits. It is possible (but not very likely) for carbon deposits to raise the compression enough to compensate for the effects of leakage past rings or valves. Refer to Chapter 2, remove the cylinder head and carefully decarbonize the combustion chamber.

19   Valve clearances - check and adjustment

Refer to illustrations 19.7a, 19.7b, 19.8, 19.9, 19.11 and 19.12

1   The engine must be cool to the touch for this maintenance procedure, so if possible let the machine sit overnight before beginning.

2   Refer to Chapter 7 and remove the seat.

3   If you're working on a 2WD model, remove the handlebar (see Chapter 5), the front cargo rack and the front fender (see Chapter 7).

4   Disconnect the cable from the negative terminal of the battery (see Section 4, if necessary).

5   Refer to Chapter 3 and remove the fuel tank.

6   Refer to Section 17 and remove the spark plug. This will make it easier to turn the engine.

7   Remove the valve adjusting hole covers (there's one on each side of the cylinder head **(see illustrations)**.

8   Remove the timing hole plug **(see illustration)**.

9   Position the piston at Top Dead Center (TDC) on the compression stroke. Do this by turning the crankshaft until the mark on the rotor is aligned with the timing notch on the crankcase **(see illustration)**. You should be able to wiggle both rocker arms - if not (if the exhaust valve

19.11 Measure valve clearance with a feeler gauge; to adjust it, loosen the locknut and turn the adjusting screw - the Yamaha special tool shown is convenient to use . . .

19.12 . . . but you can also use a box-end wrench on the locknut (left arrow) and an open-end wrench on the adjusting screw (right arrow)

is open), the engine is positioned at TDC on the exhaust stroke; turn the crankshaft one complete revolution and realign the marks.

10   With the engine in this position, both of the valves can be checked.

11   To check, insert a feeler gauge of the thickness listed in this Chapter's Specifications between the valve stem and rocker arm **(see illustration)**. Pull the feeler gauge out slowly - you should feel a slight drag. If there's no drag, the clearance is too loose. If there's a heavy drag, the clearance is too tight.

12   If the clearance is incorrect, loosen the adjuster locknut with a box-end wrench (ring spanner). Turn the adjusting screw with a wrench or special valve adjusting tool until the correct clearance is achieved, then tighten the locknut **(see illustration)**.

13   After adjusting, recheck the clearance with the feeler gauge to make sure it wasn't changed when the locknut was tightened.

14   Now measure the other valve, following the same procedure you used for the first valve. Make sure to use a feeler gauge of the specified thickness.

15   With both of the clearances within the Specifications, install the valve adjusting hole covers and timing hole plug. Use new O-rings on the covers and plug if the old ones are hardened, deteriorated or damaged.

16   Install all components removed for access.

20   Idle speed - check and adjustment

1   Before adjusting the idle speed, make sure the valve clearances and spark plug gap are correct. Also, turn the handlebars back-and-forth and see if the idle speed changes as this is done. If it does, the throttle cable may not be adjusted correctly, or it may be worn out. Be sure to correct this problem before proceeding.

2   The engine should be at normal operating temperature, which is usually reached after 10 to 15 minutes of stop and go riding. Make sure the transmission is in Neutral.

YFM350ER, YFM350FW and 1996 through 1998 YFM350U models

3   Turn the throttle stop screw **(see illustration 15.9)** until the idle speed listed in this Chapter's Specifications is obtained.

4   Snap the throttle open and shut a few times, then recheck the idle speed. If necessary, repeat the adjustment procedure.

5   If a smooth, steady idle can't be achieved, the fuel/air mixture may be incorrect. Refer to Chapter 3 for additional carburetor information.

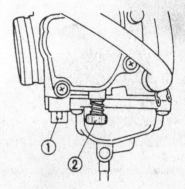

20.6 Pilot screw (1) and throttle stop screw (2) (YFM350FWB and 1999 YFM350U models)

1999 YFM350U and all YFM350FWB models

Refer to illustration 20.6

6   Turn the pilot screw clockwise until it seats lightly, then back it out the number of turns listed in this Chapter's Specifications **(see illustration)**. **Caution:** *Don't overtighten the screw or it will be damaged.*

7   Turn the throttle stop screw to obtain the specified idle speed.

21   Fasteners - check

1   Since vibration of the machine tends to loosen fasteners, all nuts, bolts, screws, etc. should be periodically checked for proper tightness. Also make sure all cotter pins or other safety fasteners are correctly installed.

2   Pay particular attention to the following:

Spark plug
Engine oil, transfer case and differential drain plugs
Oil filter cover bolts
Gearshift lever
Brake pedal
Footpegs
Engine mount bolts
Shock absorber mount bolts
Front axle nuts
Rear axle nuts
Skid plate bolts

3   If a torque wrench is available, use it along with the torque specifications at the beginning of this, or other, Chapters.

1

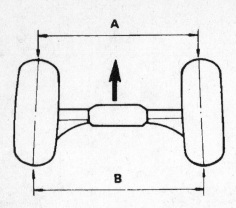

23.10 Toe-in measurement (B minus A = toe-in)

22   Suspension - check

1   The suspension components must be maintained in top operating condition to ensure rider safety. Loose, worn or damaged suspension parts decrease the vehicle's stability and control.
2   Lock the front brake and push on the handlebars to compress the front shock absorbers several times. See if they move up-and-down smoothly without binding. If binding is felt, the shocks should be inspected as described in Chapter 6.
3   Check the tightness of all front suspension nuts and bolts to be sure none have worked loose.
4   Inspect the rear shock absorber for fluid leakage and tightness of the mounting nuts and bolts. If leakage is found, the shock should be replaced.
5   Support the vehicle securely upright with its rear wheel off the ground. Grab the swingarm on each side, just ahead of the axle. Rock the swingarm from side to side - there should be no discernible movement at the rear. If there's a little movement or a slight clicking can be heard, make sure the swingarm pivot shaft is tight. If the pivot shaft is tight but movement is still noticeable, the swingarm will have to be removed and the bearings replaced as described in Chapter 5.
6   Inspect the tightness of the rear suspension nuts and bolts.

23   Steering system - inspection and toe-in adjustment

Inspection

1   This vehicle is equipped with a ball bearing (4WD) or bushings (2WD) at the lower end of the steering shaft and plastic bushings at the upper end. These can become dented, rough or loose during normal use of the machine. In extreme cases, worn or loose parts can cause steering wobble that is potentially dangerous.
2   To check, block the rear wheels so the vehicle can't roll, jack up the front end and support it securely on jackstands.
3   Point the wheel straight ahead and slowly move the handlebar from side-to-side. Dents or roughness in the bearing or bushing will be felt and the bars will not move smoothly. **Note:** *Make sure any hesitation in movement is not being caused by the cables and wiring harnesses that run to the handlebar.*
4   If the handlebar doesn't move smoothly, or if it moves horizontally, refer to Chapter 5 to remove and inspect the steering shaft bushing and bearing.
5   Look at the tie-rod ends (inner and outer) while slowly turning the

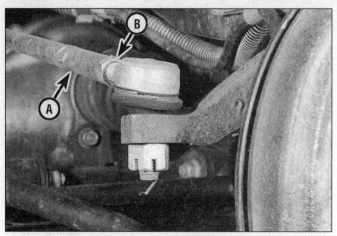

23.11a Hold and turn the tie-rod by placing an open-end wrench on the flats (A); loosen the locknuts (B) at the outer end . . .

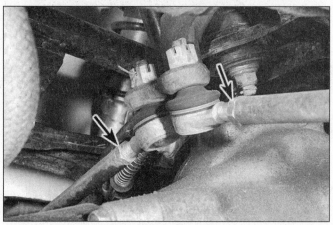

23.11b . . . and at the inner end (arrows) so the tie-rod can be turned

handlebar from side-to-side. If there's any vertical movement in the tie-rod ball-joints, refer to Chapter 5 and replace them.

Toe-in adjustment

Refer to illustrations 23.10, 23.11a and 23.11b
6   Roll the vehicle forward onto a level surface and stop it with the front wheels pointing straight ahead.
7   Make a mark at the front and center of each tire, even with the centerline of the front hub.
8   Measure the distance between the marks with a toe-in gauge or steel tape measure.
9   Have an assistant push the vehicle backward while you watch the marks on the tires. Stop pushing when the tires have rotated exactly one-half turn, so the marks are at the backs of the tires.
10   Again, measure the distance between the marks. Subtract the front measurement from the rear measurement to get toe-in **(see illustration)**.
11   If toe-in is not as specified in this Chapter's Specifications, hold each tie-rod with a wrench on the flats and loosen the locknuts **(see illustrations)**. Turn the tie-rods an equal amount to change toe-in. When toe-in is set correctly, tighten the locknuts to the torque listed in this Chapter's Specifications.

Chapter 2
Engine, clutch and transmission

Contents

Specifications

2

YFM350ER, YFM350FW and 1996 through 1998 YFM350U models

General
Bore	83 mm (3.268 inches)
Stroke	64.5 mm (2.539 inches)
Displacement	348 cc

Rocker arms
Rocker arm inside diameter	
Standard	12.000 to 12.018 mm (0.4724 to 0.4731 inch)
Limit	12.078 mm (0.4755 inch)
Rocker shaft outside diameter	
Standard	11.981 to 11.991 mm (0.4717 to 0.4721 inch)
Limit	11.951 mm (0.4705 inch)
Shaft-to-arm clearance	
Standard	0.009 to 0.037 mm (0.0004 to 0.0015 inch)
Limit	0.08 mm (0.0032 inch)

Camshaft
Lobe height	
Intake	
Standard	40.29 to 40.39 mm (1.586 to 1.590 inches)
Limit	40.26 mm (1.585 inches)
Exhaust	
Standard	40.28 to 40.38 mm (1.586 to 1.590 inches)
Limit	40.25 mm (1.585 inches)
Camshaft runout limit	0.03 mm (0.012 inch)

YFM350ER, YFM350FW and 1996 through 1998 YFM350U models (continued)

Cylinder head, valves and valve springs

Cylinder head warpage limit	0.03 mm 0.0012 inch)
Valve stem runout	0.02 mm (0.0008 inch)
Valve stem diameter	
Intake	
Standard	6.975 to 6.990 mm (0.2746 to 0.2752 inch)
Limit	6.95 mm (0.274 inch)
Exhaust	
Standard	6.955 to 6.970 mm (0.2738 to 0.2744 inch)
Limit	6.915 mm (0.2722 inch)
Valve guide inside diameter	
Standard	7.000 to 7.012 mm (0.2756 to 0.2761 inch)
Limit	7.03 mm (0.277 inch)
Stem-to-guide clearance	
Intake	
Standard	0.010 to 0.037 mm (0.0004 to 0.0015 inch)
Limit	0.08 mm (0.0031 inch)
Exhaust	
Standard	0.030 to 0.057 mm (0.0012 to 0.0022 inch)
Limit	0.02 mm (0.0008 inch)
Valve seat width	
Standard	1.0 to 1.2 mm (0.039 to 0.047 inch)
Limit	1.6 mm (0.063 inch)
Valve spring free length	
Inner spring	
Standard	39.9 mm (1.57 inch)
Limit	37.9 mm (1.49 inch)
Outer spring	
Standard	43.27 mm (1.70 inch)
Limit	41.27 mm (1.62 inch)
Valve spring bend limit	1.6 mm (0.063 inch)

Cylinder

Bore diameter	82.97 to 83.02 mm (3.267 to 3.268 inches)
Out-of-round limit	0.01 mm (0.0004 inch)
Taper limit	not specified
Measuring point	40 mm (1.57 inches) from top of bore

Piston

Diameter	82.92 to 82.97 mm (3.265 to 3.267 inches)
Measuring point	5.5 mm (7/32 inch) from bottom of skirt
Piston-to-cylinder clearance	0.04 to 0.06 mm (0.0016 to 0.0024 inches)
Oversize pistons and rings	
First oversize	83.50 mm (3.287 inches)
Second oversize	84.00 mm (3.307 inches)
Piston pin bore	Not specified
Piston pin outer diameter	Not specified
Piston pin-to-piston clearance	Not specified
Ring side clearance	
Top	
Standard	0.04 to 0.08 mm (0.0016 to 0.0031 inch)
Limit	0.12 mm (0.0047 inch)
Second	
Standard	0.03 to 0.07 mm (0.0012 to 0.0028 inch)
Limit	0.12 mm (0.0047 inch)
Ring end gap	
Top	
Standard	0.2 to 0.4 mm (0.008 to 0.016 inch)
Limit	0.5 mm (0.02 inch)
Second	
Standard	0.2 to 0.4 mm (0.008 to 0.016 inch)
Limit	0.5 mm (0.02 inch)
Oil	
Standard	0.3 to 0.9 mm (0.012 to 0.035 inch)
Limit	not specified

Primary (centrifugal) clutch
Weight lining thickness
    Standard .... 2.0 mm (0.08 inch)
    Limit .... 1.5 mm (0.06 inch)
Clutch weight spring free length............................... 31.1 mm (1.22 inches)

Secondary clutch
Spring free length
    Standard.. 47.8 mm (1.88 inches)
    Limit
        All except 1990 and later 2WD model) .... 45.8 mm (1.80 inches)
        1990 and later 2WD models .... 46.5 mm (1.831 inches)
Metal plate thickness
    Nominal 2.0 mm plates .... 1.9 to 2.1 mm (0.059 to 0.067 inch)
    Nominal 1.6 mm plates .... 1.5 to 1.7 mm (0.059 to 0.067 inch)
Friction plate thickness
    Standard.. 2.94 to 3.06 mm (0.116 to 0.120 inch)
    Limit.. 2.8 mm (0.110 inch)
Friction and metal plate warpage limit .... 0.20 mm (0.008 inch)
Cushion spring height.. 3.15 to 3.45 mm (0.12 to 0.14 inch)

Oil pump
Outer rotor-to-body clearance .... 0.04 to 0.09 mm (0.0016 to 0.0035 inch)
Inner-to-outer rotor clearance
    Standard.. 0.15 mm (0.006 inch) or less
    Limit.. 0.20 mm (0.008 inch)

Transmission
Main axle and driveaxle runout limit .... 0.08 mm (0.0031 inch)

Crankshaft and connecting rod
Runout limit
    At sprocket (left) end .... 0.02 mm (0.0008 inch)
    At right end .... 0.06 mm (0.0024 inch)
Assembly width .... 58.95 to 59.00 mm (2.321 to 2.323 inches)
Connecting rod big-end side clearance
    Standard.. 0.35 to 0.85 mm (0.014 to 0.033 inch)
    Limit.. 0.90 mm (0.035 inch)
Connecting rod small-end endplay
    Standard.. 0.8 to 1.0 mm (0.03 to 0.04 inch)
    Limit.. 2.0 mm (0.08 inch)

Torque specifications
Cylinder head Allen bolts... 20 Nm (168 in-lbs) (1)
Cylinder head bolts.. 40 Nm (29 ft-lbs) (1)
Cylinder base Allen bolt .... 10 Nm (84 in-lbs)
Cam sprocket cover Allen bolts .... 10 Nm (84 in-lbs)
Oil check bolt .... 7 Nm (61 inch-lbs)
Camshaft bearing retainer bolts .... 8 Nm (70 inch-lbs)
Cam chain guide bolts... 10 Nm (84 in-lbs) (2)
Camshaft sprocket bolt .... 60 Nm (43 ft-lbs)
Cam chain tensioner body bolts .... 10 Nm (84 in-lbs)
Cam chain tensioner cap bolt .... 23 Nm (184 in-lbs)
Crankcase bolts... 10 Nm (84 in-lbs)
Crankcase cover bolts .... 10 Nm (84 in-lbs)
Main axle bearing retainer screws .... 10 Nm (84 in-lbs) (3)
Balancer shaft bearing retainer screws .... 7 Nm (61 inch-lbs) (3)
Shift cam segment screw .... 12 Nm (108 in-lbs) (3)
Oil pump screws.. 7 Nm (61 inch-lbs)
Clutch boss nut .... 80 Nm (58 ft-lbs) (1)
Clutch spring plate bolts.. 8 Nm (70 inch-lbs)
Primary clutch nut.. 78 Nm (56 ft-lbs) (1)
Balancer shaft and driven gear nut............................ 60 Nm (43 ft-lbs) (1)
Middle driveaxle bearing retainer screws .... 25 Nm (18 ft-lbs) (4)
Middle driveaxle pinion gear nut .... 120 Nm (85 ft-lbs) (5)
Middle driven shaft bearing housing bolts .... 25 Nm (18 ft-lbs)

2

YFM350ER, YFM350FW and 1996 through 1998 YFM350U models (continued)

Torque specifications (continued)

Oil cooler hose nuts... 35 Nm (25 ft-lbs)
Oil cooler hose retainer screw .... 7 Nm (61 inch-lbs)

1 *Apply engine oil to the threads.*
2 *Use a new lockwasher.*
3 *Apply non-permanent thread locking agent to the screws.*
4 *Stake the screws after tightening.*
5 *Stake the nut after tightening.*

YFM350FWB and 1999 YFM350U models

Note: *The following section contains only the specifications that are unique to these models. If a specification isn't listed, use the specification for YFM350ER, YFM350FW and 1996 through 1998 YFM350U models, listed earlier in this table.*

Top ring side clearance
    Standard .... 0.03 to 0.09 mm (0.001 to 0.004 inch)
Primary clutch spring free length... 42.5 mm (1.67 inch)
Secondary clutch spring free length
    Standard .... 40.1 mm (1.58 inch)
    Limit .... 38 mm (1.50 inch)

Torque specifications

Crankcase bolts
    M6 .... 10 Nm (84 in-lbs)
    M8 .... 26 Nm (19 ft-lbs)
Crankcase bearing retainer screws .... 8 Nm (70 in-lbs) (3)
Crankcase cover bearing retainer Torx screws .... 10 Nm (84 in-lbs) (3)
Oil pump screws .... 8 Nm (70 in-lbs)
Clutch boss nut .... 90 Nm (65 ft-lbs)
Clutch pressure plate spring bolts... 8 Nm (70in-lbs)
Primary clutch nut.. 140 Nm (100 ft-lbs) (5)
Middle drive shaft bearing housing bolts .... 32 Nm (23 ft-lbs)
Middle drive shaft bearing retainer Torx screws .... 25 Nm (18 ft-lbs) (3)

1   General information

The engine/transmission unit is of the air-cooled, single-cylinder four-stroke design. The two valves are operated by an overhead camshaft which is chain driven off the crankshaft. The engine/transmission assembly is constructed from aluminum alloy. The crankcase is divided vertically.

The crankcase incorporates a wet sump, pressure-fed lubrication system which uses a gear-driven rotor-type oil pump, an oil filter and separate strainer screen and an oil temperature warning switch.

Power from the crankshaft is routed to the transmission via two clutches. The primary (centrifugal) clutch, which engages as engine speed is increased, connects the crankshaft to the secondary clutch, which is of the wet, multi-plate type. The secondary clutch transmits power to the transmission; it's engaged and disengaged automatically when the shift lever is moved from one gear position to another. The transmission has five forward gears and one reverse gear. YFM350ER, YFM350FW and 1996 through 1998 models have a low range (for a total of ten forward speeds).

2   Operations possible with the engine in the frame

The components and assemblies listed below can be removed without having to remove the engine from the frame. If, however, a number of areas require attention at the same time, removal of the engine is recommended.

Recoil starter (if equipped)
Starter motor
Starter reduction gears
Starter clutch

Alternator rotor and stator
Primary and secondary clutches
External shift mechanism
Cam chain tensioner
Camshaft
Rocker arms and shafts
Cylinder head
Cylinder and piston
Oil pump
Balancer gears

3   Operations requiring engine removal

It is necessary to remove the engine/transmission assembly from the frame and separate the crankcase halves to gain access to the following components:

Crankshaft and connecting rod
Transmission shafts
Shift drums and forks

4   Major engine repair - general note

1   It is not always easy to determine when or if an engine should be completely overhauled, as a number of factors must be considered.
2   High mileage is not necessarily an indication that an overhaul is needed, while low mileage, on the other hand, does not preclude the need for an overhaul. Frequency of servicing is probably the single most important consideration. An engine that has regular and frequent oil and filter changes, as well as other required maintenance, will most likely give many miles of reliable service. Conversely, a neglected

engine, or one which has not been broken in properly, may require an overhaul very early in its life.

3   Exhaust smoke and excessive oil consumption are both indications that piston rings and/or valve guides are in need of attention. Make sure oil leaks are not responsible before deciding that the rings and guides are bad. Refer to Chapter 1 and perform a cylinder compression check to determine for certain the nature and extent of the work required.

4   If the engine is making obvious knocking or rumbling noises, the connecting rod and/or main bearings are probably at fault.

5   Loss of power, rough running, excessive valve train noise and high fuel consumption rates may also point to the need for an overhaul, especially if they are all present at the same time. If a complete tune-up does not remedy the situation, major mechanical work is the only solution.

6   An engine overhaul generally involves restoring the internal parts to the specifications of a new engine. During an overhaul the piston rings are replaced and the cylinder walls are bored and/or honed. If a rebore is done, then a new piston is also required. Generally the valves are serviced as well, since they are usually in less than perfect condition at this point. While the engine is being overhauled, other components such as the carburetor and the starter motor can be rebuilt also. The end result should be a like-new engine that will give as many trouble-free miles as the original.

7   Before beginning the engine overhaul, read through all of the related procedures to familiarize yourself with the scope and requirements of the job. Overhauling an engine is not all that difficult, but it is time consuming. Plan on the vehicle being tied up for a minimum of two (2) weeks. Check on the availability of parts and make sure that any necessary special tools, equipment and supplies are obtained in advance.

8   Most work can be done with typical shop hand tools, although a number of precision measuring tools are required for inspecting parts to determine if they must be replaced. Often a dealer service department or repair shop will handle the inspection of parts and offer advice concerning reconditioning and replacement. As a general rule, time is the primary cost of an overhaul so it doesn't pay to install worn or substandard parts.

9   As a final note, to ensure maximum life and minimum trouble from a rebuilt engine, everything must be assembled with care in a spotlessly clean environment.

---

5   Engine - removal and installation

Note: *Engine removal and installation should be done with the aid of an* *assistant to avoid damage or injury that could occur if the engine is dropped.*

Removal

Refer to illustrations 5.10, 5.18a, 5.18b, 5.18c, 5.18d and 5.19

1   Drain the engine oil (and transfer case oil on YFM350FW models) (see Chapter 1).

2   Disconnect the ground cable from the engine and disconnect both battery cables.

3   Remove the seat, both footrests, the front and rear cargo racks and the front and rear fenders (see Chapter 7). Remove the front and rear fender stays as well.

4   Remove the fuel tank, carburetor, air cleaner air duct, intake manifold and exhaust system (see Chapter 3).

5   Remove the shift linkage cable(s) (see Chapter 1).

6   Remove the rear brake pedal rod and cable and the pedal (see Chapter 6).

7   Disconnect the odometer/speedometer cable. Remove the indicator bulb assembly and the odometer/speedometer (see Chapter 8).

8   Remove the starter motor (see Chapter 8).

9   If you're working on a YFM350ER model, remove the handlebar (see Chapter 5).

10   Disconnect the crankcase breather hose. On YFM350ER, YFM350FW and 1996 through 1998 YFM350U models, it's attached to the crankcase **(see illustration)**. On 1999 YFM350U and all YFM350FWB models, it's attached to the cam sprocket cover on the side of the cylinder head.

11   If you're working on a YFM350ER model, disconnect the oil cooler hoses from the engine. On all others, remove the oil filter cover (the hoses are attached to the cover). On all models, remove the oil cooler hose retainer (see Section 14).

12   Disconnect the spark plug wire (see Chapter 1).

13   Label and disconnect the following wires (see Chapters 4 or 8 for component locations if necessary):

> *CDI magneto and alternator*
> *Oil temperature, reverse and neutral switches*

14   Remove the shift pedal (see Section 21).

15   Remove the final drive unit and swingarm (see Chapter 5). Make sure the rear of the vehicle is securely supported so it can't be knocked over when the engine is removed.

16   Remove the front driveshaft (see Chapter 5). If you're working on a YFM350FW model, remove the transfer case and middle driven gear.

17   Support the engine securely from below.

18   Remove the engine mounting bolts, nuts and brackets at the upper front, lower front, lower rear and upper rear **(see illustrations)**.

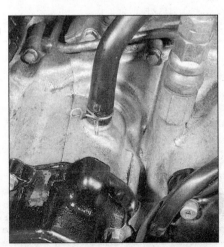

5.10 **Disconnect the breather hose from the crankcase**

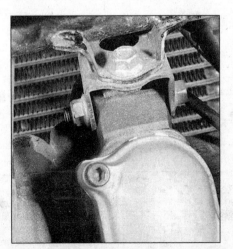

5.18a **With the engine securely supported, remove the upper front engine mounting bolt . . .**

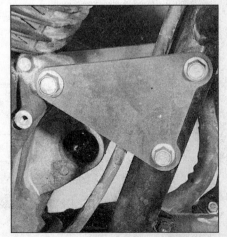

5.18b **. . . the lower front engine mounting brackets . . .**

5.18c ... the lower rear engine mounting bolt ...

5.18d ... and the upper rear engine mounting bolt

19   Have an assistant help you lift the engine. Remove the engine to the left side of the vehicle **(see illustration)**.
20   Slowly lower the engine to a suitable work surface.

Installation (YFM350ER and YFM350FW models)

21   Check the engine supports for wear or damage and replace them if necessary before installing the engine.
22   Make sure the rear of the vehicle is securely supported so it can't be knocked over during the remainder of this procedure.

YFM350FW models

23   Lubricate the splines of the front driveshaft with moly-based grease. Install the driveshaft in the front differential (see Chapter 5). Install the front driveshaft protector. Install the rear driveshaft protector, then install its lower bolt and finger-tighten it. Don't install the rear protector's Allen bolts yet.

YFM350ER and YFM350FW models

24   With the help of an assistant, lift the engine up into the frame. Install the mounting nuts and bolts at the rear, front and top. The heads of all the mounting bolts face the right side of the vehicle. Finger-tighten the mounting bolts, but don't tighten them to the specified torque yet.

YFM350FW models

25   Install the transfer case and middle driven gear (see Chapter 5), engaging the lower universal joint with the front driveshaft. Install the hex and Allen bolts that secure the transfer case and gear case cover as well as the top portion of the front driveshaft's rear protector. Finger-tighten the bolts nut don't torque them yet.

5.19 Have an assistant help you lift the engine out to the left

26   Jack up the front of the vehicle so the wheels are off the ground. Make sure it's securely supported at the front and rear.
27   Rotate the front wheels forward and backward and check the operation of the front driveshaft. It should rotate smoothly, without binding or rough movement. If not, make sure it's installed correctly. If driveshaft movement is correct, tighten the transfer case hex and Allen bolts.

YFM350ER and YFM350FW models

28   Install the rear driveshaft and swingarm (see Chapter 5). Finger-tighten the shock absorber lower bolt (YFM350ER) and the swingarm pivots, but don't torque them yet.
29   If you're working on a YFM350ER, install the rear wheels.
30   If you're working on a YFM350FW, the front of the vehicle should still be jacked up.
31   Rotate the rear wheels (YFM350ER) or front wheels (YFM350FW) forward and backward and check the operation of the rear axle (on YFM350FW models, the 4WD system will cause the rear axle to turn when the front wheels are turned). The axle should rotate smoothly, without binding or rough movement. If not, make sure it's installed correctly.
32   If axle movement is correct, tighten the swingarm pivots and locknuts (and the lower shock absorber bolt on YFM350ER models) to the torques listed in the Chapter 5 Specifications.
33   Tighten the engine mounting bolts and nuts to the torques listed in this Chapter's Specifications.
34   The remainder of installation is the reverse of the removal steps, with the following additions:
a) Use new gaskets at all exhaust pipe connections.
b) Adjust the throttle cable, rear brake cables and shift linkage following the procedures in Chapter 1.
c) Fill the engine (and the transfer case on YFM350FW models) with oil, also following the procedures in Chapter 1. Run the engine and check for leaks.

Installation (YFM350U and YFM350FWB models)

35   Check the engine supports for wear or damage and replace them if necessary before installing the engine.
36   Make sure the rear of the vehicle is securely supported so it can't be knocked over during the remainder of this procedure.
37   With the help of an assistant, lift the engine up into the frame. Don't install the mounting bolts yet.
38   If you're working on a YFM350FWB, lubricate the splines of the front driveshaft with moly-based grease. Install the driveshaft in the front differential (see Chapter 5). You'll probably need to rotate the engine clockwise to provide clearance for installation of the driveshaft.
39   Install the mounting nuts and bolts at the rear, front and top. The heads of all the mounting bolts face the right side of the vehicle. Finger-tighten the mounting bolts, but don't tighten them to the specified torque yet.

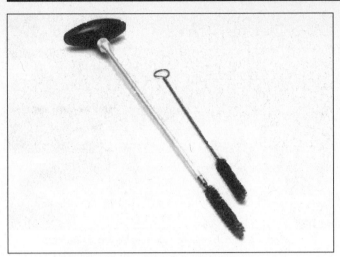

6.2 A selection of brushes is required for cleaning holes and passages in the engine components

6.3 An engine stand can be made from short lengths of lumber and lag bolts or nails

40   Tighten the mounting bolts to the torque listed in this Chapter's Specifications in the following sequence:

 a) *Top bracket to frame*
 b) *Rear mounting bolts*
 c) *Front mounting bracket to frame*
 d) *Front mounting bracket to engine*
 e) *Top mounting bracket to engine*

41   The remainder of installation is the reverse of the removal steps, with the following additions:

 a) *Use new gaskets at all exhaust pipe connections.*
 b) *Adjust the throttle cable, rear brake cables and shift linkage following the procedures in Chapter 1.*
 c) *Fill the engine with oil, also following the procedures in Chapter 1. Run the engine and check for leaks.*

6   Engine disassembly and reassembly - general information

Refer to illustrations 6.2 and 6.3

1   Before disassembling the engine, clean the exterior with a degreaser and rinse it with water. A clean engine will make the job easier and prevent the possibility of getting dirt into the internal areas of the engine.

2   In addition to the precision measuring tools mentioned earlier, you will need a torque wrench, a valve spring compressor, oil gallery brushes **(see illustration)**, a piston ring removal and installation tool, a piston ring compressor and a clutch holder tool (which is described in Section 8). Some new, clean engine oil of the correct grade and type, some engine assembly lube (or moly-based grease) and a tube of RTV (silicone) sealant will also be required.

3   An engine support stand made from short lengths of 2 x 4's bolted together will facilitate the disassembly and reassembly procedures **(see illustration)**. If you have an automotive-type engine stand, an adapter plate can be made from a piece of plate, some angle iron and some nuts and bolts.

4   When disassembling the engine, keep "mated" parts together (including gears, rocker arms and shafts, etc.) that have been in contact with each other during engine operation. These "mated" parts must be reused or replaced as an assembly.

5   Engine/transmission disassembly should be done in the following general order with reference to the appropriate Sections.

Remove the cam chain tensioner
Remove the cylinder head, rocker arms and camshaft
Remove the cylinder

Remove the piston
Remove the primary and secondary clutches
Remove the balancer gears
Remove the oil pump
Remove the external shift mechanism
Remove the alternator rotor and starter reduction gears
Separate the crankcase halves
Remove the shift drums and forks
Remove the transmission gears and shafts
Remove the balancer shaft
Remove the crankshaft and connecting rod

6   Reassembly is accomplished by reversing the general disassembly sequence.

7   Cam chain tensioner - removal and installation

Removal

Refer to illustrations 7.1 and 7.2

Caution: *Once you start to remove the tensioner bolts you must remove the tensioner all the way and reset it before tightening the bolts. The tensioner extends and locks in place, so if you loosen the bolts partway and then tighten them, the tensioner or cam chain will be damaged.*

1   Loosen the tensioner cap bolt **(see illustration)**.

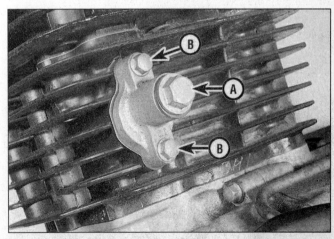

7.1 Loosen the tensioner cap bolt (A), then remove the tensioner bolts (B) and take the tensioner off

7.2 Valve train details

1 Valve adjuster locknut
2 Valve adjuster screw
3 Rocker arm
4 Rocker shaft
5 O-ring
6 Valve keepers (collets)
7 Valve spring retainer
8 Valve springs
9 Valve stem oil seal
10 Valve spring seat
11 Valve
12 Cam chain tensioner
13 Intake (rear) cam chain guide
14 Camshaft bearings
15 Camshaft
16 Cam chain
17 Camshaft dowel
18 Exhaust (front) cam chain guide

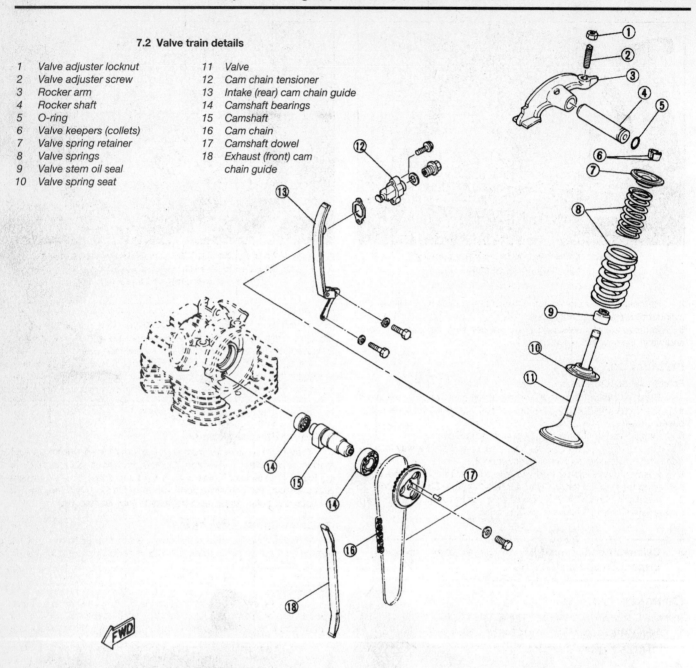

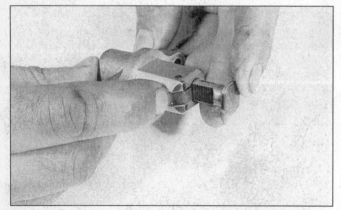

7.7a Lift the latch, press the piston into the tensioner and release the latch

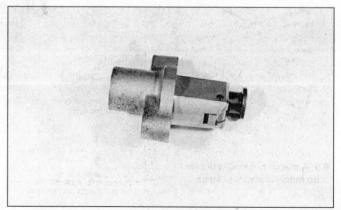

7.7b The piston should be retracted like this when the tensioner is installed

8.3 Remove the Allen bolts from the camshaft sprocket cover (arrows)

8.4 With the engine at TDC compression, the sprocket line should be even with the cast indicator in the cylinder head (arrows)

2   Remove the tensioner mounting bolts and detach it from the cylinder block **(see illustration)**.
3   Remove the cap bolt and sealing washer from the tensioner body and wash them with solvent.

Installation

Refer to illustrations 7.7a and 7.7b

4   Clean all old gasket material from the tensioner body and engine.
5   Lubricate the friction surfaces of the components with moly-based grease.
6   Install a new tensioner gasket on the cylinder.
7   Lift the latch, compress the tensioner piston all the way into the body and release the latch **(see illustrations)**.
8   Position the tensioner body on the cylinder and install the bolts, tightening them to the torque listed in this Chapter's Specifications.
9   Install the cap bolt with a new sealing washer and tighten it to the torque listed in this Chapter's Specifications.

---

8   Cylinder head, camshaft and rocker arms - removal, inspection and installation

---

Camshaft removal

Refer to illustrations 8.3, 8.4, 8.5, 8.7a, 8.7b and 8.8

1   Remove the engine from the frame (see Section 5).

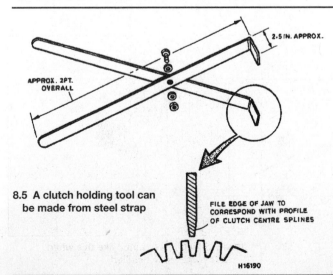

8.5 A clutch holding tool can be made from steel strap

2.5 IN. APPROX.

APPROX. 2 FT.
OVERALL

FILE EDGE OF JAW TO
CORRESPOND WITH PROFILE
OF CLUTCH CENTRE SPLINES

H16190

2   Remove the valve adjusting hole covers (see Chapter 1).
3   If you're working on a YFM350FWB or a 1999 YFM350U, disconnect the crankcase breather hose from the cam sprocket cover. Remove the Allen bolts and take the cover off **(see illustration)**.
4   Refer to *Valve clearances - check and adjustment* in Chapter 1 and place the engine at top dead center on the compression stroke. The cam sprocket mark will align with the indicator cast into the cylinder head and the rocker arms will be loose when the cylinder is at TDC compression **(see illustration)**.

Models with recoil starter

5   Prevent the crankshaft from turning. To do this, remove the recoil starter as described in Section 20. Hold the recoil starter pulley (if equipped) with a clutch holder tool. If the factory tool or an equivalent isn't available, you can make your own from some steel strap, bent at the ends and bolted together in the middle **(see illustration)**.

Models without recoil starter

6   Remove the alternator outer cover (see Chapter 8) and place a wrench on the flats of the rotor (the rotor that fits into the outer cover, not the alternator rotor).

All models

7   Unbolt the cam sprocket and take it off the camshaft **(see illustration)**. Disengage the sprocket from the chain and support the chain with wire so it doesn't fall down off the crankshaft sprocket. Unbolt the

8.7a The camshaft dowel aligns with the sprocket line and the cast indicator

8.7b Bend back the lockwasher tabs, remove the two bolts and take off the lockwasher and retainer

8.8 Thread a 10 mm bolt into the camshaft and pull on it to remove the camshaft and outer bearing

8.9 Thread a bolt into each rocker shaft and pull it out

camshaft retainer from the head **(see illustration)**.

8   Thread a 10 mm bolt into the end of the camshaft and use it as a handle to pull the camshaft out of the cylinder head **(see illustration)**. **Caution:** *The camshaft should come out easily. If it seems stuck, make sure it isn't caught on the rocker arms.*

8.10 Remove the two Allen bolts

Rocker arm removal

Refer to illustration 8.9

9   Thread a 6 mm bolt into the end of each rocker arm shaft **(see illustration)**. Support the rocker and use the bolt as a handle to pull out the shaft. **Note:** *If the shaft is stuck, it may be necessary to use a slide hammer. These can be rented from equipment rental yards (some auto parts stores also rent tools).*

Cylinder head removal

Refer to illustrations 8.10, 8.11 and 8.12

10   Remove the cylinder head Allen bolts **(see illustration)**.

11   Loosen the cylinder head bolts in several stages, in the reverse order of the tightening sequence **(see illustration)**.

12   Lift the cylinder head off the cylinder **(see illustration)**. If it's stuck, don't attempt to pry it off - tap around the sides of it with a plastic hammer to dislodge it. Be careful not to tap against the cooling fins; they're easily broken.

13   Locate the cover dowels **(see illustration 8.12)**. They may be in the cylinder or they may have come off with the head.

Cam chain and guide removal

Refer to illustrations 8.14a and 8.14b

14   Lift the front cam chain guide out of the cylinder **(see illustrations)**. The rear guide is bolted at the bottom, so the primary clutch will have to be removed for access if the guide or the cam chain need to be removed.

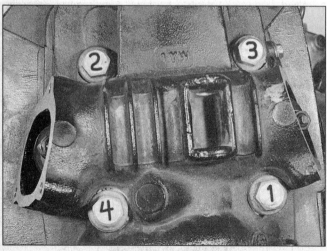

8.11 Cylinder head bolt TIGHTENING sequence

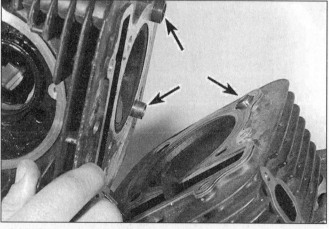

8.12 Lift the head off; the dowels and the O-ring that surrounds one of the dowels may come off with the head or stay in the cylinder (arrows)

8.14a Lift the front chain guide (arrow) . . .

8.14b . . . out of its cup (left arrow); to unbolt the rear chain guide (right arrows), you'll need to remove the primary clutch

15   Stuff clean rags into the cam chain openings so dirt, small parts or tools can't fall into them.

Inspection

Camshaft, chain and guides

Refer to illustrations 8.17a and 8.17b

Note: *Before replacing camshafts or the cylinder head because of damage, check with local machine shops specializing in ATV or motorcycle engine work. In the case of the camshaft, it may be possible for cam lobes to be welded, reground and hardened, at a cost far lower than that of a new camshaft. If the bearing surfaces in the cylinder head are damaged, it may be possible for them to be bored out to accept bearing inserts. Due to the cost of a new cylinder head it is recommended that all options be explored before condemning it as trash!*

16   Rotate the cam bearings and check for roughness, looseness or noise. Check the sealed side of the outer bearing for signs of leakage. Replace the bearing(s) if problems are found.

17   Check the camshaft lobes for heat discoloration (blue appearance), score marks, chipped areas, flat spots and spalling **(see illustration)**. Measure the height of each lobe with a micrometer **(see illustration)** and compare the results to the minimum lobe height listed in this Chapter's Specifications. If damage is noted or wear is excessive, the camshaft must be replaced. Check the bearing surfaces for scoring or wear. Also, be sure to check the condition of the rocker arms, as described below.

18   Except in cases of oil starvation, the camshaft chain wears very little. If the chain has stretched excessively, which makes it difficult to maintain proper tension, replace it with a new one. To remove the chain from the crankshaft sprocket, remove the primary clutch (see hex Section 15).

19   Check the sprocket for wear, cracks and other damage, replacing

8.17a Check the cam lobes for wear - here's a good example of damage which will require replacement (or repair) of the camshaft

it if necessary. If the sprocket is worn, the chain is also worn, and possibly the sprocket on the crankshaft. If wear this severe is apparent, the entire engine should be disassembled for inspection.

20   Check the chain guides for wear or damage. If they are worn or damaged, replace them.

Rocker arms, shafts and decompression lever

Refer to illustrations 8.21 and 8.22

21   Check the rocker arms for wear at the cam contact surfaces, inside the shaft bores and at the tips of the valve adjusting screws **(see illustration)**. Try to twist the rocker arms from side-to-side on the shafts. If

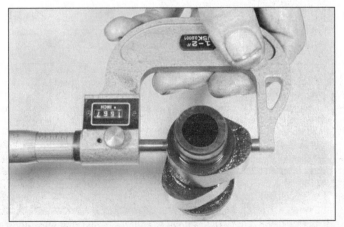

8.17b Measure the height of the cam lobes with a micrometer

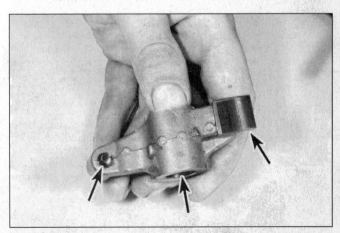

8.21 Check rocker arms for wear on the adjuster surface, inside the bore and on the cam contact surface (arrows)

2

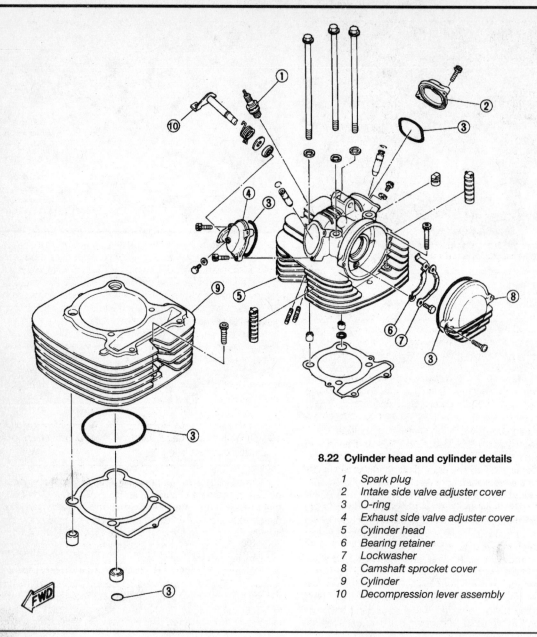

8.22 Cylinder head and cylinder details

1   Spark plug
2   Intake side valve adjuster cover
3   O-ring
4   Exhaust side valve adjuster cover
5   Cylinder head
6   Bearing retainer
7   Lockwasher
8   Camshaft sprocket cover
9   Cylinder
10 Decompression lever assembly

they're loose on the shafts or if there's visible wear, measure the rocker arm shaft diameter and bore diameter with a micrometer and hole gauge. If the parts are worn beyond the limits listed in this Chapter's Specifications, replace them. Replace the rocker arm and shaft as a set.

22   Check the decompression lever (if equipped) and its shaft for wear, damage or a broken spring **(see illustration)**. If any problems are found, pull the lever/shaft out of the cover, together with the spring. Pry the shaft oil seal out of its bore.

Cylinder head

23   Check the cylinder head gasket and the mating surfaces on the cylinder head and cylinder for leakage, which could indicate warpage. Refer to Section 10 and check the flatness of the cylinder head.

24   Clean all traces of old gasket material from the cylinder head and cylinder. Be careful not to let any of the gasket material fall into the crankcase, the cylinder bore or the bolt holes.

Installation

25   If the decompression lever/shaft was removed, press a new oil seal into the bore with a seal driver or a socket the same diameter as the seal. Install the shaft and engage its spring with the cover and the

lever, then install the retaining bolt in the cover **(see illustration 8.22)**.

26   Coat the rocker shafts and rocker arm bores with moly-based grease. Install the rocker shafts and rocker arms in the cylinder head. Be sure to install the intake and exhaust rocker arms and shafts in the correct sides of the head.

27   Install the inner camshaft bearing in the cylinder head and the outer bearing on the camshaft (if they were removed). The sealed side of the outer bearing faces out (away from the cylinder head). Lubricate the camshaft bearings with engine oil.

28   Install the camshaft in the cylinder head with its lobes pointing down. The camshaft dowel should be up, so it aligns with the cast indicator in the cylinder head, when the camshaft is installed **(see illustration 8.4)**.

29   Install the bearing retainer and a new lockwasher **(see illustrations 8.7b and 8.22)**. Tighten the bearing retainer bolts to the torque listed in this Chapter's Specifications.

30   Install the three dowel pins and the O-ring that surrounds one of the dowels, then place the new head gasket on the cylinder **(see illustration 8.12)**. Never reuse the old gasket and don't use any type of gasket sealant.

31   Install the exhaust side cam chain damper, fitting the lower end

10.7a Compress the valve springs with a valve spring compressor

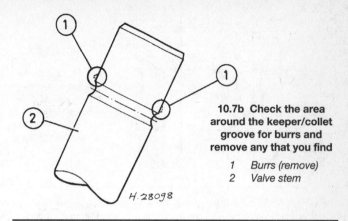

10.7b Check the area around the keeper/collet groove for burrs and remove any that you find

1   *Burrs (remove)*
2   *Valve stem*

into its notch **(see illustration 8.14b)**.

32   Carefully lower the cylinder head over the dowels and O-ring, guiding the cam chain through the slot in the cylinder head. It's helpful to have an assistant support the cam chain with a piece of wire so it doesn't fall and become kinked or detached from the crankshaft. When the head is resting on the cylinder, wire the cam chain to another component to keep tension on it.

33   Lubricate the threads of the cylinder head bolts with engine oil, then install them finger-tight. Tighten the four hex bolts in the correct sequence **(see illustration 8.11)**, in several stages, to the torque listed in this Chapter's Specifications. After the hex bolts are tightened, tighten the two Allen bolts to the torque listed in this Chapter's Specifications.

34   Refer to the valve adjustment procedure in Chapter 1 and make sure the timing mark with the T next to it is aligned with the notch in the timing hole. If it's necessary to turn the crankshaft, hold the cam chain up so it doesn't fall off the crankshaft sprocket and become jammed.

35   Engage the camshaft sprocket with the timing chain so its dowel hole aligns with the dowel **(see illustration 8.7a)**. Slip the sprocket onto the camshaft over the dowel, then install the sprocket bolt finger-tight. The line on the cam sprocket should be aligned with the cast indicator in the cylinder head **(see illustration 8.4)**.

36   Twist the cam sprocket in both directions to remove the slack from the cam chain. Insert a screwdriver in the cam chain tensioner hole and push against the cam chain guide. With the guide pushed in, the cam sprocket line and cast indicator should line up **(see illustration 8.4)**. If they don't, remove the cam sprocket from the chain, reposition it and try again. Don't continue with assembly until the marks are lined up correctly.

37   Tighten the cam sprocket bolt to the torque listed in this Chapter's Specifications.

38   Apply engine oil to a new O-ring for the cam sprocket cover. Install the O-ring and cover and tighten the Allen bolts to the torque listed in this Chapter's Specifications.

39   Install the cam chain tensioner (see Section 7).

40   Change the engine oil (see Chapter 1).

41   Adjust the valve clearances (see Chapter 1).

42   The remainder of installation is the reverse of removal.

9   Valves/valve seats/valve guides - servicing

1   Because of the complex nature of this job and the special tools and equipment required, servicing of the valves, the valve seats and the valve guides (commonly known as a valve job) is best left to a professional.

2   The home mechanic can, however, remove and disassemble the head, do the initial cleaning and inspection, then reassemble and deliver the head to a dealer service department or properly equipped vehicle repair shop for the actual valve servicing. Refer to Section 10

for those procedures.

3   The dealer service department will remove the valves and springs, recondition or replace the valves and valve seats, replace the valve guides, check and replace the valve springs, spring retainers and keepers (as necessary), replace the valve seals with new ones and reassemble the valve components.

4   After the valve job has been performed, the head will be in like-new condition. When the head is returned, be sure to clean it again very thoroughly before installation on the engine to remove any metal particles or abrasive grit that may still be present from the valve service operations. Use compressed air, if available, to blow out all the holes and passages.

10   Cylinder head and valves - disassembly, inspection and reassembly

1   As mentioned in the previous Section, valve servicing and valve guide replacement should be left to a dealer service department or other repair shop. However, disassembly, cleaning and inspection of the valves and related components can be done (if the necessary special tools are available) by the home mechanic. This way no expense is incurred if the inspection reveals that service work is not required at this time.

2   To properly disassemble the valve components without the risk of damaging them, a valve spring compressor is absolutely necessary. If the special tool is not available, have a dealer service department or vehicle repair shop handle the entire process of disassembly, inspection, service or repair (if required) and reassembly of the valves.

Disassembly

Refer to illustrations 10.7a and 10.7b

3   Remove the carburetor intake tube from the cylinder head (see Chapter 3).

4   Before the valves are removed, scrape away any traces of gasket material from the head gasket sealing surface. Work slowly and do not nick or gouge the soft aluminum of the head. Gasket removing solvents, which work very well, are available at most ATV shops and auto parts stores.

5   Carefully scrape all carbon deposits out of the combustion chamber area. A hand held wire brush or a piece of fine emery cloth can be used once most of the deposits have been scraped away. Do not use a wire brush mounted in a drill motor, or one with extremely stiff bristles, as the head material is soft and may be eroded away or scratched by the wire brush.

6   Before proceeding, arrange to label and store the valves along with their related components so they can be kept separate and reinstalled in the same valve guides they are removed from (again, plastic bags work well for this).

7   Compress the valve spring(s) on the first valve with a spring compressor, then remove the keepers/collets and the retainer from the

2

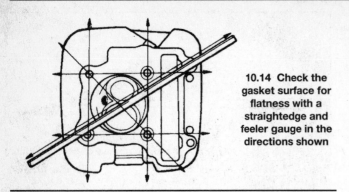

10.14 Check the gasket surface for flatness with a straightedge and feeler gauge in the directions shown

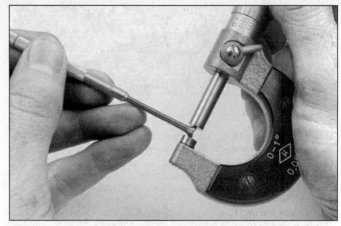

10.16 Measure the valve guide inside diameter with a hole gauge, then measure the gauge with a micrometer

valve assembly **(see illustration 7.2 and the accompanying illustration)**. Do not compress the spring(s) any more than is absolutely necessary. Carefully release the valve spring compressor and remove the spring(s), spring seat and valve from the head. If the valve binds in the guide (won't pull through), push it back into the head and deburr the area around the keeper/collet groove with a very fine file or whetstone **(see illustration)**.

8   Repeat the procedure for the remaining valve. Remember to keep the parts for each valve together so they can be reinstalled in the same location.

9   Once the valves have been removed and labeled, pull off the valve stem seals with pliers and discard them (the old seals should never be reused).

10   Next, clean the cylinder head with solvent and dry it thoroughly. Compressed air will speed the drying process and ensure that all holes and recessed areas are clean.

11   Clean all of the valve springs, keepers/collets, retainers and spring seats with solvent and dry them thoroughly. Do the parts from one valve at a time so that no mixing of parts between valves occurs.

12   Scrape off any deposits that may have formed on the valve, then use a motorized wire brush to remove deposits from the valve heads and stems. Again, make sure the valves do not get mixed up.

Inspection

Refer to illustrations 10.14, 10.16, 10.17, 10.18a, 10.18b, 10.19a and 10.19b

13   Inspect the head very carefully for cracks and other damage. If cracks are found, a new head will be required. Check the cam bearing surfaces for wear and evidence of seizure. Check the camshaft for wear as well (see Section 8).

14   Using a precision straightedge and a feeler gauge, check the head gasket mating surface for warpage. Lay the straightedge lengthwise, across the head and diagonally (corner-to-corner), intersecting the head bolt holes, and try to slip a feeler gauge under it, on either side of each

combustion chamber **(see illustration)**. The feeler gauge thickness should be the same as the cylinder head warpage limit listed in this Chapter's Specifications. If the feeler gauge can be inserted between the head and the straightedge, the head is warped and must either be machined or, if warpage is excessive, replaced with a new one.

15   Examine the valve seats in each of the combustion chambers. If they are pitted, cracked or burned, the head will require valve service that is beyond the scope of the home mechanic. Measure the valve seat width and compare it to this Chapter's Specifications. If it is not within the specified range, or if it varies around its circumference, valve service work is required.

16   Clean the valve guides to remove any carbon buildup, then measure the inside diameters of the guides (at both ends and the center of the guide) with a small hole gauge and a micrometer **(see illustration)**. Record the measurements for future reference. The guides are measured at the ends and at the center to determine if they are worn in a bell-mouth pattern (more wear at the ends). If they are, guide replacement is an absolute must.

17   Carefully inspect each valve face for cracks, pits and burned spots. Check the valve stem and the keeper groove area for cracks **(see illustration)**. Rotate the valve and check for any obvious indication that it is bent. Check the end of the stem for pitting and excessive wear and make sure the bevel is the specified width. The presence of any of the above conditions indicates the need for valve servicing.

18   Measure the valve stem diameter **(see illustration)**. If the diameter is less than listed in this Chapter's Specifications, the valves will have to be replaced with new ones. Also check the valve stem for bending. Set the valve in a V-block with a dial indicator touching the middle of the stem **(see illustration)**. Rotate the valve and look for a

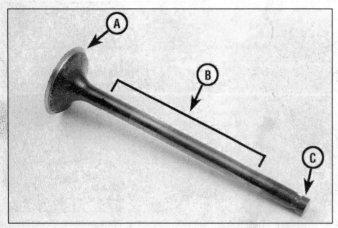

10.17 Check the valve face (A), stem (B) and keeper/collet groove (C) for wear and damage

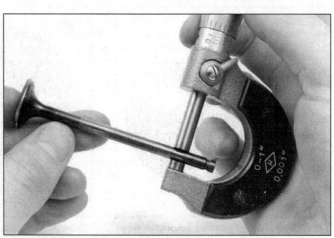

10.18a Measuring valve stem diameter

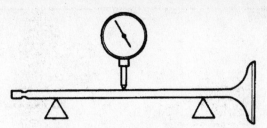

10.18b Check the valve stem for bends with a V-block (or V-blocks, as shown here) and a dial indicator

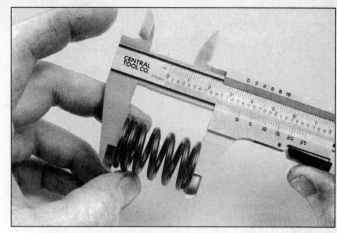

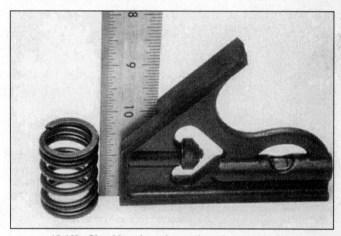

10.19a Measuring the free length of the valve springs

reading on the gauge (which indicates a bent stem). If the stem is bent, replace the valve.

19 Check the end of each valve spring for wear and pitting. Measure the free length **(see illustration)** and compare it to this Chapter's Specifications. Any springs that are shorter than specified have sagged and should not be reused. Stand the spring on a flat surface and check it for squareness **(see illustration)**.

20 Check the spring retainers and keepers/collets for obvious wear and cracks. Any questionable parts should not be reused, as extensive damage will occur in the event of failure during engine operation.

21 If the inspection indicates that no service work is required, the valve components can be reinstalled in the head.

Reassembly

Refer to illustrations 10.23, 10.24, 10.26 and 10.27

22 If the valve seats have been ground, the valves and seats should be lapped before installing the valves in the head to ensure a positive seal between the valves and seats. This procedure requires coarse and fine valve lapping compound (available at auto parts stores) and a valve lapping tool. If a lapping tool is not available, a piece of rubber or plastic hose can be slipped over the valve stem (after the valve has been installed in the guide) and used to turn the valve.

23 Apply a small amount of coarse lapping compound to the valve face **(see illustration)**, then slip the valve into the guide. **Note:** *Make sure the valve is installed in the correct guide and be careful not to get any lapping compound on the valve stem.*

24 Attach the lapping tool (or hose) to the valve and rotate the tool between the palms of your hands. Use a back-and-forth motion rather than a circular motion. Lift the valve off the seat and turn it at regular intervals to distribute the lapping compound properly. Continue the lapping procedure until the valve face and seat contact area is of uniform width and unbroken around the entire circumference of the valve face and seat **(see illustration)**. Once this is accomplished, lap the valves again with fine lapping compound.

25 Carefully remove the valve from the guide and wipe off all traces

10.19b Checking the valve springs for squareness

of lapping compound. Use solvent to clean the valve and wipe the seat area thoroughly with a solvent soaked cloth. Repeat the procedure for the remaining valves.

26 Lay the spring seat in place in the cylinder head, then install new valve stem seals on both of the guides **(see illustration)**. Use an appropriate size deep socket to push the seals into place until they are properly seated. Don't twist or cock them, or they will not seal properly against the valve stems. Also, don't remove them again or they will be damaged.

2

10.23 Apply the lapping compound very sparingly, in small dabs, to the valve face only

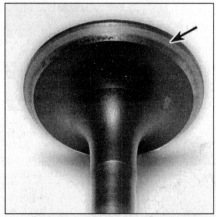

10.24 After lapping, the valve face should exhibit a uniform, unbroken contact pattern (arrow)

10.26 Push the oil seal onto the valve guide (arrow)

10.27 A small dab of grease will help hold the keepers/collets in place on the valve while the spring compressor is released

11.3 Remove the Allen bolt that attaches the cylinder to the crankcase (arrow)

11.4 Lift the cylinder off; the dowel inside the gasket loop has an O-ring (arrow) . . .

27 Coat the valve stems with assembly lube or moly-based grease, then install one of them into its guide. Next, install the spring seat, springs and retainers, compress the springs and install the keepers/collets. **Note:** *Install the springs with the tightly wound coils at the bottom (next to the spring seat).* When compressing the springs with the valve spring compressor, depress them only as far as is absolutely necessary to slip the keepers/collets into place. Apply a small amount of grease to the keepers/collets **(see illustration)** to help hold them in place as the pressure is released from the springs. Make

certain that the keepers/collets are securely locked in their retaining grooves.
28 Support the cylinder head on blocks so the valves can't contact the workbench top, then very gently tap each of the valve stems with a soft-faced hammer. This will help seat the keepers in their grooves.
29 Once all of the valves have been installed in the head, check for proper valve sealing by pouring a small amount of solvent into each of the valve ports. If the solvent leaks past the valve(s) into the combustion chamber area, disassemble the valve(s) and repeat the lapping procedure, then reinstall the valve(s) and repeat the check. Repeat the procedure until a satisfactory seal is obtained.

11.5 . . . there's also another dowel (left arrow); the dowels may stay in the crankcase or come off with the cylinder - the cylinder base O-ring (right arrow) should be replaced whenever the cylinder is removed

---

11 Cylinder - removal, inspection and installation

Removal

Refer to illustrations 11.3, 11.4 and 11.5

1 Following the procedure given in Section 8, remove the cylinder head. Make sure the crankshaft is positioned at Top Dead Center (TDC).
2 Lift out the cam chain front guide **(see illustration 8.14a)**.
3 Remove the Allen bolt that secures the base of the cylinder to the crankcase **(see illustration)**.
4 Lift the cylinder straight up to remove it **(see illustration)**. If it's stuck, tap around its perimeter with a soft-faced hammer (but don't tap on the cooling fins or they may break). Don't attempt to pry between the cylinder and the crankcase, as you'll ruin the sealing surfaces.
5 Locate the dowel pins (they may have come off with the cylinder or still be in the crankcase) **(see illustration 11.4 and the accompanying illustration)**. Be careful not to let these drop into the engine. Stuff rags around the piston and remove the gasket and all traces of old gasket material from the surfaces of the cylinder and the crankcase.

Inspection

Refer to illustration 11.8

6 Don't attempt to separate the liner from the cylinder.
7 Check the cylinder walls carefully for scratches and score marks.
8 Using the appropriate precision measuring tools, check the cylinder's diameter. Measure parallel to the crankshaft axis and across the crankshaft axis, at the depth from the top of the cylinder listed in this Chapter's Specifications **(see illustration)**. Average the two measurements and compare the results to this Chapter's Specifications. If the cylinder walls are tapered, out-of-round, worn beyond the specified limits, or badly scuffed or scored, have the cylinder rebored and honed by a dealer service department or an ATV repair shop. If a rebore is done, an oversize piston and rings will be required as well. **Note:** *Yamaha supplies pistons in two oversizes.*

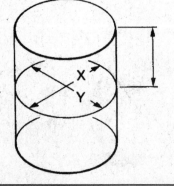

11.8 Measure the cylinder diameter in two directions, at the specified distance from the top of the cylinder

11.16 If you're experienced and very careful, the cylinder can be installed over the rings without a ring compressor, but a compressor is recommended

9   As an alternative, if the precision measuring tools are not available, a dealer service department or repair shop will make the measurements and offer advice concerning servicing of the cylinder.

10   If it's in reasonably good condition and not worn to the outside of the limits, and if the piston-to-cylinder clearance can be maintained properly, then the cylinder does not have to be rebored; honing is all that is necessary.

11   To perform the honing operation you will need the proper size flexible hone with fine stones as shown in Maintenance techniques, tools and working facilities at the front of this book, or a "bottle brush" type hone, plenty of light oil or honing oil, some shop towels and an electric drill motor. Hold the cylinder block in a vise (cushioned with soft jaws or wood blocks) when performing the honing operation. Mount the hone in the drill motor, compress the stones and slip the hone into the cylinder. Lubricate the cylinder thoroughly, turn on the drill and move the hone up and down in the cylinder at a pace which will produce a fine crosshatch pattern on the cylinder wall with the crosshatch lines inter-secting at approximately a 60-degree angle. Be sure to use plenty of lubricant and do not take off any more material than is absolutely necessary to produce the desired effect. Do not withdraw the hone from the cylinder while it is running. Instead, shut off the drill and continue moving the hone up and down in the cylinder until it comes to a complete stop, then compress the stones and withdraw the hone. Wipe the oil out of the cylinder and repeat the procedure on the remaining cylinder. Remember, do not remove too much material from

the cylinder wall. If you do not have the tools, or do not desire to perform the honing operation, a dealer service department or vehicle repair shop will generally do it for a reasonable fee.

12   Next, the cylinder must be thoroughly washed with warm soapy water to remove all traces of the abrasive grit produced during the honing operation. Be sure to run a brush through the bolt holes and flush them with running water. After rinsing, dry the cylinder thoroughly and apply a coat of light, rust-preventative oil to all machined surfaces.

Installation

Refer to illustration 11.16

13   Lubricate the cylinder bore with plenty of clean engine oil. Apply a thin film of moly-based grease to the piston skirt.

14   Install the dowel pins, then lower a new cylinder base gasket over them **(see illustrations 11.4 and 11.5)**.

15   Attach a piston ring compressor to the piston and compress the piston rings. A large hose clamp can be used instead - just make sure it doesn't scratch the piston, and don't tighten it too much.

16   Install the cylinder and carefully lower it down until the piston crown fits into the cylinder liner **(see illustration)**. While doing this, pull the camshaft chain up, using a hooked tool or a piece of stiff wire. Push down on the cylinder, making sure the piston doesn't get cocked sideways, until the bottom of the cylinder liner slides down past the piston rings. A wood or plastic hammer handle can be used to gently tap the cylinder down, but don't use too much force or the piston will be damaged.

17   Remove the piston ring compressor or hose clamp, being careful not to scratch the piston.

18   The remainder of installation is the reverse of the removal steps.

12 Piston - removal, inspection and installation

1   The piston is attached to the connecting rod with a piston pin that's a slip fit in the piston and rod.

2   Before removing the piston from the rod, stuff a clean shop towel into the crankcase hole, around the connecting rod. This will prevent the snap-rings from falling into the crankcase if they are inadvertently dropped.

Removal

Refer to illustrations 12.3a, 12.3b, 12.4a and 12.4b

3   The piston should have an arrow mark on its crown that points toward the exhaust (front) side of the engine **(see illustration)**. If this mark is not visible due to carbon buildup, scribe an arrow into the piston crown before removal. Support the piston and pry the snap-ring out with a pointed tool **(see illustration)**.

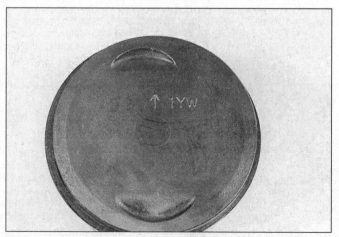

12.3a The arrow mark on top of the piston faces the exhaust (front) side of the engine

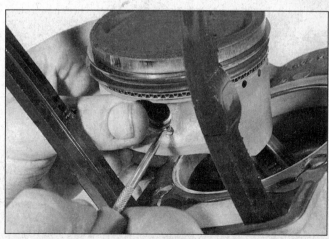

12.3b Wear eye protection and pry the snap-ring out of its groove with a pointed tool

2

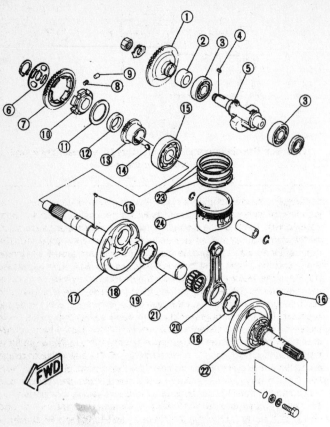

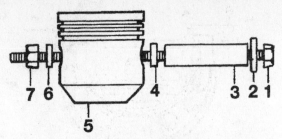

**12.4b The piston pin should come out with hand pressure -
if it doesn't, this removal tool can be fabricated
from readily available parts**

1	Bolt	7	Nut (B)
2	Washer	A	Large enough for piston
3	Pipe (A)		pin to fit inside
4	Padding (A)	B	Small enough to fit
5	Piston		through piston pin bore
6	Washer (B)		

4   Push the piston pin out from the opposite end to free the piston from the rod **(see illustration)**. You may have to deburr the area around the groove to enable the pin to slide out (use a triangular file for this procedure). If the pin won't come out, you can fabricate a piston pin removal tool from a long bolt, a nut, a piece of tubing and washers **(see illustration)**.

Inspection

Refer to illustrations 12.6, 12.11, 12.13, 12.14, 12.15 and 12.16

5   Before the inspection process can be carried out, the piston must be cleaned and the old piston rings removed.

6   Using a piston ring removal and installation tool, carefully remove the rings from the piston **(see illustration)**. Do not nick or gouge the piston in the process.

7   Scrape all traces of carbon from the top of the piston. A hand-held wire brush or a piece of fine emery cloth can be used once the majority of the deposits have been scraped away. Do not, under any circumstances, use a wire brush mounted in a drill motor to remove deposits from the piston; the piston material is soft and will be eroded away by the wire brush.

8   Use a piston ring groove cleaning tool to remove any carbon deposits from the ring grooves. If a tool is not available, a piece broken off the old ring will do the job. Be very careful to remove only the carbon deposits. Do not remove any metal and do not nick or gouge the sides of the ring grooves.

9   Once the deposits have been removed, clean the piston with solvent and dry them thoroughly. Make sure the oil return holes below

12.4a Piston, crankshaft and balancer details

1	Balancer driven gear	13	Oil pump drive gear
2	Collar	14	Woodruff key
3	Bearing	15	Bearing
4	Woodruff key (with	16	Woodruff key
	straight sides)	17	Crankshaft right half
5	Balancer shaft	18	Washer
6	Holding plate	19	Crankpin
7	Balancer drive gear	20	Connecting rod
8	Compression spring	21	Connecting rod
9	Dowel pin (inside		needle roller bearing
	compression spring)	22	Crankshaft left half
10	Buffer boss	23	Piston rings
11	Plain washer	24	Piston
12	Collar		

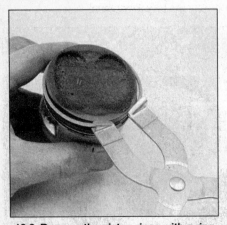

12.6 Remove the piston rings with a ring removal and installation tool

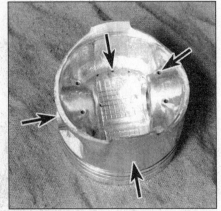

12.11 Check the piston pin bore and the piston skirt for wear, and make sure the internal holes are clear (arrows)

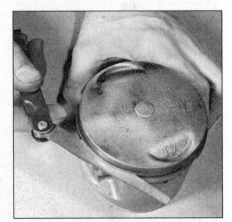

12.13 Measure the piston ring-to-groove clearance with a feeler gauge

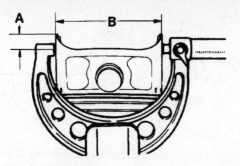

12.14 Measure the piston diameter with a micrometer

    A   *Specified distance from bottom of piston*
    B   *Piston diameter*

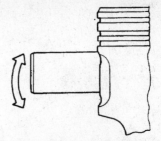

12.15 Slip the pin into the piston and try to wiggle it back-and-forth to check for looseness

the oil ring grooves are clear.

10   If the piston is not damaged or worn excessively and if the cylinder is not rebored, a new piston will not be necessary. Normal piston wear appears as even, vertical wear on the thrust surfaces of the piston and slight looseness of the top ring in its groove. New piston rings, on the other hand, should always be used when an engine is rebuilt.

11   Carefully inspect each piston for cracks around the skirt, at the pin bosses and at the ring lands **(see illustration)**.

12   Look for scoring and scuffing on the thrust faces of the skirt, holes in the piston crown and burned areas at the edge of the crown. If the skirt is scored or scuffed, the engine may have been suffering from overheating and/or abnormal combustion, which caused excessively high operating temperatures. The oil pump should be checked thoroughly. A hole in the piston crown, an extreme to be sure, is an indication that abnormal combustion (pre-ignition) was occurring. Burned areas at the edge of the piston crown are usually evidence of spark knock (detonation). If any of the above problems exist, the causes must be corrected or the damage will occur again.

13   Measure the piston ring-to-groove clearance (side clearance) by laying a new piston ring in the ring groove and slipping a feeler gauge in beside it **(see illustration)**. Check the clearance at three or four locations around the groove. Be sure to use the correct ring for each groove; they are different. If the clearance is greater than specified, a new piston will have to be used when the engine is reassembled.

14   Check the piston-to-bore clearance by measuring the bore (see Section 11) and the piston diameter **(see illustration)**. Measure the piston across the skirt on the thrust faces at a 90-degree angle to the piston pin, at the specified distance up from the bottom of the skirt. Subtract the piston diameter from the bore diameter to obtain the clearance. If it is greater than specified, the cylinder will have to be rebored and a new oversized piston and rings installed. If the appropriate precision measuring tools are not available, the piston-to-cylinder clearance can be obtained, though not quite as

accurately, using feeler gauge stock. Feeler gauge stock comes in 12-inch lengths and various thicknesses and is generally available at auto parts stores. To check the clearance, slip a piece of feeler gauge stock of the same thickness as the specified piston clearance into the cylinder along with appropriate piston. The cylinder should be upside down and the piston must be positioned exactly as it normally would be. Place the feeler gauge between the piston and cylinder on one of the thrust faces (90-degrees to the piston pin bore). The piston should slip through the cylinder (with the feeler gauge in place) with moderate pressure. If it falls through, or slides through easily, the clearance is excessive and a new piston will be required. If the piston binds at the lower end of the cylinder and is loose toward the top, the cylinder is tapered, and if tight spots are encountered as the piston/feeler gauge is rotated in the cylinder, the cylinder is out-of-round. Be sure to have the cylinder and piston checked by a dealer service department or a repair shop to confirm your findings before purchasing new parts.

15   Apply clean engine oil to the pin, insert it into the piston and check for freeplay by rocking the pin back-and-forth **(see illustration)**. If the pin is loose, a new piston and possibly new pin must be installed.

16   Repeat Step 15, this time inserting the piston pin into the connecting rod **(see illustration)**. If the pin is loose, measure the pin diameter and the pin bore in the rod (or have this done by a dealer or repair shop). A worn pin can be replaced separately; if the rod bore is worn, the rod and crankshaft must be replaced as an assembly.

17   Refer to Section 13 and install the rings on the piston.

Installation

Refer to illustration 12.18

18   Install the piston with its arrow mark toward the exhaust side (front) of the engine. Lubricate the pin and the rod bore with moly-based grease. Install a new snap-rings in the groove in one side of the piston (don't reuse the old snap-rings). Push the pin into position from the opposite side and install another new snap-ring. Compress the snap-rings only enough for them to fit in the piston. Make sure the clips are properly seated in the grooves **(see illustration)**.

2

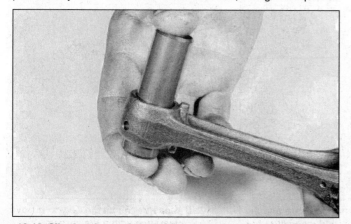

12.16 Slip the piston pin into the rod and try to rock it back-and-forth to check for looseness

12.18 Make sure both piston pin snap-rings are securely seated in the piston grooves

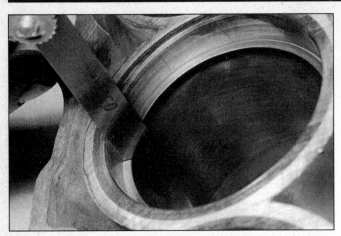

13.2 Check the piston ring end gap with a feeler gauge at the bottom of the cylinder

13.4 If the end gap is too small, clamp a file in a vise and file the ring ends (from the outside in only) to enlarge the gap slightly

13 Piston rings - installation

Refer to illustrations 13.2, 13.4, 13.7a, 13.7b, 13.9a, 13.9b, 13.10 and 13.12

1   Before installing the new piston rings, the ring end gaps must be checked.

2   Insert the top (No. 1) ring into the bottom of the first cylinder and square it up with the cylinder walls by pushing it in with the top of the piston. The ring should be about one-half inch above the bottom edge of the cylinder. To measure the end gap, slip a feeler gauge between the ends of the ring **(see illustration)** and compare the measurement to the Specifications.

3   If the gap is larger or smaller than specified, double check to make sure that you have the correct rings before proceeding.

4   If the gap is too small, it must be enlarged or the ring ends may come in contact with each other during engine operation, which can cause serious damage. The end gap can be increased by filing the ring ends very carefully with a fine file **(see illustration)**. When performing this operation, file only from the outside in.

5   Repeat the procedure for the second compression ring (ring gap is not specified for the oil ring rails or spacer).

6   Once the ring end gaps have been checked/corrected, the rings can be installed on the piston.

7   The oil control ring (lowest on the piston) is installed first. It is composed of three separate components. Slip the spacer into the groove, then install the upper side rail **(see illustrations)**. Do not use a piston ring installation tool on the oil ring side rails as they may be damaged. Instead, place one end of the side rail into the groove between the spacer expander and the ring land. Hold it firmly in place and slide a finger around the piston while pushing the rail into the groove (taking care not to cut your fingers on the sharp edges). Next, install the lower side rail in the same manner.

8   After the three oil ring components have been installed, check to make sure that both the upper and lower side rails can be turned smoothly in the ring groove.

9   Install the no. 2 (middle) ring next with its identification mark facing up **(see illustration)**. Do not mix the top and middle rings; they

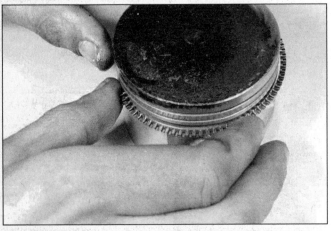

13.7a Installing the oil ring expander - make sure the ends don't overlap

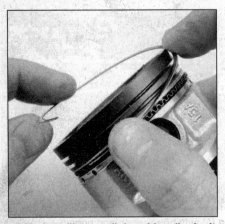

13.7b Installing an oil ring side rail - don't use a ring installation tool to do this

13.9a Install the middle ring with its identification mark up

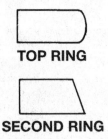

TOP RING

SECOND RING

13.9b The top and middle (second) rings can be identified by their profiles

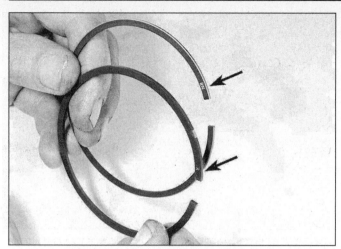

13.10 The top and middle rings have identification marks (arrows); these must be up when the rings are installed

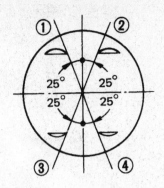

13.12 Arrange the ring gaps like this

1   *Top compression ring*
2   *Oil ring lower rail*
3   *Oil ring upper rail*
4   *Second compression ring*

can be identified by their profiles **(see illustration)**.

10   To avoid breaking the ring, use a piston ring installation tool and make sure that the identification mark is facing up **(see illustration)**. Fit the ring into the middle groove on the piston. Do not expand the ring any more than is necessary to slide it into place.

11   Finally, install the no. 1 (top) ring in the same manner. Make sure the identifying mark is facing up. Be very careful not to confuse the top and second rings.

12   Once the rings have been properly installed, stagger the end gaps, including those of the oil ring side rails **(see illustration)**.

---

14   External oil pipe and oil cooler - removal and installation

Removal

External oil pipe

Refer to illustration 14.1

1   Remove the union bolt and sealing washers on the right side of the engine **(see illustration)**.

2   At the other end of the pipe, remove the oil temperature switch (see Chapter 8), union bolt and sealing washers. Detach the pipe from the engine and take it out.

Oil cooler

Refer to illustration 14.3

3   Hold the fitting at one of the oil cooler hoses with a wrench and loosen the nut with a second wrench **(see illustration)**. Unscrew the nut from the oil cooler.

4   Remove the oil cooler mounting nuts, lower the oil cooler so the top post clears its grommet and take the oil cooler out of the vehicle.

5   To remove the oil cooler hoses from the vehicle, remove the hose retainer. Detach the hoses from the oil filter outer housing on the left side of the engine in the same way they were disconnected from the oil cooler.

Installation

6   Installation is the reverse of the removal steps, with the following additions:

a)   *Replace the sealing washers whenever the union bolts or hose fittings are loosened.*

b)   *Tighten the union bolts or hose fittings to the torques listed in this Chapter's Specifications.*

---

15   Primary clutch - removal, inspection and installation

Removal

Refer to illustrations 15.5a, 15.5b, 15.6, 15.7, 15.8, 15.9a and 15.9b

1   Place the shift pedal in the Neutral position.

2   Drain the engine oil (see Chapter 1).

3   Remove the union bolt from the external oil pipe **(see illustration 14.1)**.

14.1 There's a sealing washer on each side of the banjo fitting (arrows)

14.3 Hold the fitting (A) with one wrench and undo the nut (B); remove the mounting nuts (C), then slide the cooler off the studs and lower it clear

15.5a Loosen the clutch cover bolts in a criss-cross pattern - this is the YFM350ER, YFM350FW and 1996 through 1998 YFM350U engine . . .

15.6a There's a cover dowel at the rear (arrow) . . .

15.6b . . . and one at the front (arrow)

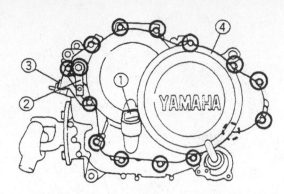

15.5b . . .and this is the YFM350FWB and 1999 YFM350U engine

4   If necessary for access, remove the right footrest (see Chapter 7).

5   If you're working on a YFM350FWB or 1999 YFM350U model, remove the reverse control lever and cable bracket from the right crankcase cover. On all models, unbolt the cover from the engine **(see illustrations)**. If you're working on a YFM350ER, YFM350FW or 1996 through 1998 YFM350U model, carefully pull the cover off so the clutch release mechanism isn't pulled from its hole in the crankcase. If the cover is stuck, tap it gently with a soft hammer to free it - don't pry it loose or the gasket surfaces will be damaged.

6   Locate the cover dowels **(see illustrations)**. Set them aside for safekeeping.

7   If you're working on a YFM350ER, YFM350FW or 1996 through 1998 YFM350U model, bend back the lockwasher tab; on YFM350FWB and 1999 YFM350U models, bend back or grind away the staked portion of the locknut.

8   Wedge a rag between the gears of the primary clutch and the secondary clutch to prevent the primary clutch from turning, then unscrew the locknut. If you're working on a YFM350ER, YFM350FW or 1996 through 1998 YFM350U model, remove the lockwasher.

9   Turn the secondary clutch so one of its cutouts aligns with the gear on the primary clutch housing **(see illustration)**, then pull the primary clutch off the crankshaft and remove the washer **(see illustration)**.

Inspection

Refer to illustrations 15.10, 15.11, 15.12 and 15.16

10   Take the weight assembly out of the drum. If you're working on a

15.7 On YFM350ER, YFM350FW and 1996 through 1998 YFM350U models, bend back the lockwasher tab; on all others, grind away the staked portion of the locknut

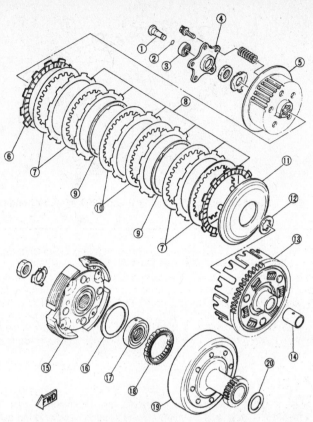

15.8a Primary and secondary clutches (YFM350ER, YFM350FW and 1996 through 1998 YFM350U models)

1	Pushrod
2	O-ring
3	Bearing
4	Spring plate
5	Clutch boss
6	Friction plate (with notch)
7	Metal plates (1.6 mm thick)
8	Friction plates (without notch)
9	Cushion springs
10	Clutch plates (2.0 mm thick)
11	Pressure plate
12	Thrust washer
13	Clutch housing (secondary clutch)
14	Collar
15	Clutch weight assembly
16	Plain washer
17	Bearing retainer
18	One-way clutch
19	Clutch housing (primary clutch)
20	Plain washer

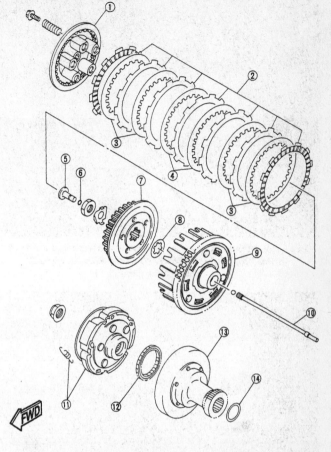

15.8b Primary and secondary clutches (YFM350FWB and 1999 YFM350U) - exploded view

1	Pressure plate	8	Thrust washer
2	Friction plates	9	Secondary clutch housing
3	Thin metal plates (1.6 mm - four total)	10	Long pushrod
4	Thick metal plates (2.0 mm - two total)	11	Primary clutch weight assembly
5	Short pushrod	12	One-way clutch bearing
6	O-ring	13	Primary clutch housing
7	Clutch boss	14	Plain washer

2

15.9a Align one of the cutouts in the secondary clutch housing with the gear on the primary clutch housing, then pull it off the crankshaft

15.9b Remove the plain washer

15.10 On YFM350ER, YFM350FW and 1996 through 1998 YFM350U engines, there's a plain washer behind the weight assembly

15.11 Check the one-way clutch for wear or damage

YFM350ER, YFM350FW or 1996 through 1998 YFM350U model, remove the plain washer as well **(see illustration)**.

11   Check the one-way clutch rollers for signs of wear or scoring **(see illustration)**. The rotors should be unmarked with no signs of wear such as pitting or flat spots. Replace the one-way clutch together with the drum if it's worn.

12   Measure the thickness of the lining material on the weights **(see illustration)**. If it's thinner than the minimum listed in this Chapter's Specifications, replace the weights as a set.

13   Check the springs for breakage and the weights for wear or damage. Replace the weight assembly if problems are found.

14   Check the inside of the drum and replace it if it's worn or damaged.

15   Install the weight assembly in the drum.

16   Rotate the inner race of the ball bearing inside the crankcase cover with a finger **(see illustration)**. If the bearing is rough, loose or noisy, remove the Torx screws and retainer and install a new bearing. Apply non-permanent thread locking agent to the threads of the Torx screws and tighten them securely.

Installation

Refer to illustrations 15.21 and 15.22

17   Slip the washer onto the crankshaft **(see illustration 15.9b)**.

Position one of the cutouts in the secondary clutch to make room, then install the primary clutch **(see illustration 15.9a)**.

18   If you're working on a YFM350ER, YFM350FW and 1996 through 1998 YFM350U, install a new lockwasher.

19   Install the nut. Wedge a rag between the gears of the primary and secondary clutches to prevent the primary clutch from turning, then tighten the nut to the torque listed in this Chapter's Specifications.

20   If you're working on a YFM350ER, YFM350FW and 1996 through 1998 YFM350U, bend the lockwasher against the nut. If you're working on a YFM350FWB or 1999 YFM350U, stake the lip of the locknut with a hammer and punch.

21   Make sure the dowels are in position and install a new gasket **(see illustrations 15.6a and 15.6b)**. Position the cover on the crankcase. If the vehicle is equipped with a speedometer, make sure the pin in the speedometer gear drive aligns with the slot in the speedometer gear **(see illustration)**. **Caution:** *Don't force the cover on if it won't go easily. The speedometer drive may not be properly aligned and it will be broken if force is used.*

22   Thread the cover bolts into their holes. On YFM350ER, YFM350FW and 1996 through 1998 YFM350U models, one of the bolts has a copper washer **(see illustration)**. Tighten the cover bolts in two or three stages, in a criss-cross pattern, to the torque listed in this Chapter's Specifications.

23   The remainder of installation is the reverse of the removal steps.

24   Refill the engine with oil (see Chapter 1).

15.12 Measure the thickness of the friction material (arrow)

15.16 Remove the Torx screws and retainer to remove the bearing

15.21 Be sure the speedometer/odometer drive pin (upper arrow) engages the slot in the speedometer/odometer drive gear; make sure the shift guide is over the stopper bolt (lower arrow)

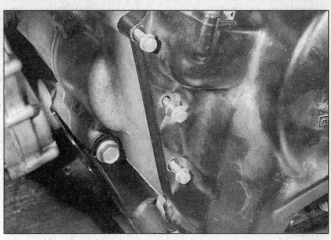

15.22 One case bolt has a copper washer

16 Secondary clutch and release mechanism - removal, inspection and installation

Release mechanism (YFM350ER, YFM350FWB and 1996 through 1998 YFM350U models)

Removal

Refer to illustrations 16.2a through 16.2h

1   Remove the right crankcase cover (see Section 15).
2   Remove the release mechanism components from the crankcase **(see illustrations)**.

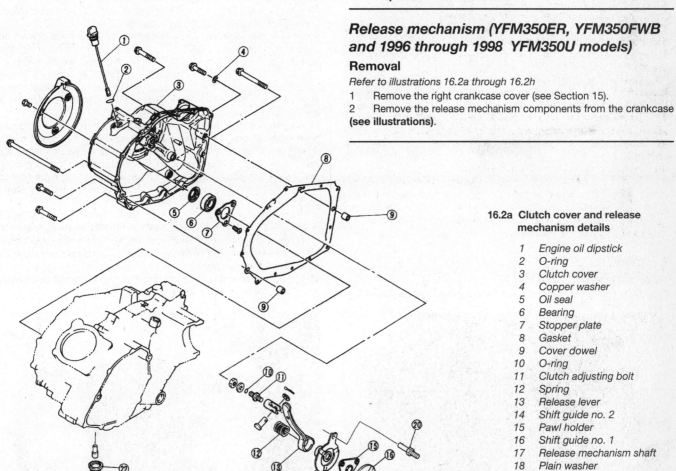

16.2a Clutch cover and release mechanism details

1   *Engine oil dipstick*
2   *O-ring*
3   *Clutch cover*
4   *Copper washer*
5   *Oil seal*
6   *Bearing*
7   *Stopper plate*
8   *Gasket*
9   *Cover dowel*
10   *O-ring*
11   *Clutch adjusting bolt*
12   *Spring*
13   *Release lever*
14   *Shift guide no. 2*
15   *Pawl holder*
16   *Shift guide no. 1*
17   *Release mechanism shaft*
18   *Plain washer*
19   *Thrust bearing*
20   *Stopper bolt*
21   *Shift shaft*
22   *Oil strainer*
23   *Spring*
24   *O-ring*
25   *Engine oil drain plug*

2

16.2b Pull off the no. 2 shift guide . . .

16.2c . . . the pawl holder . . .

16.2d . . . the no. 1 shift guide - make sure
its dots (arrows) are lined up with
each other on installation . . .

16.2e . . . a plain washer . . .

16.2f . . . the thrust bearing . . .

16.2g . . . a second plain washer . . .

Inspection

Refer to illustration 16.3

3   Check for visible wear or damage at the contact points of the lever and no. 1 shift guide and the friction points of the no. 1 shift guide, pawl holder and no. 2 shift guide. Check the spring for bending or distortion. Replace any parts that show problems. If the lever needs to be replaced, remove its cotter pin, washer and clevis pin and detach it from the cover **(see illustration)**. Replace the adjusting bolt O-ring in the crankcase cover whenever it's removed.

Installation

4   Installation is the reverse of the removal steps.
5   Refill the engine oil and adjust the clutch (see Chapter 1).

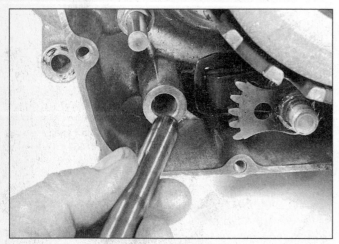

16.2h . . . and the shaft

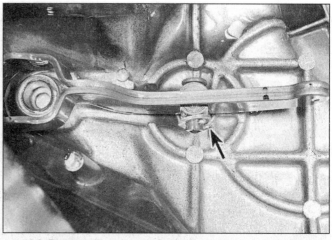

16.3 Remove the cotter pin (arrow), washer and pivot pin to
remove the clutch release lever; use a new cotter pin on installation

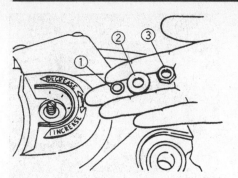

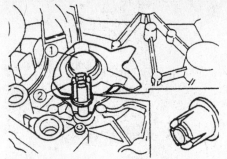

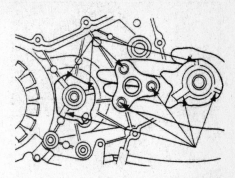

**16.8 Clutch adjuster details (YFM350FWB
and 1999 YFM350U)**

1 O-ring   2 Washer   3 Locknut

**16.9a Release mechanism (1) and the
stopper collar (2); on assembly, slide the
stopper collar just past the end of its shaft
as shown**

**16.9b On assembly, lubricate the release
mechanism friction points (arrows)**

Release mechanism (YFM350FWB and 1999 YFM350U models)

Refer to illustrations 16.8, 16.9a and 16.9b

Removal

6   The release mechanism on these models is mounted to the inside of the left crankcase cover.

7   Remove the left crankcase cover (see Chapter 8).

8   Unscrew the clutch adjuster locknut from the screw, then remove the washer and O-ring **(see illustration)**.

9   Remove the stopper collar from its shaft. Remove the three parts of the shift guide assembly **(see illustrations)**.

Inspection

10   Check all parts for wear and damage, especially at the contact points **(see illustration 16.9b)**. Replace any worn, cracked or bent parts. It's a good idea to replace all three parts of the shift guide assembly, even if only one shows problems.

Installation

11   Installation is the reverse of the removal steps. Lubricate the friction points with moly-based grease **(see illustration 16.9b)**.

Secondary clutch (YFM350ER, YFM350FWB and 1996 through 1998 YFM350U models)

Removal

Refer to illustrations 16.13a through 16.13g

12   Remove the right crankcase cover and the primary clutch (see

16.13a Remove the pushrod and O-ring . . .

Section 15).

13   Refer to the accompanying illustrations to remove the clutch components **(see illustration 15.8a and the accompanying illustra-tions)**. To prevent the clutch from turning while the nut is loosened, temporarily reinstall the primary clutch on the end of the crankshaft. Wedge a rag between the gears on the primary clutch and the secondary clutch drum, bend back the lockwasher and loosen the nut, then remove the rag and the primary clutch.

**16.13b . . . undo the spring plate bolts evenly,
in a criss-cross pattern . . .**

16.13c . . . and remove the spring plate, bolts and springs

2

16.13d Bend back the lockwasher and undo the nut as described in the text

16.13e Pull off the clutch boss, plates, cushion springs and pressure plate as a pack

Inspection

Refer to illustrations 16.17, 16.18 and 16.19

14   Check the bolt posts and the friction surface on the pressure plate for damaged threads, scoring or wear. Replace the pressure plate if any defects are found.

15   Check the edges of the slots in the clutch housing for indenta-

16.13f Remove the thrust washer (arrow) . . .

tions made by the friction plate tabs. If the indentations are deep they can prevent clutch release, so the housing should be replaced with a new one. If the indentations can be removed easily with a file, the life of the housing can be prolonged to an extent. Also, check the driven gear teeth for cracks, chips and excessive wear and the springs on the back side for breakage. If the gear is worn or damaged or the springs are broken, the clutch housing must be replaced with a new one. Check the bearing surface in the center of the clutch housing for score marks, scratches and excessive wear.

16   Check the splines of the clutch boss for indentations made by the tabs on the metal plates. Check the clutch boss friction surface for wear or scoring. Replace the clutch boss if problems are found.

17   Measure the free length of the clutch springs **(see illustration)** and compare the results to this Chapter's Specifications. If the springs have sagged, or if cracks are noted, replace them with new ones as a set.

18   If the lining material of the friction plates smells burnt or if it is glazed, new parts are required. If the metal clutch plates are scored or discolored, they must be replaced with new ones. Measure the thickness of the friction plates **(see illustration)** and replace with new parts any friction plates that are worn.

19   Lay the metal plates, one at a time, on a perfectly flat surface (such as a piece of plate glass) and check for warpage by trying to slip a feeler gauge between the flat surface and the plate **(see illustration)**. The feeler gauge should be the same thickness as the maximum warp listed in this Chapter's Specifications. Do this at several places around the plate's circumference. If the feeler gauge can be slipped under the plate, it is warped and should be replaced with a new one.

6.13g . . . then pull off the clutch housing and remove the collar

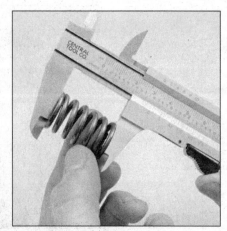

16.17 Measure the clutch spring free length

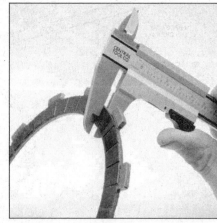

16.18 Measure the thickness of the friction plates

16.19 Check the metal plates for warpage

16.27 Align the arrows on clutch boss and pressure plate

20   Check the tabs on the friction plates for excessive wear and mushroomed edges. They can be cleaned up with a file if the deformation is not severe. Check the friction plates for warpage as described in Step 13.

21   Check the clutch collar for score marks, heat discoloration and evidence of excessive wear.

22   Check the clutch spring plate for wear and damage. Rotate the inner race of the bearing and check for roughness, looseness or excessive noise.

Installation

Refer to illustration 16.27

23   Lubricate the inner and outer surfaces of the clutch collar with moly-based grease and install it on the crankshaft.

24   Install the collar, clutch housing and thrust washer **(see illustrations 16.13g and 16.13f)**.

25   There are two different types of friction plate, one with a notch in one of its tabs and six without. The friction plate marked with a notch in one of its tabs goes next to the clutch boss flange **(see illustration 16.13e)**. There are two thicknesses of metal plate, two of them 2.0 mm thick and four of them 1.6 mm thick **(see illustration 15.8a)**.

26   Coat the friction plates with engine oil, then install the friction plates, metal plates and cushion springs on the clutch boss. Be sure to install them in the correct order **(see illustrations 15.8a and 16.13e)**.

27   Install the pressure plate on the last friction plate, aligning the arrows on clutch boss and pressure plate **(see illustration)**.

28   Install a new lockwasher and the nut on the mainshaft. Hold the clutch as described in Step 8 and tighten the locknut to the torque listed in this Chapter's Specifications.

29   Bend one of the locknut tabs over to secure the nut.

30   Install the clutch springs and the spring plate **(see illustrations 18.7b and 18.7a)**. Tighten the bolts to the torque listed in this Chapter's Specifications in two or three stages, in a criss-cross pattern.

31   The remainder of installation is the reverse of the removal steps.

Secondary clutch (YFM350FWB and 1999 YFM350U models)

Removal

Refer to illustrations 16.37a and 16.37b

32   Remove the right crankcase cover and the primary clutch (see Section 15).

33   Undo the pressure plate spring bolts evenly, in a criss-cross pattern **(see illustration 15.8b)**. Take off the bolts, springs and pressure plate.

34   Remove the short pushrod, steel ball and long pushrod, using a pencil magnet if necessary.

35   Remove the friction plates and metal plates. You can usually slide these off in a pack, but if they're stuck together you may need to pry them loose and remove them individually.

36   Bend back the tabs on the clutch locknut with a hammer and punch.

37   Using a clutch holding tool to keep the clutch boss from turning **(see illustrations)**, unscrew the clutch locknut.

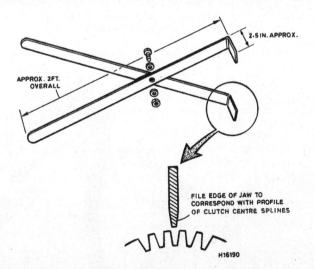

16.37a You can make a clutch holder from steel strap ...

16.37b ... or by bolting together an old metal plate and friction plate

17.3a Remove the bolt . . .

38   Remove the lockwasher, then pull off the clutch boss, thrust washer and clutch housing.

Inspection

39   Refer to Steps 14 through 22 above to inspect the clutch.

Installation

40   Lubricate the clutch housing bearing surface with clean engine oil and install the clutch housing on the transmission mainshaft.

41   Lubricate the thrust washer, then install it and the clutch boss.

42   Install a new lockwasher and the clutch locknut. Hold the clutch housing with one of the tools described in Step 37 and tighten the locknut to the torque listed in this Chapter's Specifications. Bend the tabs of the lockwasher against the flats on the nut.

43   Coat the ends of the long pushrod, the steel ball and the end of the short pushrod with moly-based grease, then install them in the mainshaft and clutch housing.

44   Coat the friction plates with clean engine oil, then install the friction and metal plates on the clutch boss. There are four thin metal plates and two thick metal plates. The installation sequence is as follows:

   a) Friction plate
   b) Thin metal plate
   c) Friction plate
   d) Thin metal plate
   e) Friction plate
   f) Thick metal plate
   g) Friction plate
   h) Thick metal plate
   i) Friction plate

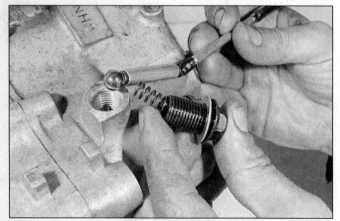

17.4 Remove the bolt and sealing washer, then pull out the spring and remove the detent ball with a magnet

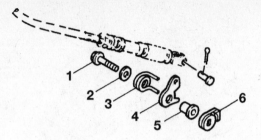

17.3b . . . and detach the lever components from the engine

1	Bolt	4	Outer lever
2	Washer	5	Collar
3	Spring	6	Inner lever

   j) Thin metal plate
   k) Friction plate
   l) Thin metal plate
   m) Friction plate

45   Install the pressure plate, aligning its punch mark with the punch mark on the clutch boss. Install the spring and spring bolts and tighten the bolts evenly in a criss-cross pattern to the torque listed in this Chapter's Specifications.

46   The remainder of installation is the reverse of the removal steps. Be sure to fill the engine with oil as described in Chapter 1.

17   Reverse shift mechanism - removal, inspection and installation

YFM350ER, YFM350FW and 1996 through 1998 YFM350U models

Refer to illustrations 17.3a, 17.3b and 17.4

1   The reverse lock lever and shift cam detent ball are accessible from outside the engine. The crankcase must be disassembled for access to the reverse shift cam and forks.

2   To remove the reverse lockout lever, disconnect its cable (see Chapter 1).

3   Remove the bolt, washer, spring, outer lever, inner lever and collar **(see illustrations)**.

4   At the right rear corner of the engine, remove the bolt and sealing washer. Lift out the spring and detent ball with a magnet **(see illustration)**.

5   Installation is the reverse of the removal steps, with the following additions:

   a) Tighten the lever bolt securely, but don't overtighten it.
   b) Use a new sealing washer on the detent ball bolt if the old one is worn or damaged. Tighten the detent ball bolt to the torque listed in this Chapter's Specifications.

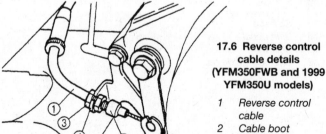

17.6 Reverse control cable details (YFM350FWB and 1999 YFM350U models)

1   Reverse control cable
2   Cable boot
3   Locknut
4   Cable bracket

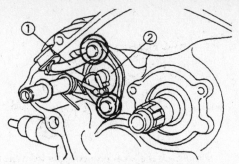

17.8 Detach the harness (1) from the crankcase notch and remove the gear position switch (2)

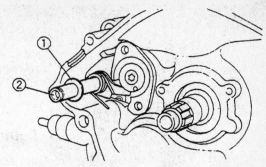

17.9a Remove the washer (1) and reverse shift bracket (2)

YFM350FWB and 1999 YFM350U models

Refer to illustrations 17.6, 17.8, 17.9a and 17.9b

6   Slide back the rubber boot on the reverse control cable, then unscrew the locknut all the way **(see illustration)**. Detach the cable from the bracket, then rotate the cable and slide its end plug out of the reverse shift arm.

7   Remove the right crankcase cover, then remove the primary and secondary clutches (see Sections 15 and 16).

8   Remove the gear position switch **(see illustration)**.

9   Remove the washer from the reverse shift bracket. Note how the spring ends engage the crankcase and the arm on the reverse shift bracket, then remove the bracket from the engine **(see illustrations)**.

10   Installation is the reverse of the removal steps, with the following additions:

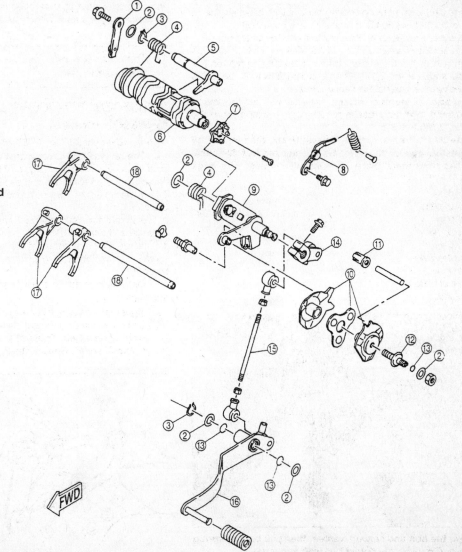

17.9b Shift and release mechanisms (YFM350FWB and 1999 YFM350U models) – exploded view

1   *Reverse control lever*
2   *Washer*
3   *Circlip*
4   *Spring*
5   *Reverse shift bracket*
6   *Shift cam*
7   *Shift cam segment*
8   *Stopper lever*
9   *Shift shaft*
10   *Shift guide assembly*
11   *Stopper collar*
12   *Adjuster*
13   *O-ring*
14   *Shift pedal link*
15   *Shift rod*
16   *Shift pedal*
17   *Shift fork*
18   *Shift fork guide bar*

2

18.2a Balancer alignment marks (YFM350ER, YFM350FW and 1996 through 1998 YFM350U models)

a) *Engage the ends of the spring on the reverse shift bracket with the bracket's arm and the crankcase. Engage the end of the arm on the reverse shift bracket with the shaft cam* (see illustration **17.9a**).
b) *Fit the grommet on the gear position switch's wiring harness securely into its notch in the crankcase* (see illustration **17.6**).

18   Balancer gears - removal, inspection and installation

Removal

Refer to illustrations 18.2a, 18.2b, 18.2c, 18.3, 18.4, 18.5, 18.6a, 18.6b, 18.7a, 18.7b, 18.8, 18.9a, 18.9b and 18.9c

1   Remove the primary and secondary clutches (see Sections 15 and 16). If you're working on a YFM350FWB or 1999 YFM350U model, remove the oil pipe and pump for access to the balancer drive gear (see Section 19).
2   Turn the crankshaft so the match marks on the balancer boss and the balancer drive and driven gears align **(see illustrations)**.
3   Bend back the tab on the balancer gear lockwasher **(see illustration 12.4 and the accompanying illustration)**. Wedge a rag between the teeth of the balancer drive and driven gears to prevent them from turning, undo the nut and remove the lockwasher.
4   Pull off the driven gear and remove the Woodruff key **(see illustration)**.

18.2b YFM350FWB and 1999 YFM350U models have alignment marks for the balancer boss and the drive gear . . .

| 1 | Drive gear | 3 | Springs |
| 2 | Pins | a | Alignment marks |

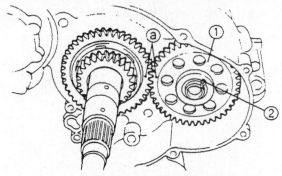

18.2c . . . and for the drive gear and driven gear

| 1 | Driven gear | a | Alignment marks |
| 2 | Woodruff key | | |

5   Slide the collar off the end of the balancer **(see illustration)**.
6   If you're working on a YFM350ER, YFM350FW or 1996 through 1998 YFM350U, remove the snap-ring **(see illustration)**. On all models, remove the holding plate **(see illustration)**.
7   Grasp the drive gear and pull it off the buffer boss **(see illustration)**. The six springs and three pins will fall out as you do this, so be prepared to catch them **(see illustration)**.
8   Place a puller on the buffer boss and pull it free of the crankshaft **(see illustration)**. **Note:** *Yamaha recommends replacing the buffer*

18.3 Bend back the lockwasher, wedge a rag between the gears to prevent rotation and unscrew the nut

18.4 Remove the balancer driven gear and the Woodruff key (arrow) . . .

18.5 . . . and slide off the collar

18.6a Remove the drive gear snap-ring (if equipped) . . .

18.6b . . . and the holding plate

18.7a Pull off the drive gear . . .

18.7b . . . the six springs and the three dowels; a dowel fits inside every other spring on assembly

18.8 Remove the buffer boss with a puller; replace the buffer boss and its Woodruff key with new ones whenever they're removed

boss and its Woodruff key with new ones whenever they are removed from the crankshaft.

9 Once the buffer boss is loose, remove it, the plain washer, the collar, the oil pump drive gear and two Woodruff keys - one for the buffer boss and one for the oil pump drive gear **(see illustrations)**.

Inspection

10 Check the gears for worn or damaged teeth and replace them as a set if problems are found.

11 Check the springs for distortion or fatigue and replace them as necessary.

12 Check the remaining components for wear and damage and replace any worn or damaged parts. Replace the lockwasher with a new one whenever it's removed.

13 Inspect the balancer and crankshaft ball bearings to the extent possible without disassembling the crankcase. If wear, looseness or roughness can be detected, the crankcase will have to be disassembled to replace the bearings.

18.9a Remove the plain washer and the oil pump drive gear . . .

18.9b . . . the buffer boss Woodruff key . . .

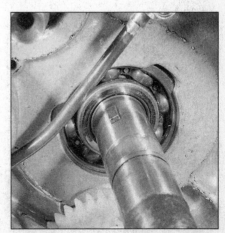

18.9c . . . and the oil pump drive gear Woodruff key

18.14 Install the lockwasher so its tab fits into the shaft slot

19.2 Remove the union bolt and two sealing washers at each end of the pipe (YFM350FW shown; others similar)

Installation

Refer to illustration 18.14

14   Installation is the reverse of the removal steps, with the following additions:

a) *Use a new buffer boss and Woodruff key.*

b) *Apply engine oil to the crankshaft after installing the oil pump drive gear Woodruff key, and again after installing the buffer boss Woodruff key.*

c) *Install the buffer boss with the same tool used to install the crankshaft (see Section 25). The basic tool is crankshaft installer set YM-90050; you'll also need pot extension YM-33280, adapter YM-33279 and buffer boss installer set 98890-04088. If you don't have the correct special tool, take the engine to a Yamaha dealer and have the buffer boss installed.*

d) *Make sure the alignment marks on the buffer boss, drive gear and driven gear are lined up* **(see illustrations 18.2a, 18.2b and 18.2c).**

e) *Use a new lockwasher and make sure its tab fits in the slot in the balancer shaft* **(see illustration).** *Tighten the nut to the torque listed in this Chapter's Specifications.*

---

19 Oil pipe and pump - removal, inspection and installation

Note: *The oil pump can be removed with the engine in the frame.*

Oil pipe

Removal

Refer to illustration 19.2

1   Remove the primary and secondary clutches (Sections 15 and 16).

2   Remove the union bolt and hex bolts that secure the oil pipe and remove the pipe **(see illustration).**

Inspection

3   Check the oil pipe for bending and for cracks, especially where the banjo fittings are brazed to the pipe. Replace it if problems are found.

4   Clean the inside of the pipe with solvent to remove any clogging.

Installation

5   Installation is the reverse of the removal steps, with the following additions:

a) *Use new sealing washers on each side of the banjo fitting at both ends of the pipe.*

b) *Tighten the bolts to the torque listed in this Chapter's Specifications.*

Oil pump

Removal

Refer to illustrations 19.8a and 19.8b

6   Remove the primary clutch (see Section 15).

7   Remove the balancer drive gear and oil pump drive gear (see Section 18).

19.8a Loosen the pump cover screw (A) if you plan to take the pump apart; remove the mounting screws (B) . . .

19.8b . . . and take the pump and gasket off the engine

19.9 Remove the oil pump assembly screw

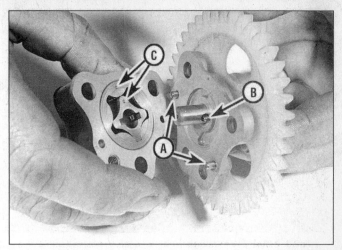

19.10 Take the cover and driven gear off the pump body and rotors; on reassembly, the dowels (A) must fit in the holes, the drive pin must fit in the slot (B) and the punch marks (C) must face the pump cover

8   Rotate the oil pump driven gear for access to the mounting screws **(see illustration)**. If you're planning to disassemble the pump, loosen the assembly screw now while the pump is secured to the engine. Remove the mounting screws and take the pump and gasket off **(see illustration)**.

Inspection

Refer to illustrations 19.9, 19.10, 19.12a, 19.12b and 19.12c

9   Remove the assembly screw **(see illustration)**.
10   Remove the driven gear, shaft and pump cover from the pump body **(see illustration)**.
11   Wash all the components in solvent, then dry them off. Check the pump body, the rotors and the cover for scoring and wear. If any damage or uneven or excessive wear is evident, replace the pump. If you are rebuilding the engine, it's a good idea to install a new oil pump.
12   Place the rotors in the pump cover. Measure the clearance between the outer rotor and body, and between the inner and outer rotors, with a feeler gauge **(see illustrations)**. Place a straightedge across the pump body and rotors and measure the gap with a feeler gauge **(see illustration)**. If any of the clearances are beyond the limits listed in this Chapter's Specifications, replace the pump.
13   Check the pump driven gear for wear or damage. The gear and its drive pin are available separately, so if either needs to be replaced, push the drive pin out of the gear shaft and pull the gear out of the pump cover.
14   Reassemble the pump by reversing the disassembly steps, with

the following additions:

a)   *Before installing the cover, pack the cavities between the rotors with petroleum jelly - this will ensure the pump develops suction quickly and begins oil circulation as soon as the engine is started.*
b)   *Make sure the cover dowels and drive pin are in position* **(see illustration 19.8b).**
c)   *Tighten the cover screw to the torque listed in this Chapter's Specifications.*

Installation

15   Installation is the reverse of removal, with the following additions:

a)   *Install a new gasket* **(see illustration 19.8b).**
b)   *Tighten the oil pump mounting screws to the torque listed in this Chapter's Specifications.*

20   Recoil starter - removal, inspection and installation

Removal

Refer to illustration 20.1

1   Unbolt the recoil starter case from the left side of the engine (see

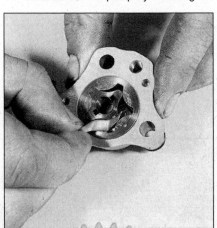

19.12a Measure the gap between the inner and outer rotors . . .

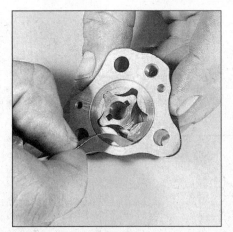

19.12b . . . and between the outer rotor and body . . .

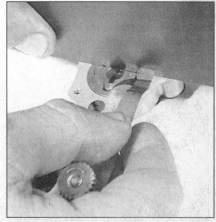

19.12c . . . and between the rotors and a straightedge; this gap isn't specified by Yamaha, but the pump should be replaced if it's significant

2

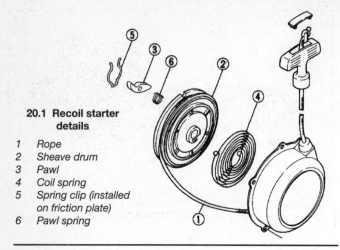

20.1 Recoil starter details

1 *Rope*
2 *Sheave drum*
3 *Pawl*
4 *Coil spring*
5 *Spring clip (installed on friction plate)*
6 *Pawl spring*

illustration). Take the starter assembly off.

2   Pull the rope partway out and tie a knot in it so it won't be pulled into the case, then remove the cap and the starter handle.

Inspection

Warning: *Rewinding the coil spring is complicated and can be potentially dangerous. If you don't have experience with recoil starters, take the job to a Yamaha dealer or other qualified shop. If you do the job yourself, wear eye protection and heavy gloves in case the recoil spring flies out.*

3   Remove the nut, then the friction plate with its spring clip, the drive pawl, pawl spring, sheave drum and coil spring.

4   Check for obvious wear or damage, such as a broken rope. Replace worn or damaged parts.

Installation

5   Tie a knot in one end of the rope and pull it through the hole in the center of the sheave drum so the rope is in the sheave drum groove. Place the sheave drum on a work surface so the slit in its outer edge is up. Wind the rope 4-1/2 turns clockwise around the sheave drum, then lodge the rope in the slit in the edge of the sheave drum.

6   Install the pawl spring and pawl in the sheave drum.

7   Engage the hook on one end of the starter spring with the slit in the case (the slit closest to the outer edge of the case), then wind the spring clockwise, from the outside in, and engage the hook on its free end with the hook in the center of the case.

8   Install the spring clip and friction plate, engaging the ends of the spring clip with the starter pawl holes.

9   With the case down on a work surface, turn the sheave drum three turns clockwise to preload the starter spring. Pull the rope out

through the starter case as you do this, then tie a temporary knot in the rope so it won't be pulled back into the case.

10   Slip the starter handle into the rope and tie a permanent knot in its end, then install the cap.

11   Untie the temporary knot in the rope and let it back into the case.

12   Install the recoil starter on the engine, engaging it with the rotor. Install the case bolts and tighten them to the torque listed in this Chapter's Specifications.

21 External shift mechanism - removal, inspection and installation

Shift pedal

Removal

Refer to illustration 21.1

1   If you're working on a YFM350ER, YFM350FW or 1996 through 1998 YFM350U, look for alignment marks on the end of the shift pedal and shift shaft **(see illustration)**. If they aren't visible, make your own marks with a sharp punch. Remove the shift pedal pinch bolt and slide the pedal off the shaft.

2   If you're working on a YFM350FWB or a 1999 YFM350U, mark and remove the shift arm as described in Step 1 **(see illustration 17.9b)**. Then remove the snap-ring that secures the shift pedal to its pivot shaft and slide the pedal off.

Inspection

3   Check the shift pedal for wear or damage such as bending. Check the splines on the shift pedal and shaft for stripping or step wear. Replace the pedal or shaft if these problems are found.

4   Check the shift shaft seal in the alternator cover for signs of leakage. If the seal has been leaking, remove the alternator cover (see Chapter 8). Pry the seal out of the cover, then tap in a new one with a seal driver or socket the same diameter as the seal.

Installation

5   Install the shift pedal. Line up its punch marks and tighten the pinch bolt to the torque listed in this Chapter's Specifications.

External shift linkage (YFM350ER, YFM350FW and 1996 through 1998 YFM350U)

Removal

Refer to illustrations 21.7, 21.8 and 21.9

6   Remove the right crankcase cover (see Section 15).

7   Pull the shift shaft and its washer out of the crankcase **(see illustration)**.

21.1 If there aren't visible alignment marks on the shift shaft and pedal, make a mark on the shaft next to the pedal gap

21.7 Pull the shift shaft out of the crankcase and remove the thrust washer (arrow)

21.8 Remove the stopper lever and spring

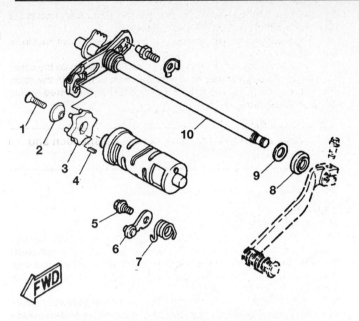

21.11 Check the shift shaft components for wear or damage

21.9 External shift mechanism details

1	Screw	6	Stopper lever
2	Washer	7	Spring
3	Segment	8	Oil seal
4	Dowel	9	Plain washer
5	Stopper lever bolt	10	Shift shaft

8   Unbolt the stopper arm, then remove the arm and its spring **(see illustration)**.

9   Remove the Torx screw from the center of the shift drum segment **(see illustration)**.

10   Remove the shift drum segment and note the location of its dowel.

Inspection

Refer to illustrations 21.11 and 21.12

11   Check the shift shaft for bends and damage to the splines **(see illustration)**. If the shaft is bent, you can attempt to straighten it, but if the splines are damaged it will have to be replaced. Check the condition of the return spring, shift arm and the pawl spring. Replace the shift shaft if they're worn, cracked or distorted.

12   Make sure the return spring post isn't loose **(see illustration)**. If it is, bend back its lockwasher and unscrew it. Apply a non-hardening

locking compound to the threads, then reinstall the post with a new lockwasher and tighten it to the torque listed in this Chapter's Specifications.

Installation

Refer to illustrations 21.15a and 21.15b

13   Position the spring on the stopper arm, then install the stopper arm on the engine and tighten its bolt to the torque listed in this Chapter's Specifications.

14   Pull down the stopper arm and install the drum segment on the shift drum, making sure its dowel is located in the drum segment notch **(see illustration 21.8)**. Apply non-permanent thread locking agent to the threads of the shift cam segment Torx screw, then install it and tighten to the torque listed in this Chapter's Specifications. Make sure the stopper arm spring is correctly installed and that the roller end of the stopper arm engages a notch in the drum center.

15   Place the washer on the shift shaft and slide it into the engine **(see illustration 21.7)**. Slide the shaft all the way in, making sure the return spring fits over the post and the pawls engage the drum segment pins **(see illustrations)**.

16   The remainder of installation is the reverse of the removal steps.

17   Check the engine oil level and add some, if necessary (see Chapter 1).

External shift linkage (YFM350FWB and 1999 YFM350U)

Removal

Refer to illustrations 21.19, 21.20 and 21.21

18   Remove the left crankcase cover (see Chapter 8).

21.12 If the return spring post is loose, unscrew it, then reinstall it with thread locking agent and a new lockwasher

21.15a Pry apart the return spring and position it over the post

21.15b Make sure the ratchet pawls engage the shift drum pins

21.19 Remove the shift shaft (1) ...

21.20 ... then unbolt the stopper lever and remove the spring (2)

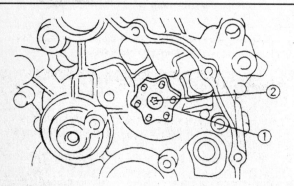

21.21 The shift cam segment (1) is secured by a Torx screw (2)

19   Disengage the shift shaft from the shift drum cam and remove it from the engine, then remove the shift shaft washer **(see illustration 17.9b and the accompanying illustration)**.

20   Note how the stopper lever spring is attached to the stopper lever and the post on the crankcase, then unbolt the stopper lever and unhook the spring **(see illustration)**.

21   If necessary, unscrew the Torx bolt and remove the shaft cam segment **(see illustration)**.

22   Installation is the reverse of the removal steps.

22 Crankcase - disassembly and reassembly

1   To examine and repair or replace the crankshaft, connecting rod, bearings and transmission components, the crankcase must be split into two parts.

22.11b ... this bolt has a copper washer

22.11a Crankcase bolts (YFM350ER, YFM350FW and 1996 through 1998 YFM350U) ...

Disassembly

Refer to illustrations 22.11a through 22.11e, 22.12a, 22.12b, 22.12c, 22.12d and 22.13

2   Remove the engine from the vehicle (see Section 5).

3   Remove the carburetor (see Chapter 3).

4   Remove the alternator rotor and the starter motor (see Chapter 8).

5   Remove the primary and secondary clutches (see Sections 15 and 16).

6   Remove the external shift mechanism (see Section 21).

7   Remove the reverse shift cam detent ball and spring (see Section 17).

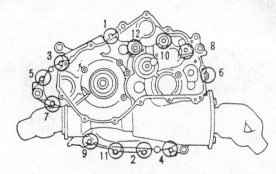

22.11c Left side crankcase bolts (YFM350FWB and 1999 YFM350U models)

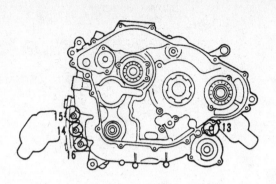

22.11d Right side crankcase bolts (YFM350FWB and 1999 YFM350U models)

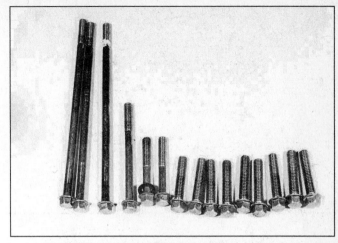

22.11e The bolts are different lengths; labeling them will speed reassembly

22.12a Using a soft face hammer, tap gently and evenly on the ends of the shafts as the case halves are separated

22.12b Pry only between the pry points . . .

8   Remove the cam chain tensioner, cylinder head, cam chain, cylinder and piston (see Sections 7, 8, 11 and 12).
9   Remove the oil pump (see Section 19).
10   Check carefully to make sure there aren't any remaining components that attach the upper and lower halves of the crankcase together.
11   Loosen the crankcase bolts in two or three stages, in a criss-cross pattern **(see illustrations)**. Remove the bolts and label them; they are different lengths **(see illustration)**. On YFM350FWB and 1999

YFM350U models, the left side bolts are M6 and the right side bolts are M8.
12   Tap gently on the ends of the transmission shafts, balancer shaft and crankshaft as the case halves are being separated **(see illustration)**. Carefully pry the crankcase apart at the pry points and lift the right half off the left half **(see illustrations)**. Don't pry against the mating surfaces or they'll develop leaks.

22.12c . . . there's one at each end of the case

22.12d Lift the right case half off the left case half

22.13 Make sure the case dowels (arrows) are in place

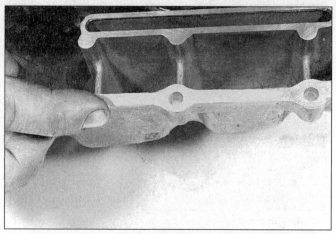

22.17 Coat both case halves with a thin film of sealant

22.18 Pour oil over the gears and shafts

23.3a Check the case bearings for roughness, looseness or noise (YFM350FW shown)

13 Locate the crankcase dowels **(see illustration)**. If they aren't secure in their holes, remove them and set them aside for safekeeping.
14 Refer to Sections 23 through 25 for information on the internal components of the crankcase.

Reassembly

Refer to illustrations 22.17 and 22.18

15 Remove all traces of old gasket and sealant from the crankcase mating surfaces with a sharpening stone or similar tool. Be careful not to let any fall into the case as this is done and be careful not to damage the mating surfaces.
16 Check to make sure the dowel pins are in place in their holes in the mating surface of the crankcase **(see illustration 22.13)**.
17 Coat both crankcase mating surfaces with Yamaha Quick Gasket (ACC-11001-05-01) or equivalent sealant **(see illustration)**.
18 Pour some engine oil over the transmission gears, balancer shaft and crankshaft bearing surfaces and the shift cams **(see illustration)**. Don't get any oil on the crankcase mating surfaces.
19 Carefully place the right crankcase half onto the left crankcase half. While doing this, make sure the transmission shafts, shift drums, crankshaft and balancer fit into their ball bearings in the right crankcase half.
20 Install the crankcase half bolts in the correct holes and tighten them so they are just snug. Then tighten them in two or three stages, in a criss-cross pattern, to the torque listed in this Chapter's Specifications (don't forget to install the copper washer).
21 Turn the transmission shafts to make sure they turn freely. Also make sure the crankshaft and balancer shaft turn freely.
22 The remainder of installation is the reverse of removal.

23 Crankcase components - inspection and servicing

Refer to illustrations 23.3a and 23.3b

1 Separate the crankcase and remove the following:

a) *Transmission shafts and gears*
b) *Middle drive gear*
c) *Crankshaft and main bearings*
d) *Shift drums and forks*

2 Clean the crankcase halves thoroughly with new solvent and dry them with compressed air. All oil passages should be blown out with compressed air and all traces of old gasket sealant should be removed from the mating surfaces. **Caution:** *Be very careful not to nick or gouge the crankcase mating surfaces or leaks will result. Check both crankcase sections very carefully for cracks and other damage.*
3 Check the bearings in the case halves **(see illustrations)**. If they don't turn smoothly, replace them. For bearings that aren't accessible from the outside, a blind hole puller will be needed for removal. Drive the remaining bearings out with a bearing driver or a socket having an outside diameter slightly smaller than that of the bearing outer race. Before installing the bearings, allow them to sit in the freezer overnight, and about fifteen-minutes before installation, place the case half in an oven, set to about 200-degrees F, and allow it to heat up. The bearings are an interference fit, and this will ease installation. **Warning:** *Before heating the case, wash it thoroughly with soap and water so no explosive fumes are present. Also, don't use a flame to heat the case. Install the bearings with a socket or bearing driver that bears against the bearing outer race.*

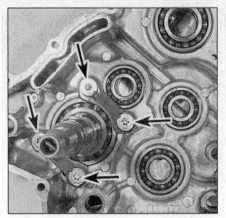

23.3b The middle drive gear bearing on early-design engines is secured by Torx screws; use new screws and stake them on reassembly

24.3a Pull out the longer guide bar (arrow) . . .

24.3b . . . and remove its shift forks

4   If any damage is found that can't be repaired, replace the crankcase halves as a set.

5   Assemble the case halves (see Section 22) and check to make sure the crankshaft and the transmission shafts turn freely.

---

24 Transmission shafts, balancer shaft and shift cam - removal, inspection and installation

---

Note: *When disassembling the transmission shafts, place the parts on a long rod or thread a wire through them to keep them in order and facing the proper direction.*

YFM350ER, YFM350FW and 1996 through 1998 YFM350U models

Removal

Refer to illustrations 24.3a, 24.3b, 24.3c, 24.3d, 24.4, 24.5, 24.8, 24.10a, 24.10b, 24.10c, 24.11a, 24.11b and 24.12

1   Remove the engine, then separate the case halves (see Sections 5 and 22).

2   The transmission components and shift cams remain in the left case half when the case is separated.

3   Pull out the longer guide bar and the two no. 1 shift forks **(see illustrations)**. Lift the shift cam out of the case half, then remove the

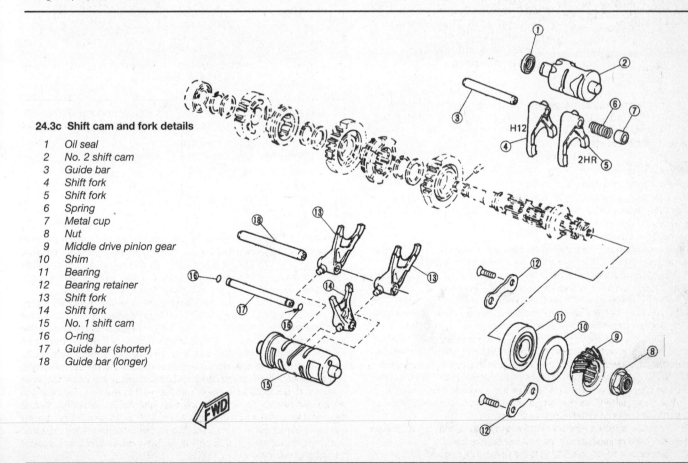

24.3c Shift cam and fork details

1   Oil seal
2   No. 2 shift cam
3   Guide bar
4   Shift fork
5   Shift fork
6   Spring
7   Metal cup
8   Nut
9   Middle drive pinion gear
10   Shim
11   Bearing
12   Bearing retainer
13   Shift fork
14   Shift fork
15   No. 1 shift cam
16   O-ring
17   Guide bar (shorter)
18   Guide bar (longer)

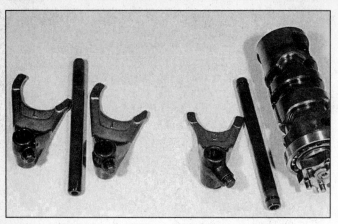

24.3d No. 1 shift cam, shift forks and shafts

24.4 Lift out the balancer shaft, then remove the plain washer (arrow), reverse wheel gear and reverse axle

shorter guide bar and no. 2 shift fork **(see illustration)**.
4   Lift the balancer shaft out of the crankcase **(see illustration)**.
5   Remove the plain washer from the reverse wheel gear, then remove the gear from the reverse axle and lift the reverse axle out of the

crankcase **(see illustration 24.4 and the accompanying illustration)**.
6   From the driveaxle, remove the plain washer, high pinion gear, first wheel gear and second plain washer.
7   From the idle axle, remove the plain washer, high wheel gear with

24.5 Transmission gears and shafts (YFM350ER, YFM350FW and 1996 through 1998 YFM350U models) - exploded view

1   Bearing
2   Plain washer
3   Reverse wheel gear
4   Snap-ring
5   Reverse axle
6   Middle driven gear
7   Middle driven gear holder
8   Middle drive gear
9   Dog clutch
10 Reverse wheel gear
11 Dowel
12 Snap-ring
13 Middle driveaxle
14 High wheel gear
15 Idle axle
16 Oil seal
17 High pinion gear (23 teeth)
18 First wheel gear (38 teeth)
19 Driveaxle
20 Fifth wheel gear (24 teeth)
21 Third wheel gear
22 Fourth wheel gear
23 Second wheel gear
24 Main axle
25 Fifth pinion gear
26 Third pinion gear
27 Fourth pinion gear
28 Second pinion gear

FWD

24.8 Remove the driveaxle (left arrow) and main axle (right arrow) from the case

24.10a Note the positions of the shift forks and the numbers cast on them

bearings and second plain washer. Remove the idle axle from the crankcase.

8   Remove the fifth wheel gear from the driveaxle, then lift the driveaxle and its remaining gears out of the case **(see illustration)**.

9   Remove the main axle with its gears from the case **(see illustration 24.8)**.

10   Note the positions of the shift forks that engage the no. 2 shift cam **(see illustration)**. Remove the snap-ring, plain washer and middle driven gear from the middle driveaxle, then remove the middle driven

gear holder **(see illustrations)**. Remove the guide bar, shift forks and no. 2 shift cam.

11   Remove another snap-ring and plain washer from the middle driveaxle, then remove the middle drive gear **(see illustration)**. Slide the dog clutch off the middle driveaxle **(see illustration)**.

12   Remove another snap-ring and plain washer, then take the no. 2 reverse wheel gear off the middle driveaxle **(see illustration)**.

13   Complete disassembly of the driveaxle and main axle by removing the snap-rings, plain washers and gears **(see illustration 24.5)**.

24.10b Remove the snap-ring, plain washer and middle driven gear . . .

24.10c . . . the middle driven gear holder . . .

24.11a . . . the snap-ring (arrow), plain washer and middle drive gear . . .

2

24.11b . . . the dog clutch . . .

24.12 . . . and the snap-ring, plain washer and reverse wheel gear

Inspection

14   Wash all of the components in clean solvent and dry them off. Rotate the middle driven shaft, feeling for tightness, rough spots, excessive looseness and listening for noises in the bearing or middle drive bevel gear. Replacement of the bevel gear or shaft will require setting up the gear backlash of the middle driven gear; take the case and middle driven gear assembly (which includes the transfer case on 4WD models) to a Yamaha dealer to have this procedure done.

15   Inspect the shift fork grooves in the gears, the middle driven gear holder and the dog clutch. If a groove is worn or scored, replace the affected part and inspect its corresponding shift fork.

16   Check the shift forks for distortion and wear, especially at the fork ears **(see illustrations 24.3c and 24.3d)**. If they are discolored or severely worn they are probably bent. Inspect the guide pins for excessive wear and distortion and replace any defective parts with new ones.

17   Check the shift fork guide bars evidence of wear, galling and other damage. Make sure the shift forks move smoothly on the guide bars. If the shafts are worn or bent, replace them with new ones.

18   Check the edges of the grooves in the shift cams for signs of excessive wear.

19   Hold the inner race of the shift cam bearing with fingers and spin the outer race. Replace the bearing if it's rough, loose or noisy. Replace the segment on the no. 1 shift cam if it's worn or damaged (see Section 21).

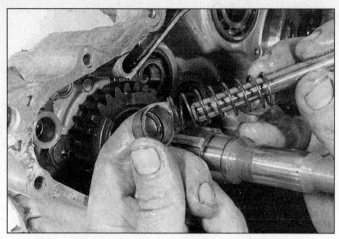

24.23 Install the metal cup and spring on the guide bar

20   Check the gear teeth for cracking and other obvious damage. Check the bushing surface in the inner diameter of the freewheeling gears for scoring or heat discoloration. Replace damaged parts.

21   Inspect the engagement dogs and dog holes on gears so

24.25 Transmission, middle drive shaft and balancer (YFM350FWB and 1999 YFM350U) – exploded view

1   Middle drive gear
2   First wheel gear
3   Drive axle
4   Fifth wheel gear
5   Third wheel gear
6   Fourth wheel gear
7   Reverse wheel gear (no. 1)
8   Second wheel gear (no. 2)
9   Middle driven gear
10   Middle drive shaft
11   Main axle
12   Fifth pinion gear
13   Third pinion gear
14   Fourth pinion gear
15   Second pinion gear
16   Reverse wheel gear no. 2

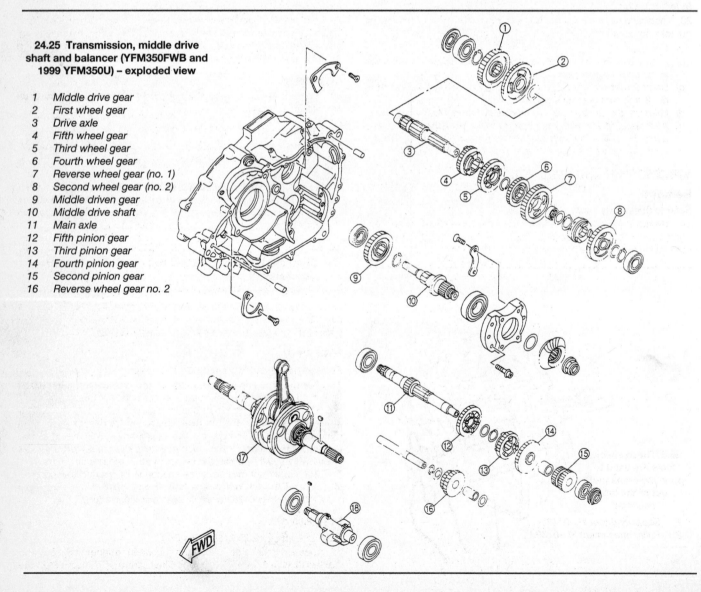

24.27 Unscrew the Allen bolts to remove the middle drive gear

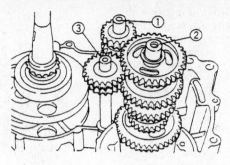

24.28 Lift out the main axle (1), drive axle (2) and reverse wheel gear (3)

25.2 If the crankshaft stays in the right case half like this, have it removed by a Yamaha dealer

equipped for excessive wear or rounding off. Replace the paired gears as a set if necessary.

22   Check the transmission shaft bearings in the crankcase for wear or heat discoloration and replace them if necessary (see Section 23).

Installation

Refer to illustration 24.23

23   Installation is the basically the reverse of the removal procedure, but take note of the following points:

   a) *Use new snap-rings.*

   b) *Align the flat on the end of the idle axle with the corresponding flat in the transmission case.*

   c) *Don't forget the metal cup and spring on the guide bar for the no. 2 shift cam* **(see illustration)**.

   d) *Lubricate the components with engine oil before assembling them.*

   e) *After assembly, check the gears to make sure they're installed correctly. Move the shift cams through the gear positions and rotate the gears to make sure they mesh and shift correctly.*

YFM350FWB and 1999 YFM350U

Removal

Refer to illustrations 24.25, 24.27 and 24.28

24   Remove the engine, then separate the case halves (see Sections 5 and 22). The transmission gears and shafts stay in the right case half when the case is separated.

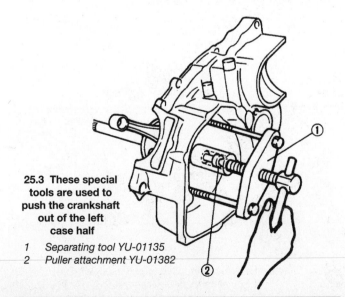

25.3 These special tools are used to push the crankshaft out of the left case half

1   *Separating tool YU-01135*
2   *Puller attachment YU-01382*

25   Pull out the balancer shaft **(see illustration)**.

26   Remove the longer shift fork guide bar, shorter shift fork guide bar, left center and right shift forks and the shift cam.

27   Remove the Allen bolts and take the middle drive shaft out of the case **(see illustration)**.

28   Remove the main axle, drive axle and reverse wheel gear as complete assemblies **(see illustration)**.

29   The reverse gear wheel assembly and drive axle can be disassembled by removing the snap-rings that hold the gears onto the shaft. The main axle is pressed together and should be disassembled by a Yamaha dealer service department or other qualified repair shop.

Inspection

30   Perform Steps 14 through 22 above to inspect the transmission and related components.

Installation

31   Installation is the basically the reverse of the removal procedure, but take note of the following points:

   a) *Use new snap-rings.*

   b) *Lubricate the components with engine oil before assembling them.*

   c) *After assembly, check the gears to make sure they're installed correctly. Move the shift cams through the gear positions and rotate the gears to make sure they mesh and shift correctly.*

---

25 Crankshaft and connecting rod - removal, inspection and installation

Note: *The procedures in this section require special tools. If you don't have the necessary equipment or suitable substitutes, have the crankshaft removed and installed by a Yamaha dealer.*

Removal

Refer to illustrations 25.2 and 25.3

1   Remove the engine and separate the crankcase halves (Sections 5, 22 and 23). The transmission shafts need not be removed.

2   Generally, the crankshaft should stay in the left half of the case when the right half is lifted off **(see illustration 22.13)**. However, if the right bearing is tight enough, the crankshaft may stay in the right case half **(see illustration)**. If this happens, have the crankshaft removed from the case half by a Yamaha dealer or other repair shop.

3   The crankshaft may be loose enough in its bearing that you can lift it out of the left crankcase half. If not, push it out with tools YU-01135 and YU-01382 or equivalent **(see illustration)**.

Inspection

Refer to illustrations 25.4, 25.6 and 25.7

4   Measure the side clearance between connecting rod and crankshaft with a feeler gauge **(see illustration)**. If it's more than the

25.4 Measure the gap between the connecting rod and the crankshaft with a feeler gauge

25.6 Check the cam chain sprocket and the ball bearing on the end of the crankshaft

25.7 Measure runout on each side of the crankshaft (A); if the assembly width (B) is greater than specified, replace the crankshaft

limit listed in this Chapter's Specifications, replace the crankshaft and connecting rod as an assembly.

5   Set up the crankshaft in V-blocks with a dial indicator contacting the big end of the connecting rod. Move the connecting rod side-to-side against the indicator pointer and compare the reading to the value listed in this Chapter's Specifications. If it's beyond the limit, the crankshaft can be disassembled and the needle roller bearing replaced. However, this is a specialized job that should be done by a Yamaha dealer or qualified machine shop.

6   Check the crankshaft splines, the cam chain sprocket, the ball bearing at the sprocket end of the crankshaft and the bearing journals for visible wear or damage **(see illustration)**. Yamaha lists the ball bearing end of the crankshaft as a separately available part, but check with your dealer first; it may be more practical to replace the entire crankshaft if the ball bearing or cam sprocket is worn or damaged. Replace the crankshaft if any of the other conditions are found.

7   Set the crankshaft in a lathe or a pair of V-blocks, with a dial indicator contacting each end **(see illustration)**. Rotate the crankshaft and note the runout. If the runout at either end is beyond the limit listed in this Chapter's Specifications, replace the crankshaft and connecting rod as an assembly.

8   Measure the assembly width of the crankshaft **(see illustration 25.7)**. If it exceeds the limit listed in this Chapter's Specifications, replace the crankshaft.

Installation

Refer to illustration 25.9

9   Start the crankshaft into the left case half. If it doesn't go in easily, pull it in the rest of the way with Yamaha tools YU-90050, YM-01383 and YM-91044 **(see illustration)**.

10   The remainder of installation is the reverse of the removal steps.

26 Initial start-up after overhaul

1   Make sure the engine oil level is correct, then remove the spark plug from the engine. Place the engine kill switch in the Off position and unplug the primary (low tension) wires from the coil.

2   Turn on the key switch and crank the engine over with the starter several times to build up oil pressure. Reinstall the spark plug, connect the wires and turn the switch to On.

3   Make sure there is fuel in the tank, then operate the choke.

4   Start the engine and allow it to run at a moderately fast idle until it reaches operating temperature. **Caution:** *If the oil temperature light doesn't go off, or it comes on while the engine is running, stop the engine immediately.*

5   Check carefully for oil leaks and make sure the transmission and

controls, especially the brakes, function properly before road testing the machine. Refer to Section 27 for the recommended break-in procedure.

6   Upon completion of the road test, and after the engine has cooled down completely, recheck the valve clearances (see Chapter 1).

27 Recommended break-in procedure

1   Any rebuilt engine needs time to break-in, even if parts have been installed in their original locations. For this reason, treat the machine gently for the first few miles to make sure oil has circulated throughout the engine and any new parts installed have started to seat.

2   Even greater care is necessary if the cylinder has been rebored or a new crankshaft has been installed. In the case of a rebore, the engine will have to be broken in as if the machine were new. This means greater use of the transmission and a restraining hand on the throttle for the first few operating days. There's no point in keeping to any set speed limit - the main idea is to vary the engine speed, keep from lugging (laboring) the engine and to avoid full-throttle operation. These recommendations can be lessened to an extent when only a new crankshaft is installed. Experience is the best guide, since it's easy to tell when an engine is running freely.

3   If a lubrication failure is suspected, stop the engine immediately and try to find the cause. If an engine is run without oil, even for a short period of time, irreparable damage will occur.

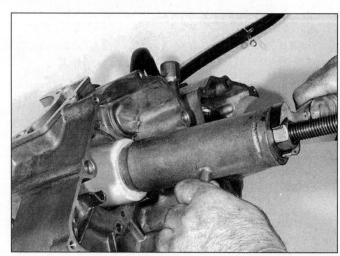

25.9 These tools are used to pull the crankshaft into the left case half

Chapter 3
Fuel and exhaust systems

Contents

Specifications

General

Fuel type .... Unleaded gasoline (petrol) subject to local regulations; minimum octane 91 RON (86 pump octane)

Carburetor

Main jet
  YFM350ER
    1987 through 1989 120
    1990 on 117.5
  YFM350FW 122.5
  YFM350U
    1996 through 1998
      Except Australia 120
      Australia 110
    1999 125
  YFM350FWB 125

Jet needle/clip position
  YFM350ER, YFM350FW 5H26/3
  YFM350U
    1996 through 1998
      Except Australia 5H26/3
      Australia 5H46/3
    1999
      Except California 4DP11/4
      California 4DP16
  YFM350FW 4DP11/4

Pilot jet
  YFM350ER, YFM350FW 45
  YFM350U
    1996 through 1998
      Except Australia 45
      Australia 42.5
    1999 .... 42.5
  YFM350FWB 42.5

Pilot screw setting (turns out from lightly seated position)
  YFM350ER 2-1/4
  YFM350FW 2-3/4
  YFM350U
    1996 through 1998
      Except Australia 2-3/8
      Australia 3-1/4
    1999 2
  YFM350FWB 2

Float height
  YFM350ER, YFM350FW, 1996 through 1998 YFM350U .... 11.4 to 13.4 mm (29/64 to 17/32 inch)
  YFM350FWB, 1999 YFM350U .... 12 to 14 mm (15/32 to 9/16 inch)

Carburetor (continued)

Fuel level
  YFM350ER
    1987 through 1989.. 3.0 to 4.0 mm (0.12 to 0.16 inch)
    1990 on.. 1.0 to 2.0 mm (0.04 to 0.08 inch)
  YFM350FW, YFM350U .... 1.0 to 2.0 mm (0.04 to 0.08 inch)
  YFM350FWB .... 3.0 to 4.0 mm (0.12 to 0.16 inch)

Tightening torques

Muffler/silencer to frame... 27 Nm (19 ft-lbs)
Muffler/silencer clamp bolts .... 20 Nm (168 in-lbs)
Exhaust pipe holder nuts.. 12 Nm (104 in-lbs)

1   General information

The fuel system consists of the fuel tank, fuel tap, filter screen, carburetor and connecting lines, hose and control cables.

The Mikuni carburetor installed on YFM350ER, YFM350FW and 1996 through 1998 YFM350U models is controlled by two cables, one that lifts the jet needle and another that operates a butterfly-type throttle valve. The two cables are controlled by a single throttle cable, which in turn is operated by a thumb lever on the right handlebar. For cold starting, an enrichment circuit is actuated by a choke knob mounted on the carburetor (early models) or a cable and a choke lever mounted on the instrument panel (later models).

A Mikuni CV carburetor is used on YFM350FW and 1999 YFM350U models. A single throttle cable operates a butterfly-type throttle valve, while vacuum through the carburetor venturi lifts the jet needle. A thumb lever on the right handlebar operates the throttle. A choke knob on the carburetor operates the enrichment circuit.

The exhaust system consists of a pipe and a muffler/silencer.

Many of the fuel system service procedures are considered routine maintenance items and for that reason are included in Chapter 1.

2   Fuel tank - removal and installation

Warning: *Gasoline (petrol) is extremely flammable, so take extra precautions when you work on any part of the fuel system. Don't smoke or allow open flames or bare light bulbs near the work area, and don't work in a garage where a natural gas-type appliance (such as a water heater or clothes dryer) with a pilot light is present. Since gasoline is carcinogenic, wear latex gloves when there's a possibility of being exposed to fuel, and, if you spill any fuel on your skin, rinse it off immediately with soap and water. Mop up any spills immediately and*

2.4 Remove the fuel tank cover screws (upper arrows) and rear mounting bolts (lower arrows) . . .

do not store fuel-soaked rags where they could ignite. When you perform any kind of work on the fuel system, wear safety glasses and have a fire extinguisher suitable for a class B type fire (flammable liquids) on hand.

1   The fuel tank is secured to a bracket by two bolts at the rear. At the front, the tank is supported by a bolt and rubber grommet on each side.

Removal

Refer to illustrations 2.4, 2.5 and 2.7

2   Remove the seat (see Chapter 7).

3   Unscrew the fuel tank filler cap and remove the trim molding from the upper edge of the fuel tank cover.

4   Remove the fuel tank cover screws and take off the cover **(see**

2.5 . . . and one front mounting bolt from each side of the tank

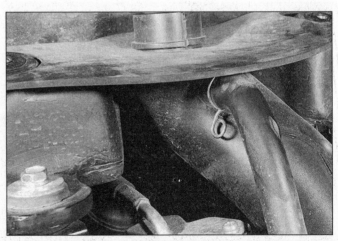

2.7 Move the mounting damper, air duct hose and breather hose out of the way

4.3 The pilot screw (arrow) adjusts idle fuel/air mixture

illustration 3.7a in Chapter 7 and the accompanying illustration).
5   Remove the fuel tank mounting bolts **(see illustration 2.4 and the accompanying illustration).**
6   Disconnect the fuel line from the fuel tap.
7   Pull the fuel tank backward off the front mounting bracket. Work it free of the bracket that contains the breather hose and air cleaner duct hose **(see illustration)** and lift it off the vehicle together with the fuel tap.

Installation

8   Before installing the tank, check the condition of the rubber mounting dampers - if they're hardened, cracked, or show any other signs of deterioration, replace them.
9   When installing the tank, reverse the removal procedure. Don't pinch any control cables or wires.

3   Fuel tank - cleaning and repair

1   The fuel tank is plastic and can't be repaired by traditional welding or brazing techniques. All repairs to the fuel tank should be carried out by a professional who has experience in this critical and potentially dangerous work. Even after cleaning and flushing of the fuel system, explosive fumes can remain and ignite during repair of the tank.
2   If the fuel tank is removed from the vehicle, it should not be placed in an area where sparks or open flames could ignite the fumes coming out of the tank. Be especially careful inside garages where a natural gas-type appliance is located, because the pilot light could cause an explosion.

4   Idle fuel/air mixture adjustment

YFM350ER, YFM350FW and 1996 through 1998 YFM350U models

Refer to illustration 4.3
1   Idle fuel/air mixture on these vehicles is preset at the factory and should not need adjustment unless the carburetor is overhauled or the pilot screw, which controls the mixture adjustment, is replaced.
2   The engine must be properly tuned up before making the adjustment (valve clearances set to specifications, spark plug in good condition and properly gapped).
3   To make an initial adjustment, turn the pilot screw clockwise until it seats lightly, then back it out the number of turns listed in this Chapter's Specifications **(see illustration). Caution:** *Turn the screw*

just far enough to seat it lightly. If it's bottomed hard, the screw or its seat may be damaged, which will make accurate mixture adjustments impossible.
4   Warm up the engine to normal operating temperature. Shut it off and connect a tune-up tachometer, following the tachometer manufacturer's instructions.
5   Restart the engine and compare idle speed to the value listed in the Chapter 1 Specifications. Adjust it if necessary.

YFM350FWN and 1999 YFM350U models

6   Fuel/air mixture adjustment is part of the routine idle speed adjustment procedure described in Chapter 1.

5   Carburetor overhaul - general information

1   Poor engine performance, hesitation, hard starting, stalling, flooding and backfiring are all signs that major carburetor maintenance may be required.
2   Keep in mind that many so-called carburetor problems are really not carburetor problems at all, but mechanical problems within the engine or ignition system malfunctions. Try to establish for certain that the carburetor is in need of maintenance before beginning a major overhaul.
3   Check the fuel tap and its strainer screen, the fuel line, the intake manifold clamps and Allen bolts, the O-ring between the intake manifold and cylinder head, the air filter element, the cylinder compression, the spark plug and the ignition timing before assuming that a carburetor overhaul is required. If the vehicle has been unused for more than a month, refer to Chapter 1, drain the float chamber and refill the tank with fresh fuel.
4   Most carburetor problems are caused by dirt particles, varnish and other deposits which build up in and block the fuel and air passages. Also, in time, gaskets and O-rings shrink or deteriorate and cause fuel and air leaks which lead to poor performance.
5   When the carburetor is overhauled, it is generally disassembled completely and the parts are cleaned thoroughly with a carburetor cleaning solvent and dried with filtered, unlubricated compressed air. The fuel and air passages are also blown through with compressed air to force out any dirt that may have been loosened but not removed by the solvent. Once the cleaning process is complete, the carburetor is reassembled using new gaskets, O-rings and, generally, a new inlet needle valve and seat.
6   Before disassembling the carburetors, make sure you have a carburetor rebuild kit (which will include all necessary O-rings and other parts), some carburetor cleaner, a supply of rags, some means of blowing out the carburetor passages and a clean place to work.

3

6   Carburetor - removal and installation

Warning: *Gasoline (petrol) is extremely flammable, so take extra precautions when you work on any part of the fuel system. Don't smoke or allow open flames or bare light bulbs near the work area, and don't work in a garage where a natural gas-type appliance (such as a water heater or clothes dryer) with a pilot light is present. Since gasoline is carcinogenic, wear latex gloves when there's a possibility of being exposed to fuel, and, if you spill any fuel on your skin, rinse it off immediately with soap and water. Mop up any spills immediately and do not store fuel-soaked rags where they could ignite. When you perform any kind of work on the fuel system, wear safety glasses and have a fire extinguisher suitable for a class B type fire (flammable liquids) on hand.*

Removal

Refer to illustrations 6.3a, 6.3b and 6.4
1   Remove the fuel tank (see Section 2).
2   Refer to Section 11 and remove the throttle cable housing or throttle valve cover.

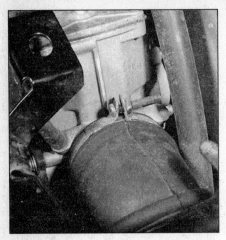

6.3a Loosen the clamping bands on the connecting tube . . .

6.3b . . . and lift the tube out

6.4 Remove the Allen bolts (right arrows) to detach the manifold from the head; the lower bolt secures a hose clip - remove the nuts (left arrows) to detach the carburetor from the manifold

3   Loosen the clamping bands on the air cleaner duct and lift it out **(see illustrations)**.

YFM350ER, YFM350FW and 1996 through 1998 YFM350U models

4   Remove the Allen bolts and detach the intake manifold from the cylinder head **(see illustration)**. Lift out the carburetor and manifold.
5   If you plan to overhaul the carburetor or replace the manifold gasket, remove the nuts and separate the intake manifold from the carburetor.

YFM350FWB and 1999 YFM350U models

6   Loosen the carburetor clamping band and work the carburetor free of the intake manifold. If you plan to replace the manifold gasket, unbolt the manifold from the cylinder.
7   Check the intake manifold and air cleaner duct for cracks, deterioration or other damage. Replace the manifold O-ring if its condition is in doubt. Since very small defects in the O-ring may affect carburetor performance, it's a good idea to replace the O-ring whenever it's removed.
8   After the carburetor has been removed, stuff clean rags into the intake port in the cylinder head to prevent the entry of dirt or other objects.

Installation

9   Installation is the reverse of the removal steps, with the following additions:
a)   *If you're working on a YFM350ER, YFM350FW or 1996 through 1998 YFM350U model, install the clip for the drive select cable on the lower Allen bolt that secures the intake manifold to the head.*
b)   *Adjust throttle lever freeplay (see Chapter 1).*

---

7   Carburetors - disassembly, cleaning and inspection

Warning: *Gasoline (petrol) is extremely flammable, so take extra precautions when you work on any part of the fuel system. Don't smoke or allow open flames or bare light bulbs near the work area, and don't work in a garage where a natural gas-type appliance (such as a water heater or clothes dryer) with a pilot light is present. Since gasoline is carcinogenic, wear latex gloves when there's a possibility of being exposed to fuel, and, if you spill any fuel on your skin, rinse it off immediately with soap and water. Mop up any spills immediately and do not store fuel-soaked rags where they could ignite. When you perform any kind of work on the fuel system, wear safety glasses and have a fire extinguisher suitable for a class B type fire (flammable liquids) on hand.*

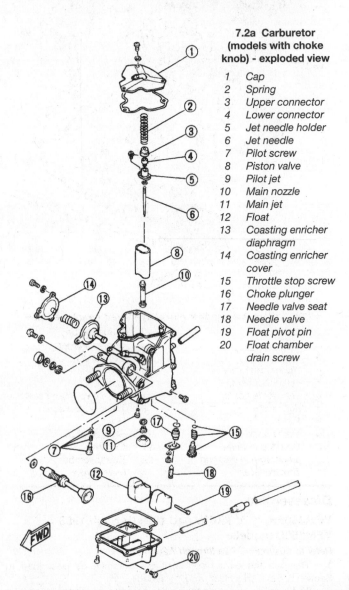

7.2a Carburetor (models with choke knob) - exploded view

1   Cap
2   Spring
3   Upper connector
4   Lower connector
5   Jet needle holder
6   Jet needle
7   Pilot screw
8   Piston valve
9   Pilot jet
10   Main nozzle
11   Main jet
12   Float
13   Coasting enricher diaphragm
14   Coasting enricher cover
15   Throttle stop screw
16   Choke plunger
17   Needle valve seat
18   Needle valve
19   Float pivot pin
20   Float chamber drain screw

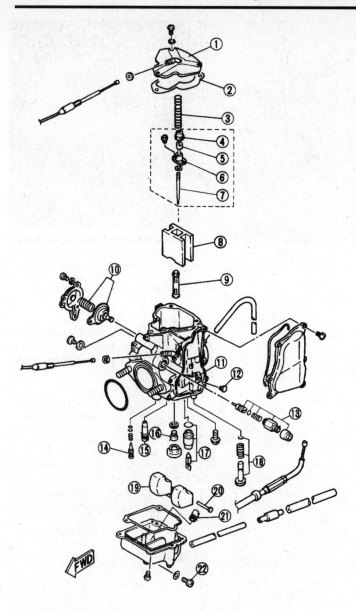

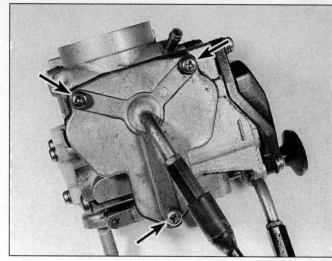

7.2c Remove the screws from the cap (arrows) . . .

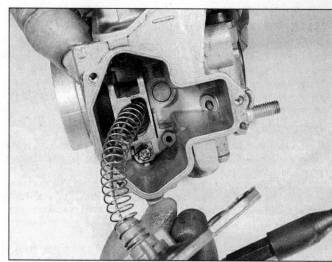

7.2d . . . and lift the cap, together with the spring, cable and jet needle components

7.2b Carburetor (models with choke lever) - exploded view

1	Cap	12	Holder guide
2	Cap gasket	13	Choke plunger
3	Spring	14	Pilot screw
4	Upper connector	15	Pilot jet
5	Lower connector	16	Main jet
6	Jet needle holder	17	Needle valve and seat
7	Jet needle	18	Throttle stop screw
8	Piston valve	19	Float
9	Main nozzle	20	Float pivot pin
10	Coasting enricher	21	Choke jet
	diaphragm and spring	22	Float chamber
11	Throttle lever		drain screw

Disassembly

YFM350ER, YFM350FW and 1996 through 1998 YFM350U models

Refer to illustrations 7.2a through 7.2u

1   Remove the carburetor from the machine as described in Section 6. Set it on a clean working surface.

2   Refer to the accompanying illustrations to disassemble the carburetor **(see illustrations)**.

7.2e Remove the cover . . .

3

7.2f ... rotate the throttle pulley ...

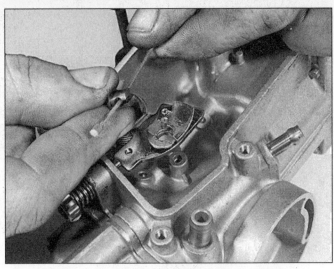

7.2g ... and disconnect the throttle valve cable

7.2h Remove the screws and take off the float chamber ...

7.2i ... remove the main jet ring ...

7.2j ... pull out the float pivot pin ...

7.2k ... and unhook the needle valve; bend the tang (arrow) if necessary to change float level

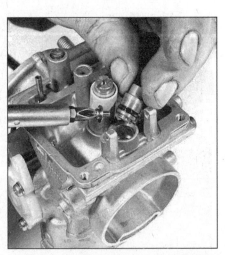

7.2l Remove the retainer screw and lift out the needle valve seat with its O-ring; the O-ring should be replaced whenever it's removed

7.2m Remove the main jet and washer . . .

7.2n . . . the pilot jet . . .

7.2o . . . and the pilot screw, together with its spring, washer and O-ring

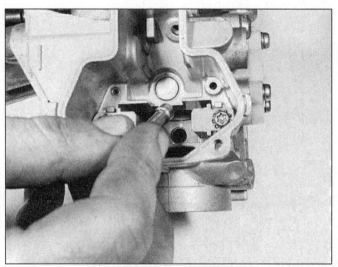

7.2p Remove the main nozzle . . .

7.2q . . . on installation, the shouldered end is up

3

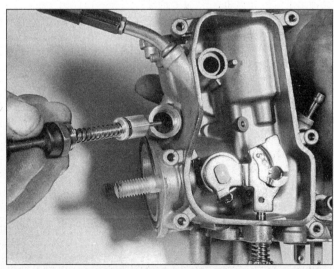

7.2r Unscrew the choke knob (or choke plunger on models equipped with a choke lever)

7.2s Remove the coasting enricher cover screws (arrows) . . .

7.2t . . . and lift out the spring and diaphragm; the locating tab (arrow) fits into the notch on installation

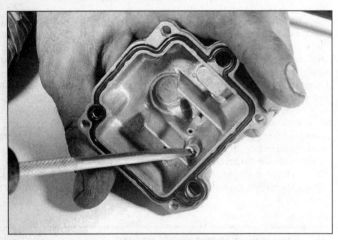

7.2u Unscrew the choke (starter) jet from the bottom of the float chamber

YFM350FWB and 1999 YFM350U models

Refer to illustration 7.3

3   Remove the throttle stop screw and spring **(see illustration)**.

4   Remove the screws securing the vacuum chamber cover to the carburetor body. Lift the cover off and remove the piston spring. Note the location of the tab on the diaphragm; it fits into a notch in the carburetor body.

5   Carefully peel the diaphragm away from the groove in the carburetor body and lift out the diaphragm/piston assembly.

6   Remove the spring and jet needle from the piston, then separate the spring, spring seat, clip and washer from the jet needle.

7   Remove the coasting enricher cover screws and take off the cover. Lift out the spring and diaphragm, noting the diaphragm tab that fits into a notch in the carburetor body.

8   Remove the float chamber screws, then detach the float chamber and remove its O-ring.

9   Push out the float pivot pin, then remove the float and unscrew the needle valve. Work the needle valve seat and O-ring out of their bore in the carburetor body.

10   Unscrew the main jet and lift it out together with its washer.

11   Unscrew the pilot jet and lift it out of the bore.

12   Unscrew the pilot screw and remove it, together with its spring, washer and O-ring.

13   Insert a screwdriver into the main jet bore and push the needle jet into the venturi, then take it out of the carburetor body.

14   Unscrew the choke plunger, pull it out of the carburetor body and remove its O-ring.

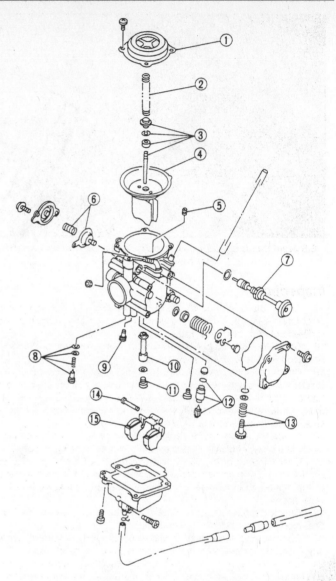

7.3 Carburetor (YFM350FWB and 1999 YFM350U) – exploded view

1	Cover	8	Pilot screw, spring,
2	Spring		washer and O-ring
3	Jet needle, clip and	9	Pilot jet
	spring seat	10	Needle jet
4	Throttle piston	11	Main jet
5	Pilot air jet	12	Needle valve and seat
6	Coasting enricher	13	Throttle stop screw and
	diaphragm		spring
7	Choke plunger	14	Float pin
		15	Float

Cleaning

Caution: *Use only a carburetor cleaning solution that is safe for use with plastic parts (be sure to read the label on the container).*

15   Submerge the metal components in the carburetor cleaner for approximately thirty minutes (or longer, if the directions recommend it).

16   After the carburetor has soaked long enough for the cleaner to loosen and dissolve most of the varnish and other deposits, use a brush to remove the stubborn deposits. Rinse it again, then dry it with compressed air. Blow out all of the fuel and air passages in the main and upper body. **Caution:** *Never clean the jets or passages with a piece of wire or a drill bit, as they will be enlarged, causing the fuel and air metering rates to be upset.*

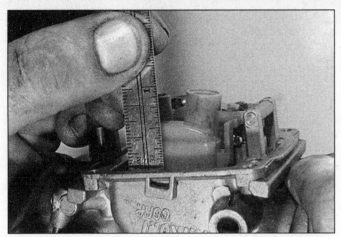

8.6 Hold the carburetor upside down and measure float height from the O-ring surface

9.2 A ruler and a clear plastic tube like this one can be used to measure fuel level if you don't have the special tool

Inspection

17   Check the operation of the choke plunger. If it doesn't move smoothly, replace it, along with the return spring. If the plunger O-ring is deteriorated or damaged, replace it.

18   Check the tapered portion of the pilot screw for wear or damage. Replace the pilot screw if necessary.

19   Check the carburetor body, float chamber and top cover for cracks, distorted sealing surfaces and other damage. If any defects are found, replace the faulty component, although replacement of the entire carburetor will probably be necessary (check with your parts supplier for the availability of separate components).

20   Check the jet needle for straightness by rolling it on a flat surface (such as a piece of glass). Replace it if it's bent or if the tip is worn.

21   Check the tip of the fuel inlet valve needle. If it has grooves or scratches in it, it must be replaced. Push in on the rod in the other end of the needle, then release it - if it doesn't spring back, replace the valve needle.

22   Check the float chamber O-ring and the drain plug (in the float chamber). Replace them if they're damaged.

23   Operate the throttle shaft to make sure the throttle butterfly valve opens and closes smoothly. If it doesn't, replace the carburetor.

24   Check the floats for damage. This will usually be apparent by the presence of fuel inside one of the floats. If the floats are damaged, they must be replaced.

25   Check the coasting enricher diaphragm for splits, holes and general deterioration. Holding it up to a light will help to reveal problems of this nature. If you're working on a YFM350FWB or 1999 YFM350U, inspect the throttle diaphragm in the same way.

26   Check the piston valve in the carburetor body for wear or damage. If it's worn or damaged, replace the carburetor.

8   Carburetors - reassembly and float height check

Refer to illustration 8.6

1   Reassembly is the reverse of disassembly, with the following additions. **Caution:** *When installing the jets, be careful not to over-tighten them - they're made of soft material and can strip or shear easily.* **Note:** *When reassembling the carburetor, be sure to use the new O-rings, gaskets and other parts supplied in the rebuild kit.*

2   Install the clip on the jet needle if it was removed. Place it in the needle groove listed in this Chapter's Specifications.

3   Install the pilot screw (if removed) along with its spring, washer and O-ring, turning it in until it seats lightly. Now, turn the screw out the number of turns listed in this Chapter's Specifications.

4   Install the coasting enricher valve into the carburetor body. Seat the bead of the diaphragm into the groove in the carburetor body, making sure the diaphragm isn't distorted or kinked **(see**

illustration 7.2t)**. If you're working on a YFM350FWB or 1999 YFM350U, install the throttle diaphragm in the same way.

5   Reverse the disassembly steps to install the jets.

6   Invert the carburetor. Attach the fuel inlet valve needle to the float. Set the float into position in the carburetor, making sure the valve needle seats correctly. Install the float pivot pin. To check the float height, hold the carburetor so the float hangs down, then tilt it back until the valve needle is just seated. Measure the distance from the float chamber gasket surface to the top of the float and compare your measurement to the float height listed in this Chapter's Specifications **(see illustration)**. If it isn't as specified, bend the tang on the float to change it **(see illustration 7.2j)**.

7   Install the O-ring into the groove in the float chamber. Place the float chamber on the carburetor and install the screws, tightening them securely.

9   Fuel level - check and adjustment

Refer to illustration 9.2

Warning: *Gasoline (petrol) is extremely flammable, so take extra precautions when you work on any part of the fuel system. Don't smoke or allow open flames or bare light bulbs near the work area, and don't work in a garage where a natural gas-type appliance (such as a water heater or clothes dryer) with a pilot light is present. Since gasoline is carcinogenic, wear latex gloves when there's a possibility of being exposed to fuel, and, if you spill any fuel on your skin, rinse it off immediately with soap and water. Mop up any spills immediately and do not store fuel-soaked rags where they could ignite. When you perform any kind of work on the fuel system, wear safety glasses and have a fire extinguisher suitable for a class B type fire (flammable liquids) on hand.*

1   Park the vehicle on a level surface and make sure the carburetor is level. If necessary, adjust its position slightly by placing a floor jack under the engine and raising it.

2   Attach Yamaha service tool YM-01312-A to the drain fitting on the bottom of the carburetor float bowl. This is a clear plastic tube graduated in millimeters. An alternative is to use a length of clear plastic tubing and an accurate ruler **(see illustration)**. Hold the graduated tube (or the free end of the clear plastic tube) vertically against the float chamber cover.

3   Unscrew the drain screw at the bottom of the float chamber a couple of turns, then start the engine and let it idle - fuel will flow into the tube. Wait for the fuel level to stabilize, then note how far the fuel level is below the line on the float chamber cover.

4   Measure the distance between the line and the top of the fuel in the tube or gauge. This distance is the fuel level.

5   Compare your reading to the value listed in this Chapter's Specifi-

3

10.2 Loosen the clamp screws (arrows) and disconnect the ducts

10.3 Remove the housing bolts (arrows)

cations. If the fuel level is not correct, remove the float chamber cover and bend the float tang up or down as necessary, then recheck the fuel level.

10 Air cleaner housing - removal and installation

Removal

Refer to illustrations 10.2 and 10.3
1   Refer to Section 2 and remove the fuel tank.

11.3 Detach the retaining band (arrow) from the throttle cable housing and move it aside

11.4 Remove the cover screws and lift off the cover

2   Loosen the clamps and detach the carburetor tube and intake tube from the air cleaner housing **(see illustration)**.
3   Remove the air cleaner housing bolts **(see illustration)**. Lift the air cleaner housing out of the frame.
4   Installation is the reverse of the removal steps.

11 Throttle cables - removal, installation and adjustment

YFM350ER, YFM350FW and 1996 through 1998 YFM350U models

1   These vehicles have three throttle cables. One runs from the throttle lever housing on the handlebar to the cable housing. Two run from the cable housing to the carburetor, one to the jet needle and one to the throttle valve.

Removal

Refer to illustrations 11.3, 11.4, 11.5, 11.8a and 11.8b
2   Remove the front fender (see Chapter 7).
3   Remove the fuel tank (see Section 2). Unhook the rubber retainer for the throttle cable housing and move it out of the way **(see illustration)**.
4   Remove the cover screws and lift the cover from the cable housing **(see illustration)**.
5   Loosen the throttle cable at the handlebar adjuster as much as possible. Lift the upper slider (the one that contains the handlebar

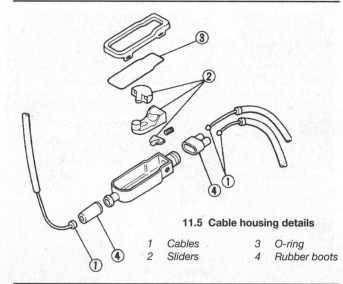

11.5 Cable housing details

1 Cables	*3 O-ring*
2 Sliders	*4 Rubber boots*

11.8a Remove the cover screws (arrows) . . .

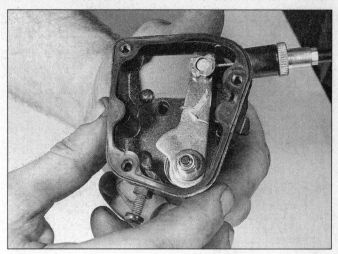

11.8b . . . and lift off the cover for access to the lever and cable

cable) and detach the cable from it (see illustration). Lift the other slider (with the two carburetor cables) and detach the cables.

6   Remove the sliders and spring.

7   Refer to Section 8 to disconnect the cables from the carburetor.

8   Remove the cover from the throttle housing on the handlebar, remove the lever components and disconnect the cable (see illustrations). Remove the cable, noting how it's routed.

9   If necessary, remove the throttle housing clamp screws and detach the throttle housing from the handlebar (see Chapter 5).

Installation

Refer to illustration 11.10

10   If the throttle housing was removed, install it on the handlebar and tighten its clamp screws loosely. Position the housing so its protrusion is aligned with the notch in the handlebar spacer (see illustration). Install the clamp and screws and tighten them securely.

11   Route the cable into place. Make sure it doesn't interfere with any other components and isn't kinked or bent sharply.

12   Lubricate the end of the cable with multi-purpose grease and connect it to the slider in the throttle housing. Do the same with the two carburetor cables.

13   Reverse the disconnection steps to connect the throttle cable to the handlebar lever. Operate the lever and make sure it returns to the idle position by itself under spring pressure. **Warning:** *If the lever doesn't return by itself, find and solve the problem before continuing with installation. A stuck lever can lead to loss of control of the vehicle.*

11.10 Align the throttle lever housing protrusion with the notch in the spacer (arrow)

Adjustment

14   Follow the procedure outlined in Chapter 1, *Throttle operation/grip freeplay - check and adjustment*, to adjust the cable.

15   Turn the handlebar back and forth to make sure the cables don't cause the steering to bind.

16   Once you're sure the cables operate properly, install the covers on the throttle lever housing and cable housing.

17   With the engine idling, turn the handlebar through its full travel (full left lock to full right lock) and note whether idle speed increases. If it does, a cable is routed incorrectly. Correct this dangerous condition before riding the vehicle.

18   Install the fuel tank and front fender.

YFM350FWB and 1999 YFM350U models

Removal

Refer to illustration 11.22

19   These models have a single throttle cable that attaches to the throttle pulley inside the carburetor.

20   Disconnect the cable from the throttle lever as described in Step 8 above.

21   Remove the throttle valve cover from the side of the carburetor (see illustration 7.3).

22   Rotate the throttle pulley to create slack in the cable, then disengage the cable and its end piece from the pulley (see illustration).

Installation

23   Installation is the reverse of the removal steps.

Adjustment

24   Adjust the cable and check its operation as described in Steps 14 through 17 above, noting that there is only one cable and no separate cable housing between the handlebar and carburetor.

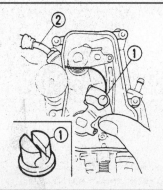

11.22 Disconnect the cable end piece (1) and remove the cable(2)

3

12   Exhaust system - removal and installation

Refer to illustration 12.1

1   Remove the exhaust pipe holder nuts and slide the holder off the mounting studs **(see illustration)**.

2   If necessary, unbolt the heat shield and remove it from the exhaust pipe.

3   Remove the muffler/silencer mounting bolts.

4   Pull the exhaust system forward, separate the pipe from the cylinder head and remove the system from the machine.

5   Installation is the reverse of removal, with the following additions:

  a) *Be sure to install a new gasket at the cylinder head.*

  b) *Tighten the muffler mounting bolts, clamp bolts, heat shield bolts and holder nuts to the torques listed in this Chapter's Specifications.*

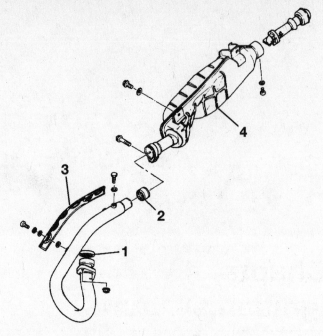

12.1 Typical exhaust system details

1	Gasket	3	Heat shield
2	Gasket	4	Muffler/silencer

Chapter 4
Ignition system

Contents

Specifications

Spark plug cap resistance

    1987 through 1989 .... Not specified

    1990 on

        YFM350ER, YFM350FWB .... 8 to 12 k-ohms

        YFM350U, YFM350FWB .... 10 k-ohms

Ignition coil resistance (at 20-degrees C/68-degrees F)

    1987 through 1989

        Primary resistance .... 0.72 to 0.98 k-ohms

        Secondary resistance .... 5.02 to 6.79 k-ohms

    1990 on

        YFM350ER, YFM350FW, 1996 through 1998 YFM350U

            Primary resistance .... 0.36 to 0.48 ohms

            Secondary resistance .... 5.44 to 7.36 k-ohms

        1999 YFM350U

            Primary resistance .... 0.32 to 0.48 ohms

            Secondary resistance .... 5.44 to 7.36 k-ohms

        YFM350FWB (1997 and 1998)

            Primary resistance .... 0.32 to 0.48 ohms

            Secondary resistance .... 5.68 to 8.52 k-ohms

        YFM350FWB (1999)

            Primary resistance .... 0.18 to 0.28 ohms

            Secondary resistance .... 6.32 to 9.48 k-ohms

Pick-up coil resistance (at 20-degrees C/68-degrees F)

    1987 through 1989 .... 180 to 200 ohms

    1990 on

        YFM350ER, YFM350FW .... 170 to 210 ohms

        YFM350FWB, YFM350U .... 459 to 561 ohms

Source coil resistance (all models) .... 270 to 330 ohms

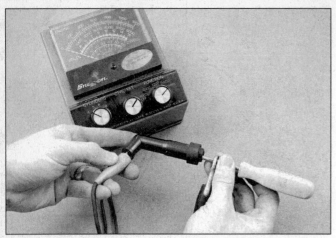

2.5 Unscrew the spark plug cap from the plug wire and measure its resistance with an ohmmeter

2.13 A simple spark gap testing fixture can be made from a block of wood, two nails, a large alligator clip, a screw and a piece of wire

1   General information

This vehicle is equipped with a battery operated, fully transistorized, breakerless ignition system. The system consists of the following components:

    CDI magneto
    CDI unit
    Battery and fuse
    Ignition coil
    Spark plug
    Engine kill (stop) and main (key) switches
    Primary and secondary (HT) circuit wiring

The transistorized ignition system functions on the same principle as a DC ignition system with the CDI magneto and CDI unit performing the tasks previously associated with the breaker points and mechanical advance system. As a result, adjustment and maintenance of ignition components is eliminated (with the exception of spark plug replacement).

Because of their nature, the individual ignition system components can be checked but not repaired. If ignition system troubles occur, and the faulty component can be isolated, the only cure for the problem is to replace the part with a new one. Keep in mind that most electrical parts, once purchased, can't be returned. To avoid unnecessary expense, make very sure the faulty component has been positively identified before buying a replacement part.

2   Ignition system - check

Refer to illustrations 2.5 and 2.13
Warning: *Because of the very high voltage generated by the ignition system, extreme care should be taken when these checks are performed.*
1   If the ignition system is the suspected cause of poor engine performance or failure to start, a number of checks can be made to isolate the problem.
2   Make sure the ignition kill (stop) switch is in the Run or On position.

Engine will not start

3   Disconnect the spark plug wire from the spark plug (refer to Chapter 1 if necessary). Connect the wire to a spare spark plug and lay the plug on the engine with the threads contacting the engine. If necessary, hold the spark plug with an insulated tool. Crank the engine over and make sure a well-defined, blue spark occurs between the spark plug electrodes. **Warning:** *Don't remove the spark plug from the*

engine to perform this check - atomized fuel being pumped out of the open spark plug hole could ignite, causing severe injury!
4   If no spark occurs, the following checks should be made:
5   Unscrew the spark plug cap from the plug wire and check the cap resistance with an ohmmeter **(see illustration)**. If the resistance is infinite, replace it with a new one.
6   Make sure all electrical connectors are clean and tight. Check all wires for shorts, opens and correct installation.
7   Check the battery voltage with a voltmeter. If the voltage is less than 12-volts, recharge the battery.
8   Check the fuse and the fuse connections (see Chapter 8). If the fuse is blown, replace it with a new one; if the connections are loose or corroded, clean or repair them.
9   Refer to Section 3 and check the ignition coil primary and secondary resistance.
10   Refer to Section 4 and check the pick-up coil and source coil resistance.
11   If the preceding checks produce positive results but there is still no spark at the plug, refer to Section 5 for information on the CDI unit.

Engine starts but misfires

12   If the engine starts but misfires, make the following checks before deciding that the ignition system is at fault.
13   The ignition system must be able to produce a spark across a six millimeter (1/4-inch) gap (minimum). A simple test fixture **(see illustration)** can be constructed to make sure the minimum spark gap can be jumped. Make sure the fixture electrodes are positioned six millimeters apart.
14   Connect one of the spark plug wires to the protruding test fixture electrode, then attach the fixture's alligator clip to a good engine ground (earth).
15   Crank the engine over with the key in the On position and see if well-defined, blue sparks occur between the test fixture electrodes. If the minimum spark gap test is positive, the ignition coil is functioning properly. If the spark will not jump the gap, or if it is weak (orange colored), refer to Steps 5 through 11 of this Section and perform the component checks described.

3   Ignition coil - check, removal and installation

Check

Refer to illustration 3.4
1   In order to determine conclusively that the ignition coil is defective, it should be tested by an authorized Yamaha dealer service department which is equipped with the special electrical tester

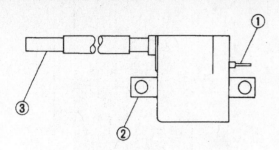

3.4 Ignition coil details

1 Primary terminal   3 Spark plug wire
2 Coil base

3.9 The coil is secured by two bolts (arrows)

required for this check.

2   However, the coil can be checked visually (for cracks and other damage) and the primary and secondary coil resistances can be measured with an ohmmeter. If the coil is undamaged, and if the resistances are as specified, it is probably capable of proper operation.

3   To check the coil for physical damage, it must be removed (see Step 9). To check the resistance, remove the fuel tank (see Chapter 3), unplug the primary circuit electrical connectors from the coil and remove the spark plug wire from the spark plug. Mark the locations of all wires before disconnecting them.

4   To check the coil primary resistance, attach one ohmmeter lead to the primary terminals and the other ohmmeter lead to the coil base **(see illustration)**.

5   Place the ohmmeter selector switch in the Rx1 position and compare the measured resistance to the value listed in this Chapter's Specifications.

6   If the coil primary resistance is as specified, check the coil secondary resistance by disconnecting the meter leads and attaching them between the spark plug wire terminal and the primary terminal **(see illustration 3.4)**.

7   Place the ohmmeter selector switch in the Rx1000 position and compare the measured resistance to the values listed in this Chapter's Specifications.

8   If the resistances are not as specified, unscrew the spark plug cap from the plug wire and check the resistance between the primary terminal and the end of the spark plug wire. If it is now within specifications, the spark plug cap is bad. If it's still not as specified, the coil is probably defective and should be replaced with a new one.

Removal and installation

Refer to illustration 3.9

9   To remove the coil, refer to Chapter 3 and remove the fuel tank, then disconnect the spark plug wire from the plug. Unplug the coil primary circuit electrical connector **(see illustration)**.

10   Support the coil with one hand and remove the coil mounting bolts, then lift the coil out. Note that one mounting bolt secures a coil primary wire.

11   Installation is the reverse of removal.

---

4   CDI magneto - check, removal and installation

Check

Refer to illustration 4.1

1   Follow the wiring harness from the engine cover on the left side of the vehicle to the electrical connectors on the frame rail inside the rear fender **(see illustration)**. Disconnect the connector.

2   Set the ohmmeter to Rx100. **Note:** During the next steps, connect the ohmmeter to the side of the connector that leads back to the engine, not to the wiring harness side.

1987 through 1989 models

3   Connect the ohmmeter between the yellow and green wire terminals in the connector, then between the gray and blue wire terminals. These are the pick-up coil wires. Compare the readings with the value listed in this Chapter's Specifications.

4   Connect the ohmmeter between the brown and red wire terminals in the connector. These are the source coil wires. Compare the readings with the value listed in this Chapter's Specifications.

1990 through 1996 models

5   Connect the ohmmeter between the blue and yellow wire terminals in the connector. These are the pick-up coil wires. Compare the readings with the value listed in this Chapter's Specifications.

6   Connect the ohmmeter between the white/green and red wire terminals in the connector. These are the source coil wires. Compare the readings with the value listed in this Chapter's Specifications.

1997 and later models

7   Connect the ohmmeter between the red and white wire terminals in the connector. These are the pick-up coil wires. Compare the readings with the value listed in this Chapter's Specifications.

8   Connect the ohmmeter between the brown and green wire terminals in the connector. These are the source coil wires. Compare the readings with the value listed in this Chapter's Specifications.

4.1 Follow the wiring harness from the engine to the connectors (YFM350FW shown)

4

All models

9   If any of the readings is incorrect, the pick-up coil(s) must be replaced. They're supplied as a unit with the alternator stator assembly, so the stator must also be replaced if the pick-up coil(s) are defective (see Chapter 8).

5   CDI unit - check, removal and installation

Check

1   The CDI unit is checked by process of elimination (when all other possible causes have been checked and eliminated, the CDI unit is at fault). Because the CDI unit is expensive and can't be returned once purchased, consider having a Yamaha dealer test the system before you buy a new CDI unit.

Replacement

Refer to illustration 5.3

2   If you're working on a YFM350FW model, refer to Chapter 7 and remove the front fender.

3   Disconnect the electrical connector from the CDI unit **(see illustration)**. Remove its mounting screws and take it off the frame.

4   Installation is the reverse of the removal steps.

6   Ignition timing - general information and check

General information

1   Ignition timing need be checked only if you're troubleshooting a problem such as loss of power. Since the ignition timing can't be adjusted and since none of the ignition system parts is subject to mechanical wear, there's no need for regular checks.

2   The ignition timing is checked with the engine running, both at idle and at a higher speed listed in this Chapter's Specifications. Inexpensive neon timing lights should be adequate in theory, but in practice may produce such dim pulses that the timing marks are hard to see. If possible, one of the more precise xenon timing lights should be used, powered by an external source of the appropriate voltage. **Note:** *Don't use the vehicle's own battery as an incorrect reading may result from stray impulses within the electrical system.*

5.3 The CDI unit on YFM350FW models (shown) is mounted under the front fender at the center of the vehicle; on all others, it's under the left rear fender forward of the battery

Check

3   Warm the engine to normal operating temperature, make sure the transmission is in Neutral, then shut the engine off.

4   Refer to *Valve clearance - check and adjustment* in Chapter 1 and remove the timing hole plug.

5   Connect the timing light and a tune-up tachometer to the engine, following manufacturer's instructions.

6   Start the engine. Make sure it idles at the speed listed in the Chapter 1 Specifications. Adjust if necessary.

7   Point the timing light into the timing window. At idle, notch at the top of the timing window should be between the two lines on either side of the F mark on the alternator rotor **(see illustration 19.9 in Chapter 1)**.

8   If the timing is incorrect and all other ignition components have tested as good, the CDI unit may be defective. Have it tested by a Yamaha dealer.

9   When the check is complete, grease the timing hole plug O-ring, then install the O-ring and plug and disconnect the test equipment.

Chapter 5
Steering, suspension and final drive

Contents

Specifications

Tie-rod balljoint spacing
YFM350ER ... 300 mm (11.8 inches)
YFM350FW ... 344.5 mm (13.6 inches)
YFM350FWB ... Not specified
YFM350U ... 344 mm (13.5 inches)
Rear axle runout (maximum) ... 1.5 mm (0.06 inch)

Torque specifications

Handlebar bracket bolts
YFM350ER, YFM350FW, YFM350U ... 20 Nm (168 in-lbs)
YFM350FWB ... 23 Nm (17 ft-lbs)
Tie-rod nuts
YFM350ER ... 40 Nm (29 ft-lbs)
YFM350FW, YFM350FWB, YFM350U ... 25 Nm (18 ft-lbs)
Tie-rod locknuts
YFM350ER, YFM350FW, YFM350FWB ... 30 Nm (22 ft-lbs)
YFM350U ... 35 Nm (25 ft-lbs)
Steering shaft nut
YFM350ER, YFM350FW, YFM350U ... 30 Nm (22 ft-lbs)
YFM350FWB ... 35 Nm (25 ft-lbs)
Steering shaft upper bracket bolts ... 23 Nm (17 ft-lbs)
Front shock absorbers ... 45 Nm (32 ft-lbs)
Rear shock absorbers
YFM350ER, YFM350FW, 1996 through 1998 YFM350U ... 50 Nm (36 ft-lbs)
YFM350FWB, 1999 YFM350U ... 59 Nm (43 ft-lbs)
Front suspension arm pivot bolts
YFM350ER ... 45 Nm (32 ft-lbs)
YFM350FW, YFM350FWB, YFM350U ... 43 Nm (31 ft-lbs)
Steering knuckle pilot bolt nut (YFM350ER) ... 35 Nm (25 ft-lbs)
Upper balljoint nut (YFM350FW, YFM350ER, YFM350U) ... 25 Nm (18 ft-lbs)
Lower balljoint pinch bolt and nut (YFM350FW, YFM350ER, YFM350U)
1987 and 1988 models ... 35 Nm (25 ft-lbs)
1989-on models ... 48 Nm (35 ft-lbs)

5

Torque specifications (continued)

Front differential
YFM350FW

Front mounting bolts	45 Nm (32 ft-lbs)
Rear mounting bolts	23 Nm (17 ft-lbs)
YFM350FWB	64 Nm (46 ft-lbs)

Middle driven gear and transfer case (YFM350ER, YFM350FW and 1996 through 1998 YFM350U)

Allen bolts	10 Nm (84 In-lbs)
Bearing housing (hex) bolts	25 Nm (18 ft-lbs)

Middle driven gear (YFM350FWB and 1999 YFM350U)

Universal joint yoke nuts	97 Nm (70 ft-lbs) (1)
Front bearing retainer ring nut (YFM350FWB)	80 Nm (58 ft-lbs) (1)
Rear bearing retainer to crankcase bolts	25 Nm(18 ft-lbs)
Middle drive gear bearing housing Allen bolts	32 Nm (23 ft-lbs) (1)

Axle nuts (YFM350ER, YFM350FW) (1)
Cogged nuts

First step (inner nut)	Finger tight (2)
Second step (inner nut)	30 Nm (22 ft-lbs) (3)
Third step (outer nut)	190 Nm (140 ft-lbs) (4)
Fourth step (inner nut)	240 Nm (170 ft-lbs) (5)

Hex nuts

First step (inner nut)	Finger tight (2)
Second step (inner nut)	55 Nm (40 ft-lbs) (3)
Third step (outer nut)	190 Nm (140 ft-lbs) (4)
Fourth step (inner nut)	240 Nm (170 ft-lbs) (5)

Rear final drive unit bolts

YFM350ER, YFM350FW, 1996 through 1998 YFM350U	45 Nm (32 ft-lbs)
YFM350FWB, 1999 YFM350U	63 Nm (45 ft-lbs)

Rear final drive unit mounting nuts
YFM350ER

1987 through 1989	23 Nm (17 ft-lbs)
1990 through 1995	45 Nm (32 ft-lbs)

YFM350FW

1987 through 1993	23 Nm (17 ft-lbs)
1994 through 1997	45 Nm (32 ft-lbs)
YFM350FWB	57 Nm (41 ft-lbs)

YFM350U

1996 through 1998	23 Nm (17 ft-lbs)
1999	57 Nm (41 ft-lbs)

Swingarm

Pivot shafts	6 Nm 51 in-lbs)
Pivot shaft locknuts	130 Nm 94 ft-lbs)

1 Apply non-permanent thread locking agent to the threads.
2 Check engagement of the final drive gears while tightening.
3 Hold the axle while tightening
4 Hold the inner nut and tighten the outer nut against it.
5 Hold the outer nut and tighten the inner nut back against it.

1   General information

The front suspension on YFM350ER models consists of a single lower control arm on each side of the vehicle, connected to the frame by a shock absorber with a concentric coil spring. On all other models, there's an upper and lower control arm on each side of the vehicle. A shock absorber with a concentric coil spring is installed between each upper suspension arm and the frame.

The rear suspension on all models consists of a single shock absorber with a concentric coil spring and a steel swingarm. Final drive is by a shaft, which passes through an integral tube on the swingarm.

The steering system consists of knuckles mounted at the outer ends of the front suspension and connected to a steering shaft by tie-rods. The steering shaft is turned by a one-piece handlebar.

2   Handlebar - removal, inspection and installation

1   The handlebar is a one-piece tube. The tube fits into a bracket, which is integral with the steering shaft. If the handlebar must be removed for access to other components, such as the steering shaft, simply remove the bolts and slip the handlebar off the bracket. It's not necessary to disconnect the cables, wires or brake hose (4WD), but it is a good idea to support the assembly with a piece of wire or rope, to avoid unnecessary strain on the cables, wires and the brake hose.

2   If the handlebar is to be removed completely, refer to Chapter 3 for the throttle housing removal procedure, Chapter 6 for the master cylinder removal procedure and Chapter 8 for the switch removal procedure.

Removal

Refer to illustrations 2.4a, 2.4b, 2.4c and 2.4d

3   Lift the indicator bulb housing off the handlebar (see Chapter 8).

4   Remove the handlebar bracket bolts and lift off the brackets **(see illustrations)**. Separate the upper and lower halves and take the handlebar out of the brackets.

Inspection

5   Check the handlebar and brackets for cracks and distortion and replace them if any undesirable conditions are found.

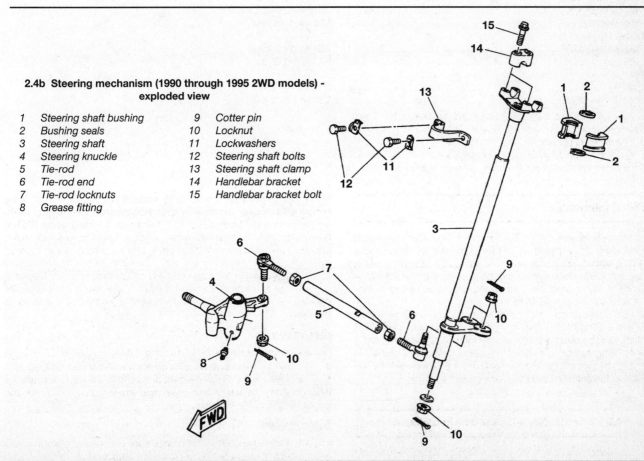

2.4a Steering mechanism (1987 through 1989 2WD models) - exploded view

1   Steering shaft bushing
2   Bushing seals
3   Steering shaft
4   Steering knuckle
5   Knuckle pivot shaft
6   Thrust cover
7   Bushing
8   Spacer
9   Tie-rod
10 Tie-rod end
11 Handlebar bracket bolt
12 Handlebar bracket
13 Steering shaft clamp
14 Lockwasher
15 Steering shaft boot
16 Washer
17 Locknut
18 Cotter pin
19 Tie rod locknuts

2.4b Steering mechanism (1990 through 1995 2WD models) - exploded view

1	Steering shaft bushing	9	Cotter pin
2	Bushing seals	10	Locknut
3	Steering shaft	11	Lockwashers
4	Steering knuckle	12	Steering shaft bolts
5	Tie-rod	13	Steering shaft clamp
6	Tie-rod end	14	Handlebar bracket
7	Tie-rod locknuts	15	Handlebar bracket bolt
8	Grease fitting		

5

Installation

Refer to illustrations 2.6a and 2.6b

6   Installation is the reverse of the removal steps, with the following additions:

a) *When installing the handlebar to the brackets, place the punch mark on each upper bracket half toward the front of the vehicle* **(see illustration).**

b) *Tighten the bracket bolts to the torques listed in this Chapter's Specifications, leaving a gap between the rear of each upper bracket half and the corresponding lower bracket half* **(see illustration).**

3   Steering shaft - removal, inspection, bushing/bearing replacement and installation

Removal

Refer to illustrations 3.6a, 3.6b, 3.8 and 3.10

1   Remove the handlebars and their brackets (see Section 2).

2   Remove the seat, front cargo rack and front fender (see Chapter 7).

3   Remove the fuel tank (see Chapter 3).

4   Remove the odometer/speedometer (see Chapter 8).

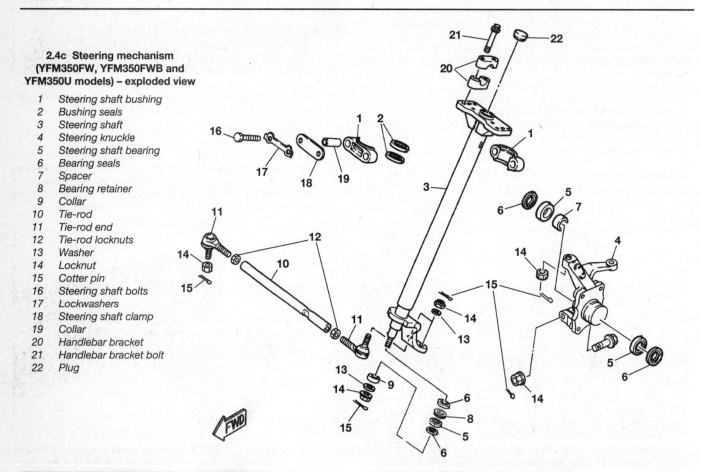

2.4c Steering mechanism (YFM350FW, YFM350FWB and YFM350U models) – exploded view

1   *Steering shaft bushing*
2   *Bushing seals*
3   *Steering shaft*
4   *Steering knuckle*
5   *Steering shaft bearing*
6   *Bearing seals*
7   *Spacer*
8   *Bearing retainer*
9   *Collar*
10   *Tie-rod*
11   *Tie-rod end*
12   *Tie-rod locknuts*
13   *Washer*
14   *Locknut*
15   *Cotter pin*
16   *Steering shaft bolts*
17   *Lockwashers*
18   *Steering shaft clamp*
19   *Collar*
20   *Handlebar bracket*
21   *Handlebar bracket bolt*
22   *Plug*

2.4d On 4WD models, the lower bracket halves can be removed from the steering shaft; place the protrusion in the hole in the steering shaft bracket on installation

2.6a Place the punch mark (arrow) on each upper bracket half toward the front of the vehicle

5　On models so equipped, remove the cover from beneath the lower end of the steering shaft.

6　Unbolt the steering shaft bracket from the frame to expose the upper bushing and seals **(see illustrations 2.4a, 2.4b, 2.4c and the accompanying illustrations)**.

7　Refer to Section 5 and disconnect the inner ends of the tie-rods.

8　Remove the cotter pin and nut from the bottom of the steering shaft **(see illustration)**.

9　Remove the steering shaft from the vehicle.

10　On 2WD models, remove the lower bushings and O-rings from the frame **(see illustration)**.

Inspection

11　Clean all the parts with solvent and dry them thoroughly, using compressed air, if available.

12　Check the steering shaft bushings and seals or O-rings for wear, deterioration or damage. Replace them if there's any doubt about their condition.

13　Check the steering shaft and its integral steering arm for bending or other signs of damage. Do not attempt to repair any steering components. Replace them with new parts if defects are found.

14　If you're working on a 4WD model, insert a finger into the steering shaft bearing and turn the inner race. If it's rough, loose or noisy, replace it as described below.

Bearing replacement (4WD models)

Refer to illustrations 3.15 and 3.16

15　Pry the upper and lower grease seals out of the bearing housing

2.6b Tighten the front bracket bolts first, then the rear brackets; tighten the bolts to Specifications and don't try to close the gap at the rear edge of each bracket

in the frame **(see illustration)**.

16　Unscrew the bearing retainer with Yamaha tool YM-01327 or equivalent **(see illustration 2.4c and the accompanying illustration)**, then remove the bearing through the top of the housing. The tool is a damper rod holder, usually used to prevent the damper rod from turning when disassembling the front forks on a motorcycle.

3.6a Bend back the lockwasher tabs and remove the bolts and clamp (YFM350FW shown) . . .

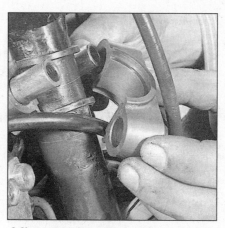

3.6b . . . to expose the bushing and seals

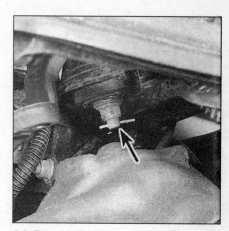

3.8 Remove the cotter pin and nut (arrow) from the bottom end of the steering shaft

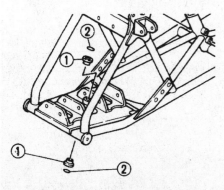

3.10 Steering shaft lower bushings (YFM350ER models)

1 Bushings　　　*2 O-rings*

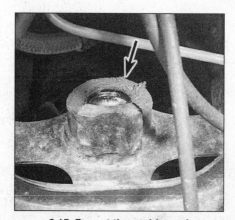

3.15 Pry out the seal (arrow)

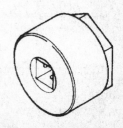

3.16 Unscrew the bearing retainer with this Yamaha special tool or equivalent

5

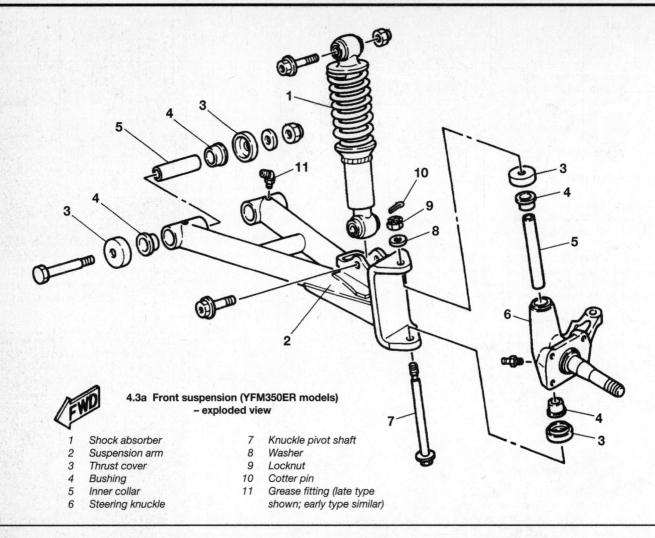

4.3a   Front suspension (YFM350ER models) – exploded view

1	Shock absorber	7	Knuckle pivot shaft
2	Suspension arm	8	Washer
3	Thrust cover	9	Locknut
4	Bushing	10	Cotter pin
5	Inner collar	11	Grease fitting (late type
6	Steering knuckle		shown; early type similar)

17   Pack a new bearing with high-quality grease (preferably a moly-based grease). Position the bearing in the housing, screw in the retainer with the Yamaha special tool and tighten it to the torque listed in this Chapter's Specifications.

18   Coat the lips of new upper and lower grease seals with grease, then tap them into the housing with a seal driver or a socket the same diameter as the seal.

Installation

19   Installation is the reverse of removal, with the following additions:

a) Lubricate the steering shaft bushings with grease.
b) Use new locknuts and cotter pins and tighten all fasteners to the torque listed in this Chapter's Specifications.
c) On 2WD models, lubricate the steering column lower bushing through the grease nipple at the bottom end of the steering column, using a grease gun.

---

4   Shock absorbers - removal, installation and adjustment

Removal and installation

Front shock absorbers

Refer to illustrations 4.3a, 4.3b, 4.3c and 4.3d

1   Securely block both rear wheels so the vehicle won't roll. Refer to Chapter 6 and remove the front wheels.

2   Support the outer ends of the front suspension with jackstands so

they won't drop when the shock absorbers are removed.

3   Remove the nuts and bolts at the upper and lower ends of the shock absorber **(see illustrations)**. Separate the shock absorber from the frame and suspension arm and lift it out.

4   Check the shock absorber for signs of wear or damage such as oil leaks, bending, a weak spring and worn bushings. Replace both shock absorbers as a pair if any problems are found.

5   Installation is the reverse of the removal steps. Tighten the nuts and bolts to the torque listed in this Chapter's Specifications.

Rear shock absorbers

Refer to illustration 4.7

6   Securely block both front wheels so the vehicle can't roll. Jack up the rear end and support it securely with the rear wheels off the ground.

7   Remove the mounting bolt and nut at the top of the shock, then the cotter pin and pivot pin at the bottom **(see illustration)**. Lift the shock out of the vehicle.

8   Installation is the reverse of the removal steps, with the following additions:

a) Tighten the nut and bolt to the torque listed in this Chapter's Specifications.
b) Use a new cotter pin.

Adjustment

Refer to illustrations 4.9a and 4.9b

9   The shock absorber is adjusted by turning the ring at the bottom of the shock with a spanner wrench **(see illustrations)**.

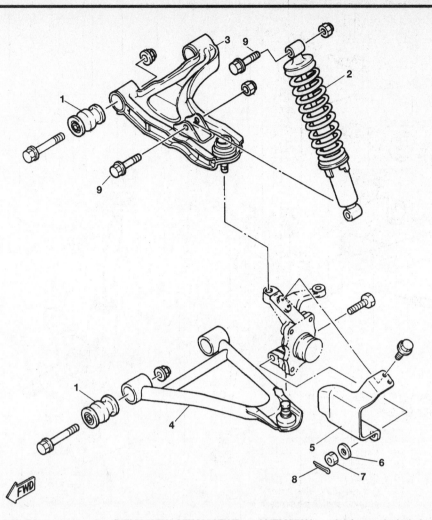

4.3c Remove the nut and bolt at the upper end of the shock absorber (YFM350FW shown) . . .

4.3d . . . and at the lower end

4.3b Front suspension (YFM350FW, YFM350FWB and YFM350U models) – exploded view

1	Bushing	6	Washer
2	Shock absorber	7	Locknut
3	Lower suspension arm	8	Cotter pin
4	Upper suspension arm	9	Shock absorber bolts (heads face rearward on YFM350FWB models)
5	Driveaxle boot protector (YFM350FW models)		

4.7 Remove the cotter pin (A), withdraw the pivot pin and remove the thrust washers; the adjuster (B) is shown on the softest setting

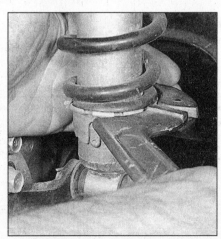

4.9a Turn the adjuster to change the setting

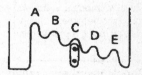

4.9b There are five settings; A is the softest and E is the stiffest

5

5.2 Remove the cotter pin and undo the locknut (4WD shown)

A   Cotter pin and locknut
B   Toe-in adjusting flat
C   Tie-rod locknut
D   Upper balljoint cotter pin and locknut
E   Lower balljoint pinch bolt

5   Tie-rods - removal, inspection and installation

Removal

Refer to illustration 5.2

1   Look for a white paint mark on the right-hand tie-rod. If you don't see one, make your own so the tie-rods don't get mixed up when both are removed.

2   Remove the cotter pin from the nut at the outer end of the tie-rod **(see illustrations 2.4a, 2.4b, 2.4c and the accompanying illustration)**.

3   Undo the nut. Separate the tie-rod stud from the knuckle with a bearing puller, power steering pump puller or "pickle-fork" balljoint separator. **Caution:** *It's very easy to damage the rubber boot on the tie-rod with a pickle-fork separator. If you're going to use the tie-rod again, it's best to use another type of tool.*

4   Repeat Steps 1 and 2 to disconnect the inner end of the tie rod **(see illustration 23.11b in Chapter 1)**.

Inspection

5   Check the tie-rod shaft for bending or other damage and replace it if any problems are found. Don't try to straighten the shaft.

6   Check the tie-rod balljoint boots for cracks or deterioration. Twist and rotate the threaded studs. They should move easily, without roughness or looseness. If a boot or stud show any problems, unscrew the tie-rod end from the tie-rod and install a new one.

Installation

Refer to illustration 5.7

7   Thread the tie-rod ends onto the tie-rods until the length between stud centerlines is as listed in this Chapter's Specifications **(see illustration)**. The length of exposed threads on each end of the tie-rod must be even. The flat on the tie-rod used to adjust toe-in goes at the outer end of the tie-rod.

8   The remainder of installation is the reverse of the removal steps, with the following additions:

a) Use new cotter pins and bend them to hold the nuts securely.
b) Check front wheel toe-in and adjust as necessary (see Chapter 1).

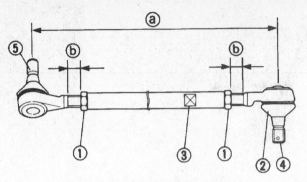

5.7 Tie-rod assembly details

1   Tie-rod locknuts
2   Tie-rod boot
3   Toe-in adjusting flat
4   Tie-rod stud
5   Tie-rod stud
a   Tie-rod length
b   Exposed threads (must be the same length)

6.7 The upper balljoint is threaded and secured to the steering knuckle by a nut. The lower balljoint is secured to the knuckle by a pinch bolt and nut

6   Steering knuckles - removal, inspection, and installation

Removal

1   Securely block both rear wheels so the vehicle won't roll. Loosen the front wheel nuts with the tires still on the ground, then jack up the front end, support it securely on jackstands and remove the front wheels.

2   Refer to Section 5 and disconnect the outer end of the tie-rod from the knuckle.

3   Remove the front brake panel (see Chapter 6). The front brake hose on 4WD models can be left connected, but be careful not to twist it and be sure to support the panel with wire or rope so it doesn't hang by the brake hose.

YFM350ER models

4   Refer to Section 5 and remove the tie-rod.

5   Remove the cotter pin, locknut and washer from the top end of the steering knuckle pivot shaft **(see illustration 4.3a)**. Lower the pivot shaft out of the knuckle and separate the knuckle from the suspension arm.

YFM350FW, YFM350FWB and YFM350U models

Refer to illustration 6.7

6   Separating the balljoint(s) from the knuckle requires a separator tool. Equivalent automotive tools can be rented, but they must be small

6.10 Turn the bearing inner races (arrows) with a finger to check for roughness

7.1 Pry the seals from the knuckle

7.2 Tap out the bearings with a hammer and drift and remove the spacer

enough for use on these vehicles. If the correct special tool isn't available, the knuckle can be removed as an assembly with the upper and lower suspension arms. This assembly can then be taken to a Yamaha dealer for balljoint removal (and knuckle bearing replacement, if necessary).

7   Remove the cotter pin and nut from the upper balljoint **(see illustration)**.

8   Separate the balljoints from the knuckle, then pull the knuckle off the end of the driveaxle.

Inspection

Refer to illustration 6.10

9   Check the knuckle carefully for cracks, bending or other damage. Replace it if any problems are found. If the vehicle has been in a collision or has been bottomed hard, it's a good idea to have the knuckle magnafluxed by a machine shop to check for hidden cracks.

10   If you're working on a 4WD model, turn the inner race of each knuckle bearing with a finger **(see illustration)**. If it's rough, loose or noisy, refer to Section 7 and replace it. Replace the bearing grease seals if they show signs of leakage or wear.

Installation

11   Installation is the reverse of the removal steps, with the following additions: Use new cotter pins and tighten the nuts to the torque listed in this Chapter's Specifications.

7   Steering knuckle bearing and seal replacement (YFM350FW, YFM350FWB and YFM350U models)

Bearing replacement

Refer to illustrations 7.1 and 7.2

1   Pry out the bearing grease seals **(see illustration)**.

2   Insert a drift through the knuckle and place it against the bearing on the opposite side **(see illustration)**. Tap around the circumference of the bearing to drive the bearing out of the knuckle, then remove the spacer and drive the other bearing out from the opposite side.

3   Pack a new bearing with grease, then drive it in with a bearing driver or socket that bears against the outer race of the bearing. Don't apply pressure to the inner race or the bearing may be damaged. Seat the bearing securely, then install the snap-ring and make sure it fits completely into its groove.

4   Install the spacer, then install the remaining bearing as described in Step 2.

5   Tap in new grease seals with a bearing driver or socket the same diameter as the seals. Make sure the seals seat squarely in their bores, then lubricate the seal lips with grease.

8   Suspension arms - removal, inspection and installation

Note: *This procedure describes removal and installation of the upper and lower suspension arms on models so equipped. If you plan to remove only the upper or lower arm, ignore the steps which don't apply.*

Removal

Refer to illustration 8.6

1   Securely block both rear wheels so the vehicle won't roll. Loosen the front wheel nuts with the tires still on the ground, then jack up the front end, support it securely on jackstands and remove the front wheels.

2   Refer to Section 6 and remove the steering knuckle.

YFM350ER models

3   Remove the pivot bolts and nuts and take the suspension arm out **(see illustration 4.3a)**.

YFM350FW, YFM350FWB and YFM350U models

4   Unbolt the bottom end of the shock absorber from the upper suspension arm (see Section 5).

5   Detach the brake fluid hose from the upper suspension arm.

6   Remove the nuts and bolts at the inner end of the suspension arm **(see illustration 4.3b and the accompanying illustration)** and pull the suspension arms out.

8.6 Remove the pivot nuts and bolts to separate the suspension arm from the frame

5

9.4a This circlip holds the inner end of the driveaxle in the differential . . .

9.4b . . . pull on the joint (not on the shaft) to free the circlip from the differential

10.3 Pry the boot clamp retaining tabs (arrow) up with a small screwdriver, open the clamps and slide them off the boot

Inspection

7   Check the suspension arm(s) for bending, cracks or other damage. Replace damaged parts. Don't attempt to straighten them.

8   Check the rubber bushings at the inner end of the suspension arm for cracks, deterioration or wear of the metal insert **(see illustration 4.3a or 4.3b)**. Check the pivot bolts for wear as well. Replace the suspension arm if any problems are visible.

9   If you're working on a 4WD model, check the balljoint boot for cracks or deterioration. Twist and rotate the threaded stud. It should move easily, without roughness or looseness. The balljoints can't be replaced separately from the suspension arm. If the boot or stud show any problems, replace the suspension arm together with the balljoint.

Installation

10   Installation is the reverse of the removal steps, with the following addition: Tighten the nuts and bolts slightly while the vehicle is jacked up, then tighten them to the torque listed in this Chapter's Specifications while the vehicle's weight is resting on the wheels.

9   Front driveaxles (4WD models) - removal and installation

Removal

Refer to illustrations 9.4a and 9.4b

1   Securely block both rear wheels so the vehicle won't roll. Loosen the front wheel nuts with the tires still on the ground, then jack up the front end, support it securely on jackstands and remove the front wheels.

2   Remove the front brake panel (see Chapter 6).

3   Remove the lower balljoint-to-steering knuckle pinch bolt and nut and separate the lower suspension arm from the steering knuckle **(see illustration 6.7)**. Swing the steering knuckle outward and pull the end of the driveaxle out. **Note:** *If you can't pull the steering knuckle out far enough, remove the shock absorber.*

4   The inner end of the driveaxle is held in the front differential unit by a circlip **(see illustration)**. With the outer end of the driveaxle free of the knuckle, grasp the joint at the inner end firmly so it won't be pulled apart, then pull the driveaxle out of the differential **(see illustration)**. **Caution:** Pull the driveaxle straight out (don't let it tilt up, down or sideways) to prevent damage to the oil seal in the differential.

Installation

5   Installation is the reverse of the removal steps. After installing the driveaxle in the differential, tug out on it to make sure the circlip is locked in place.

10.4 Pry the wire ring ball retainer out of the outer race

10   Front driveaxle (4WD) - CV joint and boot replacement

Inner CV joint and boot

Disassembly

Refer to illustrations 10.3, 10.4, 10.6 and 10.8

1   Remove the driveaxle from the vehicle (see Section 9).

2   Mount the driveaxle in a vise. The jaws of the vise should be lined with wood or rags to prevent damage to the driveaxle.

3   Pry the boot clamp retaining tabs up with a small screwdriver and slide the clamps off the boot **(see illustration)**.

4   Slide the boot back on the axleshaft and pry the wire ring ball retainer from the outer race **(see illustration)**.

5   Pull the outer race off the inner bearing assembly.

6   Remove the snap-ring from the groove in the axleshaft with a pair of snap-ring pliers **(see illustration)**.

7   Slide the inner bearing assembly off the axleshaft.

8   Make match marks on the inner and outer portions of the bearing to identify which side faces out on assembly **(see illustration)**.

Inspection

9   Clean the components with solvent to remove all traces of grease. Inspect the cage, balls and races for pitting, score marks,

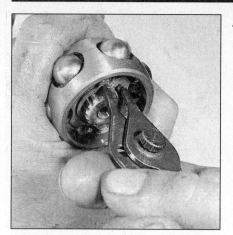

10.6 Remove the snap-ring from the end of the axle

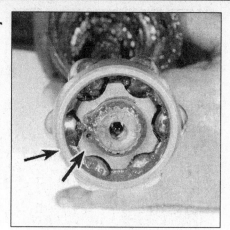

10.8 Apply match marks on the bearing (arrows) to identify which side faces out during reassembly

10.10 Wrap the splined area of the axle with tape to prevent damage to the boot when installing it

10.16 Equalize the pressure inside the boot by inserting a small, dull screwdriver between the boot and the outer race

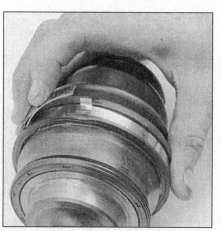

10.17a To install the new clamps, bend the tang down and . . .

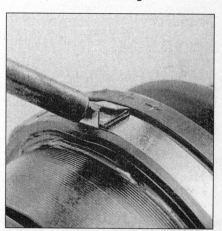

10.17b . . . fold the tabs over to hold it in place

cracks and other signs of wear and damage. Shiny, polished spots are normal and will not adversely affect CV joint performance.

Reassembly

Refer to illustrations 10.10, 10.16, 10.17a and 10.17b

10   Wrap the axleshaft splines with tape to avoid damaging the boot. Slide the small boot clamp and boot onto the axleshaft, then remove the tape **(see illustration)**.

11   Install the inner bearing assembly on the axleshaft with the previously made matchmarks facing out.

12   Install the snap-ring in the groove. Make sure it's completely seated by pushing on the inner bearing assembly.

13   Fill the outer race and boot with CV joint grease (normally included with the new boot kit). Pack the inner bearing assembly with grease, by hand, until grease is worked completely into the assembly.

14   Slide the outer race down onto the inner race and install the wire ring retainer.

15   Wipe any excess grease from the axle boot groove on the outer race. Seat the small diameter of the boot in the recessed area on the axleshaft. Push the other end of the boot onto the outer race.

16   Equalize the pressure in the boot by inserting a dull screwdriver between the boot and the outer race **(see illustration)**. Don't damage the boot with the tool.

17   Install the boot clamps **(see illustrations)**.

18   Install a new circlip on the inner CV joint stub axle.

19   Install the driveaxle as described in Section 9.

10.21 Slide the boot away from the joint and off the axleshaft

Outer CV joint and boot

Disassembly

Refer to illustration 10.21

20   Following Steps 1 through 8, remove the inner CV joint from the axleshaft.

21   Remove the outer CV joint boot clamps, using the technique described in Step 3. Slide the boot off the axleshaft **(see illustration)**.

5

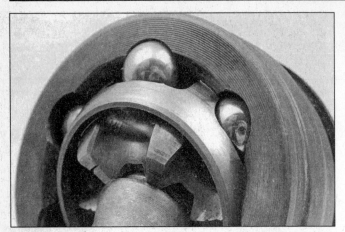

10.23 After the old grease has been rinsed away and the solvent has been blown out with compressed air, rotate the outer joint housing through its full range of motion and inspect the bearing surfaces for wear and damage - if any of the balls, the race or the cage look damaged, replace the driveaxle and outer joint assembly

Inspection

Refer to illustration 10.23

22   Thoroughly wash the inner and outer CV joints in clean solvent and blow them dry with compressed air, if available. **Note:** *Because the outer joint cannot be disassembled, it is difficult to wash away all the old grease and to rid the bearing of solvent once it's clean. But it is imperative that the job be done thoroughly, so take your time and do it right.*

23   Bend the outer CV joint housing at an angle to the driveaxle to expose the bearings, inner race and cage **(see illustration)**. Inspect the bearing surfaces for signs of wear. If the bearings are damaged or worn, replace the driveaxle.

Reassembly

24   Slide the new outer boot onto the driveaxle. It's a good idea to wrap vinyl tape around the spline of shaft to prevent damage to the boot **(see illustration 10.10)**. When the boot is in position, add the specified amount of grease (included in the boot replacement kit) to the outer joint and the boot (pack the joint with as much grease as it will hold and put the rest into the boot). Slide the boot on the rest of the way and install the new clamps **(see illustrations 10.17a and 10.17b)**.

25   Proceed to clean and install the inner CV joint and boot by following Steps 9 through 18, then install the driveaxle as outlined in Section 10.

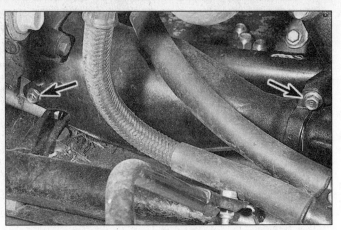

11.7a Remove the bolt at the rear of the driveshaft front protector (right arrow) and two more bolts at the front (left arrow)

11   Front differential and driveshaft - removal, inspection and installation

Removal

Refer to illustrations 11.7a, 11.7b and 11.8

1   Refer to Section 10 and remove both front driveaxles.

2   Remove the seat, front and rear cargo racks, front and rear fenders and front skid plate (see Chapter 7). Unbolt the front fender stays and remove them as well.

3   Remove the exhaust system (see Chapter 3).

4   Remove the starter motor (see Chapter 7).

5   Remove the oil cooler hose retainer and the lower oil cooler mounting bolts (see Chapter 2).

6   Remove the differential drain plugs and drain the oil (see Chapter 1).

7   Unbolt the front driveshaft cover and lift it off **(see illustration)**. Unbolt the rear driveshaft protector, but leave it in place for now **(see illustration)**.

8   Remove the forward mounting bolts **(see illustration)**, then remove the rear mounting bolts from the underneath the differential.

9   Pull the differential forward to disengage the differential U-joint from the front driveshaft, taking care not to lose the spring and spring seat in the end of the driveshaft, then lift the differential and remove it to one side of the vehicle.

10   Pull the rubber boot on the rear end of the driveshaft forward, then pull the driveshaft out of the transfer case universal joint.

11.7b Unbolt the driveshaft rear protector (arrows); the lower bolt secures a wiring harness retainer

11.8 Unbolt the differential from the mounting bracket on each side

12.4 Remove the upper cover Allen bolts (the two forward bolts have copper washers and the upper bolt secures a wiring harness retainer) . . .

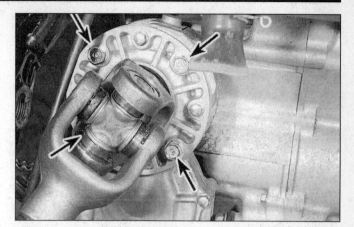

12.5 . . . and the four hex bolts at the rear (lower left bolt hidden)

Inspection

11   Check the driveshaft for bending and for worn or damaged splines. Replace it if these conditions are found.
12   Check the oil seals at the driveaxle holes and the driveshaft hole for signs of leakage (see illustration 11.8). Look into the driveaxle holes and check for obvious signs of wear and for damage such as broken gear teeth. Turn the universal joint by hand to rotate the gears so they can be inspected.
13   Differential overhaul is a complicated procedure that requires several special tools, for which there are no readily available substitutes. If there's visible wear or damage, or if the differential's rotation is rough or noisy, take it to a Yamaha dealer for disassembly and further inspection.

Installation

14   Lubricate the lips of the driveaxle seals, as well as the splines of the universal joint, with multi-purpose grease.
15   Lubricate the splines at the rear of the driveshaft and slide it into the transfer case universal joint, then pull the rubber boot into position. Make sure the spring and spring seat are in place in the front end of the driveshaft.
16   Place the differential in the frame from the right side and position it slightly forward of its installed position. Slide the differential back and slip the driveshaft into the universal joint.
17   Bolt the differential to the mounting brackets and tighten its bolts to the torque listed in this Chapter's Specifications. Install the driveaxles (see Section 10).
18   Fill the differential with the recommended type and amount of oil (see Chapter 1).
19   The remainder of installation is the reverse of the removal steps.

12 Middle driven gear and YFM350FW transfer case - removal, inspection and installation

YFM350ER, YFM350FW and 1996 through 1998 YFM350U models

Removal

Refer to illustrations 12.4, 12.5 and 12.6

1   Remove the rear cargo rack, rear fender and the skid plate from under the engine (see Chapter 7).
2   Remove the exhaust system (see Chapter 3).
3   Remove the rear final drive unit and swingarm (see Sections 14 and 16). The differential and swingarm can be removed as a unit if they're only being removed for access to the transfer case.
4   Remove the middle gear case Allen bolts, noting the locations of the copper washers, wiring harness retainer and driveshaft rear cover (see illustration). Don't try to remove the middle gear case yet.
5   Remove the four bolts that secure the middle driven gear to the middle gear case and crankcase (see illustration).
6   Pull the middle driven gear (and transfer case on YFM350FW models) back and sideways, disengaging the middle driven gear bearings from the crankcase, and take the assembly out of the frame (see illustration).

Inspection

Refer to illustrations 12.7a and 12.7b

7   Check the teeth on the middle driven gear and the middle drive gear (in the crankcase) for wear or damage (see illustrations). Replacement of the gears requires disassembly of the middle driven gear. This is a complicated procedure involving the use of a press and special Yamaha tools, and should be only be done by a Yamaha dealer

12.6 Take the middle driven gear (and the transfer case on 4WD models) out of the engine

12.7a Inspect the bearing, spring and bevel gear . . .

5

12.7b . . . and the corresponding bevel gear in the engine

A   *Bevel gear*   B   *Dowels*

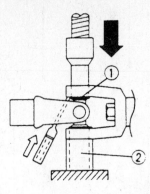

12.12a Pry out the snap-rings (1) and place the U-joint over a socket (2)

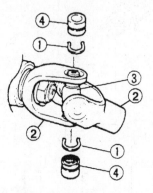

12.12b Universal joint details

1   *Snap-rings*
2   *Yokes*
3   *Spider*
4   *Bearing cups*

or qualified ATV shop.

8   Rotate the middle driven gear bearings and check for roughness, looseness or noise **(see illustration 12.7a)**. Hold one side of each universal joint and try to rotate the other side while checking for looseness. If problems are found, take the middle driven gear to a dealer or ATV shop for repairs.

9   If the middle driven gear is disassembled for repair, the backlash of the drive and driven gears will have to be adjusted by changing the number of shims. This procedure should be done, and the middle driven gear installed in the engine, by the same shop that does the repairs.

Installation

10   Installation is the reverse of the removal steps, with the following additions:

a) *Install the same number of shims that were removed (unless the gear has been repaired).*

b) *Lubricate the driveshaft splines with multipurpose grease.*

c) *Be sure the gear case dowels are reinstalled* **(see illustration 12.7b)**.

d) *Tighten the bearing housing assembly bolts and the case Allen bolts to the torques listed in this Chapter's Specifications.*

e) *Fill the engine (and transfer case on 4WD models) with the recommended amount and type of oil (see Chapter 1).*

YFM350FWB and 1999 YFM350U models

Removal

Refer to illustrations 12.12a, 12.12b, 12.16 and 12.17

11   Remove the engine. If you're planning to work on the internal components of the middle driven gear, separate the crankcase halves and remove the middle drive shaft (see Chapter 2).

12   If you're planning to replace the universal joint, place it in a sturdy vise and remove the snap-rings from the spider **(see illustrations)**. Supporting the engine, place the universal joint in position on either an arbor press or on a workbench equipped with a large vise.

13   Place a piece of pipe or a large socket over one of the bearing cups (the pipe or socket should be large enough that the bearing cap will fit inside it when pressed out of the yoke). Position a socket of slightly smaller diameter than the cup on the opposite bearing **(see illustration 13.12b)** and use the vise or press to force the cup out (inside the pipe or large socket), stopping just before it comes completely out of the yoke. Use the vise or large pliers to work the cup the rest of the way out.

14   Transfer the socket to the other and press out the opposite bearing cup, then remove the remaining two bearings in the same way.

15   Separate the spider and yoke. Hold the yoke half that's attached to the engine in a vise and remove the nut and washer, then release the vise and take the yoke off the middle driven gear.

16   **Note:** *If you haven't already separated the crankcase halves, do so now.* Unbolt the bearing housing from the engine, then remove the housing and its shim or shims **(see illustration)**. Remove the damper cam, damper spring and gear coupling from the crankcase.

17   If you're working on a YFM350FWB model, remove the front universal joint and yoke as described in Steps 12 through 15 above. Pry out the oil seal and unscrew the bearing retainer from the crankcase using a ring nut wrench (Yamaha tool YM38404 or 90890-01430) **(see illustration)**. **Note:** *The ring nut has left-hand threads (unscrews clockwise). If you don't have this tool, you can have the nut loosened by a dealer service department. You can also fabricate a tool from a socket the same diameter as the ring nut; grind the end of the socket to leave four protrusions that match the removal notches in the ring nut.* **Note:** *The ring nut is secured with Loctite and tightened to 58 ft-lbs, so the tool must be sturdy.*

18   Withdraw the front portion of the middle driven shaft from the crankcase.

Inspection

19   Inspection is basically the same as for YFM350FW models, described in Steps 7 through 9 above.

Installation

20   Installation is the reverse of the removal steps, with the following additions:

a) *Install the same number of shims that were removed (unless the gears have been replaced)*

b) *Lubricate driveshaft splines with multipurpose grease.*

c) *Secure the ring nut (YFM350FWB models) with non-permanent thread locking agent and tighten it to the torque listed in this Chapter's Specifications. Use a new oil seal next to the ring nut.*

d) *Tighten the universal joint yoke nuts and bearing retainer bolts to the torques listed in this Chapter's Specifications. Use non-permanent thread locking agent on the universal joint yoke nuts.*

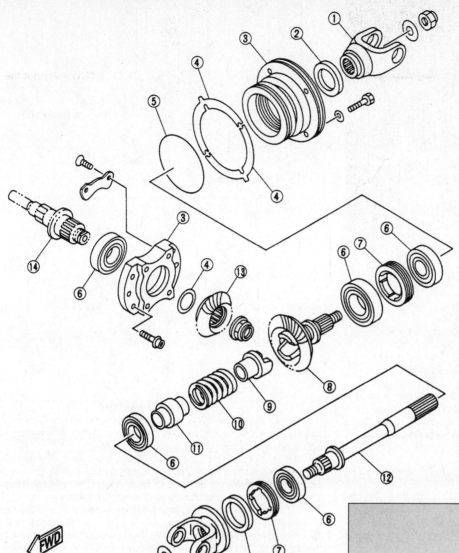

12.16 Middle drive and driven gears (YFM350FWB and 1999 YFM350U) – exploded view

1   Universal joint yoke
2   Oil seal
3   Bearing housing
4   Shim(s)
5   O-ring
6   Bearing
7   Bearing retainer
8   Middle driven pinion gear
9   Damper cam
10 Spring
11 Gear coupling
12 Middle driven shaft (YMF350FWB only)
13 Middle drive pinion gear
14 Middle drive shaft

12.17 This special tool or an equivalent is needed to unscrew the bearing retainer

13.3a These special tools are used to loosen and tighten the axle nuts - the one on the left is used for hex nuts, with a breaker bar or torque wrench fitted into its square hole; the one on the right is used for cogged nuts . . .

13   Rear axle - removal, inspection and installation

Removal

Refer to illustrations 13.3a, 13.3b, 13.5 and 13.6

1   Securely block the front wheels so the vehicle won't roll. Loosen the rear wheel nuts with the vehicle on the ground. Jack up the rear end and support it securely, positioning the jackstands so they won't obstruct removal of the axle. The supports must be secure enough so the vehicle won't be knocked off of them while the very tight axle nuts are loosened. Remove the rear wheels.

2   Remove the rear wheel hubs and the complete rear brake assembly (see Chapter 6). Remove the trailer hitch bracket.

3   The axle on YFM350ER and YFM350FW models is secured on the

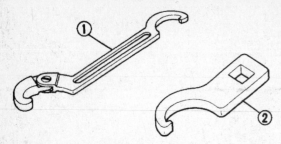

13.3b ... these tools are also used for cogged nuts

1   *Tool no. YU-01268*
2   *Tool no. YU-33975 (used with breaker bar or torque wrench)*

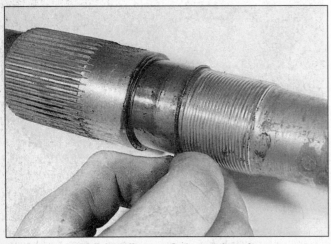

13.6 Place the hub and nut on the end of the axle and tap it gently to free it from the final drive unit

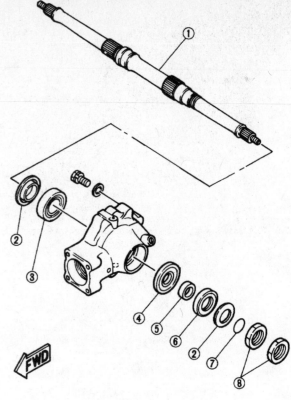

13.5 Rear axle details

1   *Rear axle*   5   *Collar*
2   *Dust cover*   6   *Grease seal*
3   *Bearing*   7   *O-ring*
4   *Bearing*   8   *Ring nut*

left side by a pair of nuts tightened against each other (YFM350FWB and YFM350U models don't use nuts). On early models, these nuts are cogged; later models use hex nuts. Loosening and retightening the nuts requires a special wrench **(see illustrations)**. Equivalent wrenches are available from aftermarket sources. Yamaha tool numbers are:

    Cogged axle nuts: YU-01268 and YU-33975
    Hex axle nuts: YM-37132

4   Use the special tool to loosen the outer nut. **Note:** *If the wrench is hard to hold (the nuts are very tight), place a breaker bar in the square hole of the wrench adapter and place it against the floor of the work area or on a solid support such as a large block of wood.*

5   Once the nuts are loose, unscrew them from the axle and remove the washers **(see illustration)**.

6   Clean any foreign material from the left side of the axle so it won't be pulled into the final drive unit during removal. Install the left wheel hub and thread the nut on until it's flush with the end of the axle to protect the threads. Tap on the left end of the axle with a soft faced hammer to free it, then pull it out of the axle housing **(see illustration)**.

Inspection

Refer to illustrations 13.7, 13.8 and 13.9

7   Check the axle for obvious damage, such as step wear of the splines or bending, and replace it as necessary. Remove the axle O-ring and install a new one **(see illustration)**.

8   Place the axle in V-blocks and set up a dial indicator to contact each of the outer ends in turn **(see illustration)**. Rotate the axle and compare runout to the value listed in this Chapter's Specifications. If runout is excessive, replace the axle.

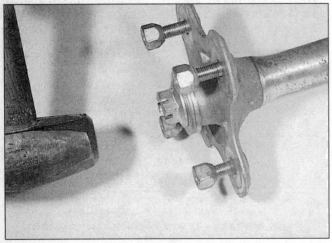

13.7 Install a new O-ring on the axle

13.8 Place the axle in a pair of V-blocks and measure runout with a dial indicator at the ends (arrows)

13.9 This bearing will come out with the axle; replace it if it's worn or damaged

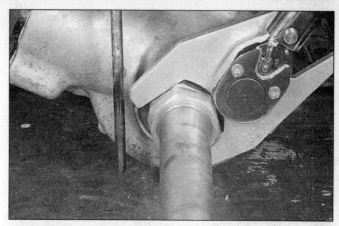

13.13 Tighten the inner axle nut to the specified torque, then hold the inner nut and tighten the outer nut to the specified torque, then hold the outer nut and tighten the inner nut back against the outer nut to the final torque

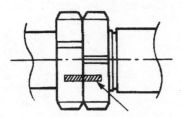

13.16a Scribe a line across the nuts . . .

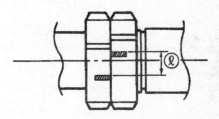

13.16b . . . when the inner nut is tightened against the outer nut, the gap between the lines (arrows) should be as specified in the text

9   Check the axle bearing for roughness, looseness or noise and replace it as necessary **(see illustration)**. If the bearing is difficult to remove from the axle shaft, have it pressed off by a Yamaha dealer or machine shop.

Installation

Refer to illustration 13.13

10   Lubricate the axle splines and the lip of the differential oil seal with multipurpose grease. Install the axle from the right side of the vehicle. Place the right hub on the axle and thread the hub nut on until it's flush with the end of the axle shaft , then tap the axle into position, aligning the splines of the axle with those of the final drive unit.

11   Install the rear brake assembly (see Chapter 6).

12   Apply non-permanent thread locking agent to the nut threads on the axle.

13   Install the inner nut and tighten it to the torque listed in this Chapter's Specifications, using the special tools described above **(see illustration)**.

14   Hold the inner nut so it can't turn and tighten the outer nut against the inner nut to the torque listed in this Chapter's Specifications.

Models with cogged nuts

15   Hold the outer nut and tighten the inner nut back against the outer nut to the final torque listed in this Chapter's Specifications.

Models with hex nuts

Refer to illustrations 13.16a and 13.16b

16   Draw a line across both nuts **(see illustration)**. Hold the outer nut and tighten the inner nut against it to the final torque listed in this Chapter's Specifications. The line on the inner nut should have moved so that there's a gap of at least 3 mm (1/8 inch) between the two lines **(see illustration)**. If the gap is too small, hold the outer nut and tighten the inner nut against it some more until the gap is as specified.

17   The remainder of installation is the reverse of the removal steps.

18   Check oil level in the final drive unit and add oil as necessary (see Chapter 1).

14   Rear final drive unit - removal, inspection and installation

Removal

Refer to illustrations 14.3a and 14.3b

1   Remove the axle shaft (see Section 13).

2   Unbolt the skid plate and remove it from under the final drive unit.

3   Disconnect the breather tube. Unbolt the final drive unit from the axle housing and remove the nuts that secure the final drive unit to the swingarm **(see illustrations)**. Pull the unit rearward to detach it and lift it away from the swingarm.

5

14.3a Disconnect the breather tube (upper arrow) and remove the four axle housing-to-final drive bolts (lower arrows) (two upper bolts shown)

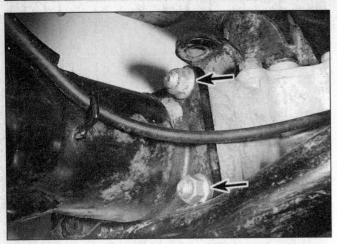

14.3b Remove the four nuts and detach the final drive unit from the swingarm

14.4a Remove the dust seal to check the bearing; if it's worn or damaged, have it replaced

Inspection

Refer to illustrations 14.4a and 14.4b

4   Look into the axle holes and check for obvious signs of wear and for damage such as broken splines **(see illustrations)**. Also check the seals for signs of leakage. Turn the pinion by hand (temporarily install the driveshaft and use it as a handle if necessary).

5   Final drive overhaul is a complicated procedure that requires several special tools, for which there are no readily available substitutes. If there's visible wear or damage, or if rotation is rough or noisy, take it to a Yamaha dealer for disassembly and further inspection.

Installation

6   Make sure the driveshaft spring (if equipped) is in place in the driveshaft **(see illustration 18.2b)**. Clean all old sealant from the mating surfaces of the final drive unit and swingarm.

7   Slide the final drive unit studs through the holes in the swingarm, align the driveshaft with the final drive pinion and push the final drive unit into position.

8   Install the final drive nuts and tighten them slightly.

9   Tighten the final drive unit bolts to the torque listed in this Chapter's Specifications.

10   Tighten the final drive unit nuts to the torque listed in this Chapter's Specifications.

11   The remainder of installation is the reverse of the removal steps.

12   Fill the final drive unit with the amount and type of oil recommended in Chapter 1.

15 Swingarm bearings - check

1   Refer to Chapter 6 and remove the rear wheels, then refer to Section 4 and remove the rear shock absorber.

2   Grasp the rear of the swingarm with one hand and place your other hand at the junction of the swingarm and the frame. Try to move the rear of the swingarm from side-to-side. Any wear (play) in the bearings should be felt as movement between the swingarm and the frame at the front. The swingarm will actually be felt to move forward and backward at the front (not from side-to-side). If any play is noted, the bearings should be replaced with new ones (see Section 16).

3   Next, move the swingarm up and down through its full travel. It should move freely, without any binding or rough spots. If it does not move freely, refer to Section 16 for servicing procedures.

16 Swingarm - removal and installation

1   If the swingarm is being removed just for bearing replacement or driveshaft removal, the brake assembly, final drive and rear axle need not be removed from the swingarm.

Removal

Refer to illustrations 16.7a, 16.7b, 16.8, 16.9, and 16.10

2   Raise the rear end of the vehicle off the ground with a jack. Support the vehicle securely so it can't be knocked over while it's

16.7a Loosen the clamp screws

14.4b Look inside the final drive unit for visible wear or damage

16.7b Swingarm details

1 Rear shock absorber
2 Thrust washers
3 Locknut
4 Pivot shaft (with O-ring on
   YFM350FWB and
   YFM350U models)
5 Collar
6 Grease seal
7 Swingarm bearing
8 Swingarm
9 Boot

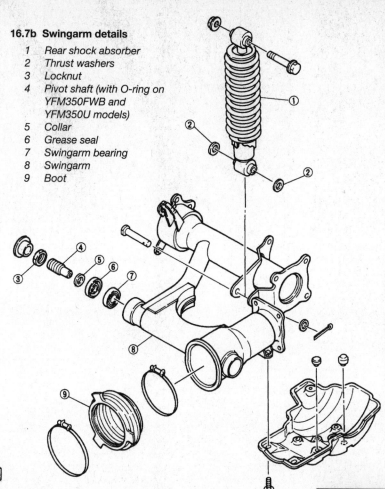

16.8 Remove the plastic cap from each side
of the swingarm . . .

16.9 . . . unscrew the locknuts, then unscrew the
pivot bolts with an Allen wrench

16.10 A spring fits inside the driveshaft (arrow) on some models

jacked up.

3   Remove the rear wheels (see Chapter 6).
4   Refer to Section 4 and detach the lower end of the shock absorber from the swingarm.
5   Disconnect the rear brake lever cable and the pedal rod/cable (see Chapter 6).
6   If you're planning to remove the rear axle, final drive unit or brake assembly, do it now (see Section 13, Section 14 or Chapter 6).
7   On the left side of the swingarm, loosen the clamps that secure the rubber boot **(see illustrations)**.
8   Pry the plastic pivot cap from each side of the swingarm **(see illustration)**.
9   Unscrew the locknut and pivot bolt from each side of the swingarm **(see illustration)**.
10   Pull the swingarm back and away from the vehicle, separating the driveshaft from the middle driven gear as you pull **(see illustration)**.
11   Check the pivot bearings in the swingarm for dryness or deterioration (see Section 17). If they're in need of lubrication or replacement, refer to Section 17.

Installation

12   If the driveshaft was removed from the swingarm, install it **(see illustration 16.10)**. Lubricate the driveshaft splines with molybdenum disulfide grease.
13   If the boot was removed from the swingarm, install it with one of its tabs down.
14   Lift the swingarm into position in the frame. Align the splines of the driveshaft with those of the output gear and align the pivot bolt

holes in the swingarm with those in the frame.
15   Install both pivot shafts to hold the swingarm in the frame, but don't tighten them yet.
16   Tighten the right pivot bolt to the torque listed in this Chapter's Specifications with an Allen wrench. Tighten the right pivot bolt's locknut to the torque listed in this Chapter's Specifications.
17   Tighten the left pivot bolt to the torque listed in this Chapter's Specifications with an Allen wrench. Tighten the left pivot bolt's locknut to the torque listed in this Chapter's Specifications.
18   Raise and lower the swingarm several times, moving it through its full travel to seat the bearings and pivot bolts.

5

17.3 Remove the collar and pry out the seal for access to the bearing (arrow)

19   Slip the boot into position and tighten the clamp.
20   The remainder of installation is the reverse of the removal steps.

17 Swingarm bearings - replacement

Refer to illustration 17.3
1   The swingarm pivot shafts ride on two tapered roller bearings.
2   Remove the swingarm (see Section 16).
3   Remove the collar and pry the seal from each side of the swingarm **(see illustration 16.7b and the accompanying illustration)**. Take the bearings out of the swingarm and clean them thoroughly with solvent.
4   Check the bearings for roughness, looseness or play. If there's any doubt about bearing condition, replace the bearings as a set.
5   Insert a long drift from the opposite side of the swingarm so it rests against the inside of the bearing outer race. Tap against the drift to remove the bearing outer race. Work around the circumference of the outer race as you tap so the bearing doesn't tilt sideways and jam.
6   Tap new outer races into position with a bearing driver or socket just slightly smaller than the diameter of the outer race.
7   Pack the bearings with waterproof lithium-based wheel bearing grease.

18 Rear driveshaft - removal, inspection and installation

Removal

Refer to illustrations 18.2a and 18.2b
1   Refer to Section 16 and remove the swingarm.
2   Pull the driveshaft (and spring, if equipped) out of the swingarm, then pull the coupling spline out of the final drive unit **(see illustrations)**.

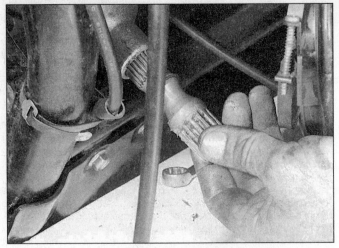

18.2a Pull out the driveshaft . . .

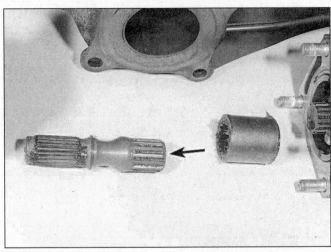

18.2b . . . and disengage the coupling spline from the final drive unit; on some models there's a spring inside the rear end of the driveshaft (arrow)

Inspection

3   Check the shaft for bending or other visible damage such as step wear of the splines. If the shaft is bent or the splines are worn, replace it.
4   Make sure the snap-ring is securely installed in its groove. If not, remove it and install a new one.

Installation

5   Installation is the reverse of the removal procedure. Make sure the snap-ring (and spring, if equipped) are in place.

Chapter 6 Brakes, wheels and tires

Contents

Specifications

Brakes

Brake fluid type	See Chapter 1
Brake shoe lining minimum thickness	See Chapter 1
Brake pad lining minimum thickness	See Chapter 1
Brake pedal height	See Chapter 1

Drum diameter

1987 through 1989 YFM350ER (front only)
- Standard: 110 mm (4.33 inches)*
- Limit: 111 mm (4.37 inches)*

All other drum brake models (front and rear)
- Standard: 160 mm (6.30 inches)*
- Limit: 161 mm (6.34 inches)*

Rear disc thickness
- Standard: 4.0 mm (0.16 inch)*
- Limit: 3.0 mm (0.12 inch)*

Rear disc runout limit: 0.5 mm (0.02 inch)

Front disc thickness
- Standard: 3.5 mm (0.14 inch)*
- Limit: 3.0 mm (0.12 inch)*

Front pad wear limit: See Chapter 1

*Refer to marks cast into the drum or disc (they supersede numbers printed here).

Wheels and tires

Tire pressures	See Chapter 1
Tire tread depth	See Chapter 1

Torque specifications

Front hub nuts
- YFM350ER: 115 Nm (85 ft-lbs)
- YFM350FW: 150 Nm (110 ft-lbs)
- YFM350FWB, YFM350U
  - Through 1998: 130 Nm (94 ft-lbs)
  - 1999: 150 Nm (110 ft-lbs)

Rear hub nuts
- YFM350ER
  - 1987 and 1988: 150 Nm (110 ft-lbs)
  - 1989 through 1995: 115 Nm (85 ft-lbs)
- YFM350FW: 130 Nm (94 ft-lbs)
- YFM350FWB, YFM350U: 150 Nm (110 ft-lbs)

Front brake fasteners (YFM350ER)
- Brake lever pinch bolt and nut: 9 Nm (78 in-lbs)
- Brake cam and anchor pin bolts (1990 on): 6 Nm (52 in-lbs)
- Brake panel bolts (1990 on): 28 Nm (20 ft-lbs)

Torque specifications (continued)

Front brake hydraulic system (YFM350FW)

Wheel cylinder bolts/nuts...	10 Nm (86 in-lbs)
Brake hose union bolts	25 Nm (18 ft-lbs) (1)
Brake hose joint mounting bolt	20 Nm (168 in-lbs)
Brake pipe flare nuts	18 Nm (156 in-lbs) (2)

Front drum brake hydraulic system (YFM350FWB, YFM350U)

Wheel cylinder bolts/nuts...	10 Nm (86 in-lbs) (3)
Brake panel mounting bolts	28 Nm (20 ft-lbs) (3)
Brake hose union bolts	27 Nm (19 ft-lbs) (1)
Brake hose joint mounting bolt	23 Nm (19 ft-lbs)
Brake pipe flare nuts	18 Nm (156 in-lbs) (2)
Wheel cylinder bleed valve..	6 Nm (52 in-lbs)
Master cylinder cover screws	Not specified
Master cylinder clamp bolts...	7 Nm (61 in-lbs)

Front disc brake hydraulic system

Pad pins	18 Nm (156 in-lbs)
Caliper mounting bolts	30 Nm (22 ft-lbs)
Disc-to-hub bolts	30 Nm (22 ft-lbs)
Brake hose union bolts	27 Nm (19 ft-lbs) (1)
Caliper bleed valve	6 Nm (52 in-lbs)

1   *Use new sealing washers each time the bolts are removed.*
2   *Replace the brake pipe with a new one each time the flare nuts are disconnected.*

1   General information

The vehicles covered by this manual include several different brake designs. YFM350ER models use front drum brakes, actuated by a cable. All YFM350FW models, as well as YFM350FWB and YFM350U models through 1998, use hydraulically actuated drum brakes at the front. All 1999 models use hydraulically actuated disc brakes at the front.

All models use a single rear brake, located at the right end of the rear axle. 1987 through 1995 models use a mechanically actuated disc brake. 1996 and later models use a mechanically actuated drum brake. The front brakes on all models are controlled by a lever on the right handlebar. The rear brake has two means of control: a lever on the left handlebar, which can be locked to provide a parking brake, and a pedal on the right side of the vehicle. The pedal and lever are connected to the rear brake assembly by a cable (lever) and rod/cable (pedal).

All models are equipped with steel wheels, which require very little maintenance and allow tubeless tires to be used. **Caution:** *Brake components rarely require disassembly. Do not disassemble components unless absolutely necessary. If any hydraulic brake line connection in the system is loosened, the entire system should be disassembled, drained, cleaned and then properly filled and bled upon reassembly. Do not use solvents on internal hydraulic brake components. Solvents will cause seals to swell and distort. Use only clean brake fluid for cleaning. Use care when working with brake fluid as it can injure your eyes and it will damage painted surfaces and plastic parts.*

2   Front brakes and wheel bearings (YFM350ER models) - removal, inspection and installation

Warning: *If a front wheel cylinder indicates the need for an overhaul (usually due to leaking fluid or sticky operation), ALL FOUR front wheel cylinders should be overhauled and all old brake fluid flushed from the system. Also, the dust created by the brake system may contain asbestos, which is harmful to your health. Never blow it out with compressed air and don't inhale any of it. An approved filtering mask should be worn when working on the brakes. Do not, under any circumstances, use petroleum-based solvents to clean brake parts. Use clean brake fluid only!*

Removal

Refer to illustrations 2.3a and 2.3b

1   Loosen the front wheel nuts. Securely block the rear wheels so the vehicle can't roll. Jack up the front end and support it securely on jackstands.
2   Remove the front wheel.

Brake drum

3   Remove the cotter pin from the front hub nut **(see illustrations)**. Remove the nut with a socket and breaker bar, then remove the washer and, on later models, the O-ring.
4   Pull the brake drum off together with the front wheel bearings and seals.

Brake shoes

5   Pull the brake shoes apart and fold them toward each other to release the spring tension. Remove the shoes and springs from the brake panel.

Brake panel

6   Unscrew the brake cable adjuster wing nut all the way. Slip the cable out of the adjuster pin, then pull the pin out of the brake adjuster lever.
7   Remove the snap-ring and detach the cable from the bracket on the brake panel.
8   If you're working on a 1987 through 1989 model, slip the brake panel off the steering knuckle.
9   If you're working on a 1990 or later model, remove the four brake panel bolts and take it off the steering knuckle.

Inspection

10   Check the linings for wear, damage and signs of contamination

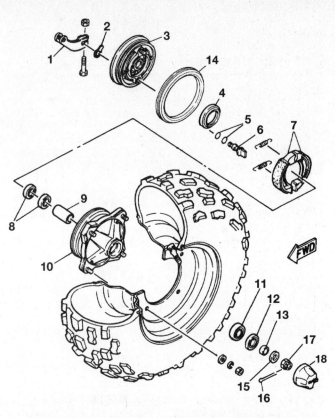

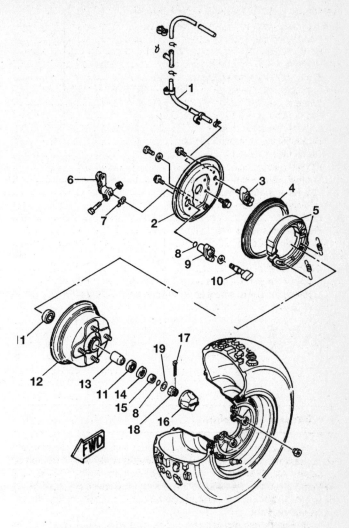

2.3a Front brakes (1988 and 1989 YFM350ER models) - exploded view

1	Brake lever	11	Outer wheel bearing
2	Wear indicator	12	Grease seal
3	Brake panel	13	Collar
4	Grease seal	14	Brake drum seal (1988
5	O-rings		and later models)
6	Brake cam	15	Washer
7	Brake shoes	16	Cotter pin
8	Inner wheel bearings	17	Locknut
9	Bearing spacer	18	Wheel cap
10	Brake drum/front hub		

2.3b Front brakes (1990 and later YFM350ER models) - exploded view

1	Breather hose	11	Inner wheel bearing
2	Brake panel	12	Brake drum/front hub
3	Anchor pin	13	Bearing spacer
4	Brake drum seal	14	Grease seal
5	Brake shoes	15	Collar
6	Brake lever	16	Wheel cap
7	Wear indicator	17	Cotter pin
8	O-ring	18	Locknut
9	Brake cam holder	19	Washer
10	Brake cam		

from road dirt or water. If the linings are visibly defective, replace them.

11   Measure the thickness of the lining material (just the lining material, not the metal backing) and compare with the value listed in the Chapter 1 Specifications. Replace the shoes if the material is worn to the minimum or less.

12   Check the ends of the shoes where they contact the brake cam and anchor pin. Replace the shoes if there's visible wear.

13   Check the anchor pin for wear or damage. On 1987 through 1989 models, it's an integral part of the brake panel, so the panel will have to be replaced if the anchor pin isn't serviceable. On 1990 and later models, unbolt it from the brake panel and install a new one.

14   If the brake cam is loose in its bore or if the O-rings show any signs of leakage, remove the brake cam from the panel. Make alignment marks on the brake cam and adjuster lever with a punch so they can be reassembled in their relative positions. Remove the lever pinch bolt, slide the lever and wear indicator off the brake cam and pull the cam out of the brake panel. Inspect the cam and its bore for wear and replace worn parts, then reverse the disassembly sequence to reinstall the brake cam and adjuster lever.

15   Check the brake drum for wear or damage. Measure the diameter at several points with a drum micrometer (or have this done by a Yamaha dealer). Very small scratches can be polished away with fine

emery cloth (polish the whole drum surface evenly). If the measurements are uneven (indicating that the drum is out-of-round) or if there are scratches deep enough to snag a fingernail, replace the drum. The drum must also be replaced if the diameter is greater than the maximum listed in this Chapter's Specifications. Yamaha doesn't recommend resurfacing the brake drums on these vehicles.

16   If you're working on a 1988 or later model, check the waterproof seal on the edge of the brake panel for wear (caused by rubbing against the brake drum). Also check for damage such as cuts and tears. If the seal is worn or damaged, replace it.

17   Remove the collar from the grease seal in the center of the brake drum. Check the seal for wear or damage. If its condition is in doubt, pry it out and drive in a new seal with a socket the same diameter as the seal. Turn the bearings in the brake drum with a finger. If their movement is rough, noisy or loose, replace them.

6

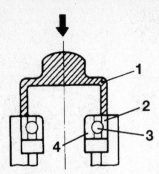

2.22 Drive the new bearings in with a socket or bearing driver the same diameter as the bearing outer race

1	Socket or bearing driver	3	Bearing balls
2	Bearing outer race	4	Bearing inner race

Wheel bearing replacement

Refer to illustration 2.22

18   The front wheel bearings on YFM350ER models are mounted in the brake drums. Early models use two inner bearings and one outer bearing; later models use one inner and one outer bearing.

19   Pry out the seal.

20   Insert a soft metal drift into the hub from the inside. Tap gently against the inner bearing, on opposite sides of the bearing, to drive it from the drum. On early models, drive out both inner bearings. On all models, insert the drift from the other side and drive the outer bearing out in the same way.

21   Pack the new bearings with multi-purpose grease. Work the grease into the spaces between the bearing balls. Hold the outer race and rotate the bearing inner race as you pack it to distribute the grease.

22   Place the new outer bearing on the brake drum with its sealed side out. Position the drum on a workbench or similar surface. Tap the bearing into position with a bearing driver or socket the same diameter as the bearing outer race **(see illustration)**.

23   Turn the drum over and install the inner bearing in the same manner.

Installation

24   Installation is the reverse of the removal steps, with the following additions:

a) *Tighten the brake panel bolts on 1990 and later models to the torque listed in this Chapter's Specifications.*

b) *If you removed the anchor pin or brake cam on 1990 and later models, apply a thin film of sealant (Yamaha Quick Gasket, Yamaha Bond 1215 or equivalent) to the surface that contacts the brake panel. Tighten the bolts to the torque listed in this Chapter's Specifications.*

c) *Apply a thin film of high-temperature brake grease to the brake cam and the pivot areas in the anchor pin, as well as to the shoe contact areas on the brake panel. Be sure not to get any grease on the brake drum or linings.*

d) *Place the shoes on the brake panel with their flat ends against the brake cam and their dished ends over the anchor pin.*

e) *Lubricate the drum seal with high temperature brake grease. Be sure not to get any grease on the inside of the drum; if you do, clean it off with a non-residue solvent such as brake cleaner or lacquer thinner.*

f) *Be sure to insert the collar in the dust seal.*

g) *Tighten the hub nut to the torque listed in this Chapter's Specifications and install a new cotter pin. If necessary, tighten the nut to align the hole in the spindle with the slots in the nut. Don't loosen the nut.*

h) *Once the nut is tightened properly, bend the cotter pin to secure it.*

i) *Refer to Chapter 1 and adjust the brakes.*

3   Front drum brakes (except YFM350ER models) – removal, inspection and installation

Warning: *If a front wheel cylinder indicates the need for an overhaul (usually due to leaking fluid or sticky operation), ALL FOUR front wheel cylinders should be overhauled and all old brake fluid flushed from the system. Also, the dust created by the brake system may contain asbestos, which is harmful to your health. Never blow it out with compressed air and don't inhale any of it. An approved filtering mask should be worn when working on the brakes. Do not, under any*

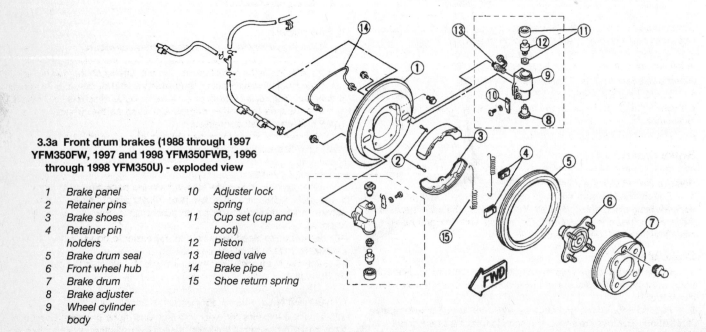

3.3a Front drum brakes (1988 through 1997 YFM350FW, 1997 and 1998 YFM350FWB, 1996 through 1998 YFM350U) - exploded view

1	Brake panel	10	Adjuster lock spring
2	Retainer pins		
3	Brake shoes	11	Cup set (cup and boot)
4	Retainer pin holders		
5	Brake drum seal	12	Piston
6	Front wheel hub	13	Bleed valve
7	Brake drum	14	Brake pipe
8	Brake adjuster	15	Shoe return spring
9	Wheel cylinder body		

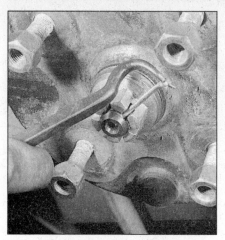

3.3b Bend back the cotter pin and pull it out

3.5 Rotate the ends of the retainer pins to align with the slot in the pin holder, then take the pin holders off

3.6 Pull the shoes apart until the ends clear the wheel cylinders, then take them off the brake panel

3.7 If you remove the brake hose union bolt, be sure to use a new sealing washer on each side of the bolt during assembly

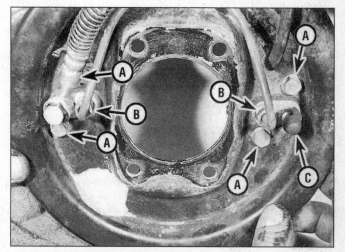

3.9 Wheel cylinder mounting details

A	Wheel cylinder bolts	C	Bleed valve
B	Brake pipe flare nuts		

circumstances, use petroleum-based solvents to clean brake parts. Use clean brake fluid or brake system cleaner only!

Removal

Refer to illustrations 3.3a, 3.3b, 3.5, 3.6, 3.7 and 3.9

1   Loosen the front wheel nuts. Securely block the rear wheels so the vehicle can't roll. Jack up the front end and support it securely on jackstands.

2   Remove the front wheel.

Brake drum

3   Remove the cotter pin from the front hub nut **(see illustrations)**. Remove the nut with a socket and breaker bar.

4   Pull the brake drum and hub off the driveaxle. On models with separate drums and hubs, separate the drum from the hub if necessary (such as for drum replacement). On models with integral hubs, the drum and hub can't be separated.

Brake shoes

5   Compress the shoe holders, turn the pins 1/4 turn to align their ends with the holder slots, then remove the holders and pins **(see illustration)**.

6   Pull the ends of the brake shoes out of the wheel cylinders **(see illustration)**. Remove the shoes and springs from the brake panel.

Brake panel

7   If you're planning to remove the wheel cylinders, remove the brake hose union bolt and sealing washers from the brake panel **(see illustration)**. Place the end of the hose in a container so the brake fluid can drain or else wrap a plastic bag over the end of the hose with a rubber band to prevent loss of brake fluid. If you're removing the brake panel for access to another component such as the driveaxle, the brake hose can be left connected.

8   Remove the four brake panel bolts and lift it off the knuckle together with the wheel cylinders.

Wheel cylinders

9   Unscrew the brake pipe fittings from the back side of the brake panel with a flare nut wrench **(see illustration)**. **Note:** *Yamaha recommends replacing the brake pipe with a new one once it's removed.*

10   Unscrew the bleed valve (this will be easier to do while the wheel cylinder is bolted to the brake panel).

11   Remove the wheel cylinder mounting bolts and take the cylinders off the panel.

Inspection

12   Check the linings for wear, damage and signs of contamination from road dirt or water. If the linings are visibly defective, replace them.

6

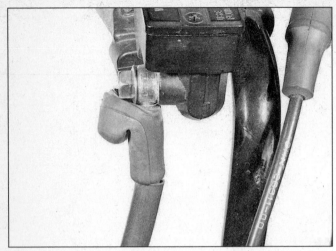

4.4 Pull back the rubber boot and remove the brake hose union bolt; use a new sealing washer on each side of the bolt during assembly

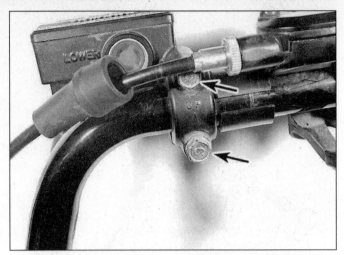

4.5 Remove the master cylinder clamp bolts (arrows); the UP mark on the clamp must be upright on installation

13   Measure the thickness of the lining material (just the lining material, not the metal backing) and compare with the value listed in the Chapter 1 Specifications. Replace the shoes if the material is worn to the minimum or less.

14   Check the ends of the shoes where they contact the wheel cylinders and replace them if they're worn or damaged.

15   Pull back the rubber cups on the wheel cylinders. Slight moisture inside the cups is normal, but if fluid runs out, overhaul the wheel cylinders as described below.

16   Check the brake drum for wear or damage. Measure the diameter at several points with a drum micrometer (or have this done by a Yamaha dealer). Very small scratches can be polished away with fine emery cloth (polish the whole drum surface evenly). If the measurements are uneven (indicating that the drum is out-of-round) or if there are scratches deep enough to snag a fingernail, replace the drum. The drum must also be replaced if the diameter is greater than the maximum listed in this Chapter's Specifications. Yamaha doesn't recommend resurfacing the brake drums on these vehicles.

17   If you're working on a 1988 or later model, check the waterproof seal on the edge of the brake panel for wear (caused by rubbing against the brake drum). Also check for damage such as cuts and tears. If the seal is worn or damaged, replace it.

Wheel cylinder overhaul

18   Remove the boot(s) from the cylinder(s) **(see illustration 3.3a)**. Remove the adjuster lock spring and pull the adjuster out of the other end of the cylinder.

19   Push the piston out of the cylinder.

20   Check the piston and cylinder bore for wear, scratches and corrosion. If there's any doubt about their condition, replace the cylinder as an assembly. Even barely visible flaws can reduce braking performance.

21   The piston cups and boots are available separately and should be replaced whenever the wheel cylinders are overhauled. Work the cup(s) off the piston(s). Dip new ones in clean brake fluid and carefully install them without stretching or damaging them. The wide side of the piston cup faces into the cylinder bore.

22   Check the adjuster components for wear or damage and replace as necessary.

23   Assembly is the reverse of the disassembly steps, with the following additions:

   a) *Coat the cylinder bore with clean brake fluid. Install the piston with the wide side of the piston cup entering the bore first. Be sure not to turn back the lip of the cup.*

   b) *Lubricate the adjuster wheel(s) with high temperature brake grease.*

Installation

24   Apply high temperature grease to the ends of the springs and to the ends of the shoes where they contact the adjusters and wheel cylinder pistons. Apply a thin smear of grease to each of the brake shoe contact points on the brake panel.

25   Hook the springs to the shoes **(see illustration 3.6)**.

26   Pull the shoes apart and position their ends in the wheel cylinders and adjusters.

27   Install the pin holders and pins. Compress the holders and turn the pins 90-degrees so the pins secure the holders **(see illustration 3.5)**.

28   The remainder of installation is the reverse of the removal steps, with the following additions:

   a) *Tighten all fasteners to the torques listed in this Chapter's Specifications.*

   b) *Replace the metal brake pipe with a new one whenever it's removed and use new sealing washers on the brake hose union bolt.*

   c) *Lubricate the drum seal with high temperature brake grease. Be sure not to get any grease on the inside of the drum; if you do, clean it off with a non-residue solvent such as brake cleaner or lacquer thinner.*

   d) *Tighten the hub nut to the torque listed in this Chapter's Specifications and install a new cotter pin. If necessary, tighten the nut to align the hole in the spindle with the slots in the nut. Don't loosen the nut. Once the nut is tightened properly, bend the cotter pin to secure it.*

   e) *Refer to Chapter 1 and adjust the brakes.*

---

4   Front brake master cylinder - removal, overhaul and installation

---

1   If the master cylinder is leaking fluid, or if the lever doesn't produce a firm feel when the brake is applied and bleeding the brakes does not help, master cylinder overhaul is recommended. Before disassembling the master cylinder, read through the entire procedure and make sure that you have the correct rebuild kit. Also, you will need some new, clean brake fluid of the recommended type, some clean rags and internal snap-ring pliers. **Note:** *To prevent damage to the finish from spilled brake fluid, always cover the fuel tank and front fender when working on the master cylinder.*

2   **Caution:** *Disassembly, overhaul and reassembly of the brake master cylinder must be done in a spotlessly clean work area to avoid contamination and possible failure of the brake hydraulic system components.*

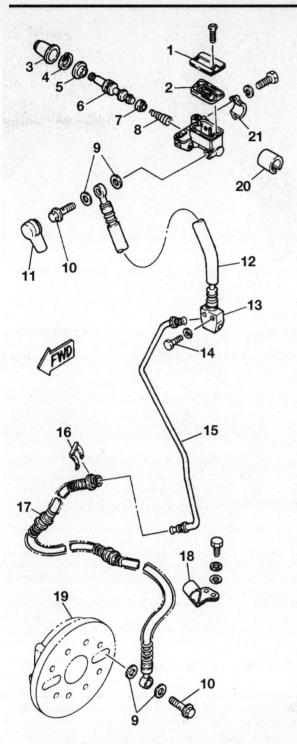

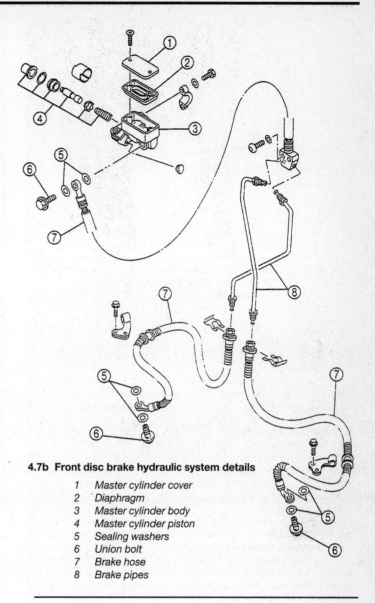

4.7b Front disc brake hydraulic system details

1   Master cylinder cover
2   Diaphragm
3   Master cylinder body
4   Master cylinder piston
5   Sealing washers
6   Union bolt
7   Brake hose
8   Brake pipes

4.7a Front drum brake hydraulic system details

1	Master cylinder cover	12	Upper brake hose
2	Diaphragm	13	Metal union (part of upper
3	Rubber boot		brake hose)
4	Snap-ring	14	Mounting bolt
5	Piston cup	15	Upper brake pipe
6	Piston	16	Clip
7	Piston cup	17	Lower brake hose
8	Spring	18	Hose retainer
9	Sealing washers	19	Brake assembly
10	Union bolt	20	Handlebar spacer
11	Rubber boot	21	Master cylinder clamp

Removal

Refer to illustrations 4.4 and 4.5

3   Loosen, but do not remove, the screws holding the reservoir cover in place.

4   Place rags beneath the master cylinder to protect the finish in case of brake fluid spills. Remove the union bolt **(see illustration)** and separate the brake hose from the master cylinder. Wrap the end of the hose in a clean rag and suspend the hose in an upright position or bend it down carefully and place the open end in a clean container. The objective is to prevent excess loss of brake fluid, fluid spills and system contamination.

5   Remove the master cylinder mounting bolts **(see illustration)** and separate the master cylinder from the handlebar.

Overhaul

Refer to illustrations 4.7a and 4.7b

6   Remove the locknut from the underside of the lever pivot screw, then remove the screw and detach the lever from the master cylinder.

7   Carefully remove the rubber dust boot from the end of the piston **(see illustration)**.

8   Using snap-ring pliers, remove the snap-ring and slide out the piston, the cup seals and the spring. Lay the parts out in the proper

6

4.14 Position the master cylinder protrusion in the notch of the handlebar spacer

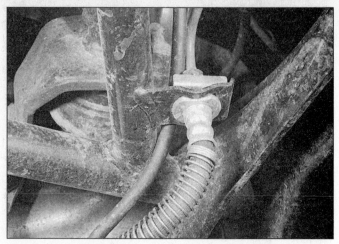

6.2 Check the hoses for cracks; pay special attention to the points where they meet the metal fittings

order to prevent confusion during reassembly.

9   Clean all of the parts with clean brake fluid. **Caution:** *Do not, under any circumstances, use a petroleum-based solvent to clean brake parts. If compressed air is available, use it to dry the parts thoroughly (make sure it's filtered and unlubricated). Check the master cylinder bore for corrosion, scratches, nicks and score marks. If damage is evident, the master cylinder must be replaced with a new one. If the master cylinder is in poor condition, then the wheel cylinders should be checked as well.*

10   Remove the old cup seals and install the new ones. Make sure the lips of the cup seals face away from the lever end of the piston. If a new piston is included in the rebuild kit, use it regardless of the condition of the old one.

11   Before reassembling the master cylinder, soak the piston and the rubber cup seals in clean brake fluid for ten or fifteen minutes. Lubricate the master cylinder bore with clean brake fluid, then carefully insert the piston and related parts in the reverse order of disassembly. Make sure the lips on the cup seals do not turn inside out when they are slipped into the bore.

12   Depress the piston, then install the snap-ring (make sure the snap-ring is properly seated in the groove with the sharp edge facing out). Install the rubber dust boot (make sure the lip is seated properly in the piston groove).

13   Install the brake lever and tighten the pivot bolt locknut.

Installation

Refer to illustration 4.14

14   Attach the master cylinder to the handlebar. Align the protrusion on the master cylinder body with the notch in the handlebar spacer **(see illustration)**.

15   Make sure the arrow and the word UP on the master cylinder clamp are pointing up, then tighten the bolts to the torque listed in this Chapter's Specifications **(see illustration 4.5)**. Tighten the top bolt fully, then tighten the lower bolt. **Caution:** *Don't try to close the gap at the lower bolt mating surface or the clamp may break.*

16   Connect the brake hose to the master cylinder, using new sealing washers. Tighten the union bolt to the torque listed in this Chapter's Specifications.

17   Refer to Section 8 and bleed the air from the system.

5   Brake system bleeding

1   Bleeding the hydraulic brakes on models so equipped is simply the process of removing all the air bubbles from the brake fluid reservoir, the lines and the wheel cylinders or calipers. Bleeding is necessary whenever a brake system hydraulic connection is loosened, when a component or hose is replaced, or when the master cylinder,

wheel cylinders or calipers are overhauled. Leaks in the system may also allow air to enter, but leaking brake fluid will reveal their presence and warn you of the need for repair.

2   To bleed the brake, you will need some new, clean brake fluid of the recommended type (see Chapter 1), a length of clear vinyl or plastic tubing, a small container partially filled with clean brake fluid, some rags and a wrench to fit the brake bleed valve.

3   Cover the fuel tank and other painted components to prevent damage in the event that brake fluid is spilled.

4   Remove the reservoir cap and slowly pump the brake lever a few times, until no air bubbles can be seen floating up from the holes at the bottom of the reservoir. Doing this bleeds the air from the master cylinder end of the line. Reinstall the reservoir cap.

5   Attach one end of the clear vinyl or plastic tubing to the wheel cylinder or caliper bleed valve **(see illustration 3.9 or 10.1)** and submerge the other end in the brake fluid in the container.

6   Check the fluid level in the reservoir. Do not allow the fluid level to drop below the lower mark during the bleeding process.

7   Carefully pump the brake lever three or four times and hold it while opening the bleed valve. When the valve is opened, brake fluid will flow out of the wheel cylinder or caliper into the clear tubing and the lever will move toward the handlebar.

8   Retighten the bleed valve, then release the brake lever gradually. Repeat the process until no air bubbles are visible in the brake fluid leaving the wheel cylinder or caliper, and the lever is firm when applied. Remember to add fluid to the reservoir as the level drops. Use only new, clean brake fluid of the recommended type. Never reuse the fluid lost during bleeding.

9   Repeat this procedure at the other wheel. Be sure to check the fluid level in the master cylinder reservoir frequently.

10   Replace the reservoir cap, wipe up any spilled brake fluid and check the entire system for leaks. **Note:** *If bleeding is difficult, it may be necessary to let the brake fluid in the system stabilize for a few hours (it may be aerated). Repeat the bleeding procedure when the tiny bubbles in the system have floated out.*

6   Brake hoses and lines - inspection and replacement

Inspection

Refer to illustration 6.2

1   Once a week, or if the vehicle is used less frequently, before every use, check the condition of the brake hoses.

2   Twist and flex the rubber hoses while looking for cracks, bulges and seeping fluid. Check extra carefully around the areas where the hoses connect with metal fittings, as these are common areas for hose failure **(see illustration)**.

6.4 Unbolt the retainer to release the hose

Replacement

Refer to illustration 6.4

3   There are three brake hoses. One hose is attached to the master cylinder and connects to the metal junction block. Two metal pipes attached to the junction block run to flexible hoses, which in turn run to the rear wheel cylinder at each wheel (drum brakes) or the caliper at each wheel (disc brakes). On drum brake models, the wheel cylinders at each wheel are connected to each other by a metal pipe. **Note:** *Yamaha recommends that all metal brake pipes, as well as the clips that attach the metal pipes to the fittings where they join the flexible hoses, be replaced with new ones whenever they're removed.*

Flexible hoses

4   Cover the surrounding area with plenty of rags and unscrew the union bolt or flare nut. Pull out the clip or detach the hose from any retainers that may be present and remove the hose **(see illustrations 4.7, 6.2 and the accompanying illustration)**.
5   Position the new hose, making sure it isn't twisted or otherwise strained, between the two components. Make sure the metal tube portion of the banjo fitting at the brake panel is located between the stoppers on the panel. Install the union bolts, using new sealing washers on both sides of the fittings, and tighten them to the torque listed in this Chapter's Specifications. If the hose is connected by a flare nut, hold it with one wrench and tighten the flare nut with another wrench.

Metal pipes

6   Unscrew the flare nut fitting at each end of the metal pipe with a flare nut wrench **(see illustration 4.7)**. Thread the fittings of the new pipe in with fingers so they won't be cross-threaded, then tighten them with the flare nut wrench.
7   Flush the old brake fluid from the system, refill the system with the recommended fluid (see Chapter 1) and bleed the air from the system (see Section 8). Check the operation of the brakes carefully before riding the vehicle.

7   Rear disc brake - removal/disassembly, inspection and assembly/installation

Removal and disassembly

Refer to illustrations 7.3a, 7.3b, 7.6, 7.7a and 7.7b
Note: *This procedure includes all steps for disassembly of the caliper. If you're only removing the caliper to replace the pads, ignore the steps which don't apply.*
1   Refer to Section 9 and remove the right rear wheel.
2   Refer to Section 11 and remove the right rear wheel hub.
3   Remove the outer cover screws and take the cover off **(see illustrations)**.

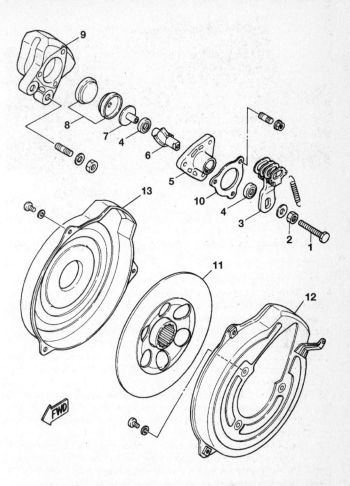

7.3a Rear disc brake - exploded view (4WD shown; 2WD similar)

1	Adjusting bolt	8	Brake pads
2	Locknut	9	Caliper
3	Brake lever	10	Support plate
4	Grease seal		(4WD models)
5	Cam holder	11	Brake disc
6	Cam	12	Outer cover
7	Backup plate	13	Inner cover

6

7.3b Remove the outer cover screws (arrows) and take off the cover

4   Refer to Section 8 and disconnect the brake lever cable and brake pedal rod from the rear brake, then unhook the caliper spring.

5   Remove the cam holder mounting nuts and take it off, together with the brake levers.

6   Set up a dial indicator with its pointer contacting the center of the brake disc **(see illustration)**. Spin the disc slowly and note the reading on the dial indicator (disc runout). If it's beyond the limit listed in this Chapter's Specifications, replace the disc.

7   Remove the caliper together with the brake disc, then separate them **(see illustration)**. Remove the inner cover screws and take the cover off **(see illustration)**.

8   Remove the pads and backup plate from the caliper **(see illustration 7.3a)**.

9   Loosen the locknut on the adjusting bolt, then unscrew the adjusting bolt from the caliper and remove the lever.

10   Pry the seals out of the cam holder and remove the cam.

Inspection

11   Inspect the brake pads for contamination with oil or grease. Measure the thickness of the lining material (just the lining material, not the metal backing) and compare it with the value listed in this Chapter's Specifications. If the pads are contaminated or worn, replace them.

12   Check the brake disc for scoring or wear. If score marks are deep enough to snag a fingernail, replace the disc. Measure its thickness with a micrometer and compare it to the minimum listed in this Chapter's Specifications. If it's less than the minimum, replace the disc.

13   Check all remaining parts for visible wear, damage or corrosion.

Assembly

14   Coat the cam with lithium-based multi-purpose grease and install it in the holder. Coat the lips of new seals with grease and press them into position with a socket the same diameter as the seal.

15   Place the lever on the end of the cam and install the washer. Make sure the locknut is on the adjusting bolt, then thread the adjusting bolt into the cam and tighten the locknut slightly to hold it in place.

16   Lubricate the post of the backup plate with multi-purpose grease and install it in the cam.

17   Move the lever back and forth to make sure the cam moves smoothly. If it doesn't, stop and find out why before continuing.

Installation

18   Installation is the reverse of the removal steps, with the following additions:

a) *Lubricate the splines in the center of the brake disc with multi-purpose grease. Lubricate the cup area inside the metal backing*

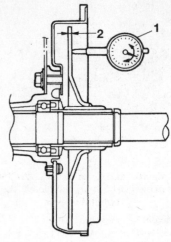

7.6 Measure disc runout with a dial indicator

1   *Dial indicator*   2   *Disc runout*

plates on the brake pads with high-temperature brake grease. Be careful not to get any grease on the pad friction material.

b) *Install the cam holder so the mark that lines up with the wear indicator pointer faces the rear (see illustration 6.15 in Chapter 1).*

c) *Tighten all fasteners to the torque listed in this Chapter's Specifications.*

d) *Refer to Chapter 1 and adjust the brake lever and pedal freeplay.*

8   Brake pedal, rear brake lever and cables - removal and installation

Brake cables

Removal

Refer to illustrations 8.1 and 8.2

1   Loosen the lockwheel at the handlebar brake lever, then loosen the adjuster all the way. Line up the adjuster slot with the slots in the lever and bracket, then rotate the cable out of the slots and lower the cable end out of the lever **(see illustration)**.

2   Unscrew the cable adjusting nut at the brake assembly all the way off the end of the cable **(see illustration)**.

3   If you're working on a 2WD front brake cable, remove the snap-ring and separate the cable from the bracket on the brake panel.

7.7a Remove the caliper together with the brake disc

7.7b Remove the inner cover screws and take off the cover

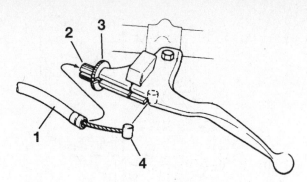

8.1 Align the adjuster and locknut slots with the lever slot and rotate the cable out of them, then lower the cable end out of the lever

1	Cable	3	Locknut
2	Adjuster	4	Cable end

4   If you're working on a rear brake cable, pull the cable out of the pin and lift it out of its bracket.
5   Thread the pin and wing nut back onto the cable so they won't be lost.

Installation

6   Installation is the reverse of the removal steps, with the following additions:
  a) *Lubricate the cable ends with multi-purpose grease.*
  b) *Make sure the cables are secure in their slots and retainers.*
  c) *Adjust brake pedal and lever play as described in Chapter 1.*

Pedal rod/cable

Removal

7   Unscrew the pedal adjusting wing nut all the way off the rod **(see illustration 8.2).**
8   At the brake pedal, remove the cotter pin and washer, then remove the clevis pin and detach the rod/cable from the brake pedal **(see illustration 8.6a in Chapter 1).** Pull the rod/cable forward out of the pin at the rear wheel and remove it.

Installation

9   Installation is the reverse of the removal steps, with the following additions:
  a) *Lubricate the clevis pin and the rear end of the rod/cable with multi-purpose grease.*
  b) *Adjust brake pedal height and freeplay as described in Chapter 1.*

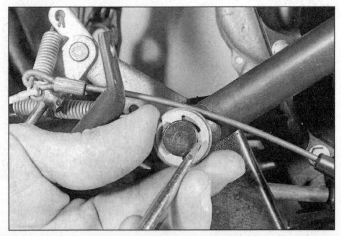

8.11 Pry the clip out of its groove

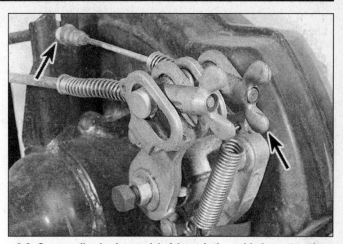

8.2 On rear disc brake models (shown), the cable is next to the brake assembly; on rear drum brake models, the rod is next to the brake assembly

Brake pedal

Removal

Refer to illustration 8.11

10   Disconnect the rod/cable from the pedal as described above. Unhook the pedal return spring and the drive select spring **(see illustration 8.6a in Chapter 1).**
11   Pry off the clip, remove the washer and slide the pedal off the pivot shaft **(see illustration).**

Installation

12   Installation is the reverse of the removal steps, with the following additions:
  a) *Lubricate the pedal shaft with multi-purpose grease.*
  b) *Refer to Chapter 1 and adjust brake pedal height and freeplay.*

Brake lever

Removal

Refer to illustration 8.16

13   The front brake lever on 4WD models is part of the master cylinder. Refer to Section 4 for removal procedures.
14   On all other models, disconnect the cable from the brake lever as described above.
15   If the machine has a brake light switch, refer to Chapter 8 and remove it.
16   Remove the lever mounting screws and take it off the handlebar **(see illustration).**

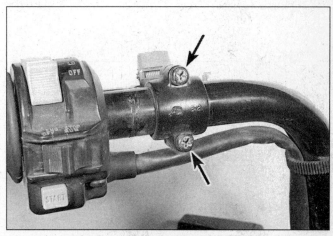

8.16 Remove the clamp screws (arrows)

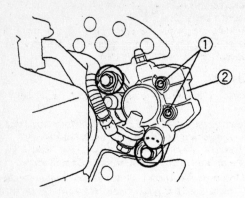

9.2 Loosen the pad pins (1), then unbolt and remove the caliper (2)

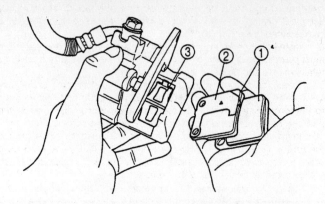

9.3 Remove the pads (1), shim (2) and spring (3)

Installation

17   Installation is the reverse of the removal steps.
18   Refer to Chapter 1 and adjust brake lever freeplay.

9   Front disc brakes – pad replacement

Refer to illustrations 9.2 and 9.3

Warning: *The dust created by the brake system may contain asbestos, which is harmful to your health. Never blow it out with compressed air and don't inhale any of it. An approved filtering mask should be worn when working on the brakes.*

1   Support the front of the vehicle securely on jackstands and remove the front wheels.

2   Loosen the pad pins while the caliper is still bolted to the steering knuckle **(see illustration)**.
3   Remove the caliper mounting bolts and lift the caliper off. Unscrew the pad pins and pull out the pads, together with the shim on the inner pad. Remove the pad spring from the caliper **(see illustration)**.
4   Inspect the pad spring and replace it if it's rusted or damaged.
5   Refer to Chapter 1 and inspect the pads.
6   Check the condition of the brake disc (see Section 11). If it's in need of machining or replacement, follow the procedure in that Section to remove it. If it's okay, deglaze it with sandpaper or emery cloth, using a swirling motion.
7   Remove the cover from the master cylinder reservoir and siphon out some fluid. Push the piston into the caliper as far as possible, while checking the master cylinder reservoir to make sure it doesn't

**10.1 Front disc brakes –
exploded view**

1   Brake disc
2   Disc shield
3   Brake pads
4   Pad shim
5   Bleed valve
6   Pad pin
7   Caliper
8   Piston
*9   Piston seal and dust
      seal*

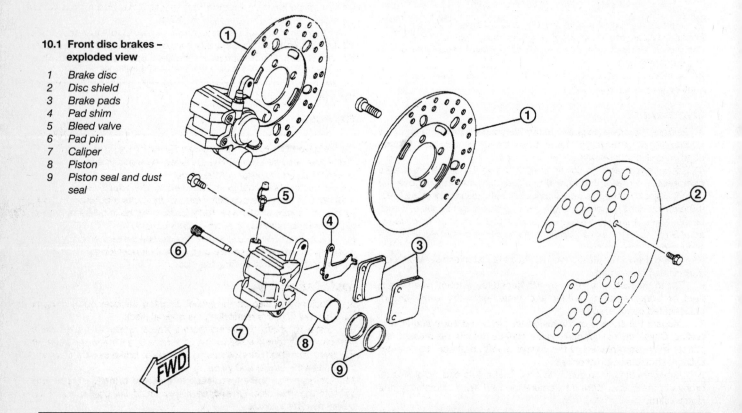

overflow. If you can't depress the pistons with thumb pressure, try using a C-clamp. If the piston sticks, remove the caliper and overhaul it as described in Section 10.

8   Install the spring and new pads. The arrow mark on the pad shim must point in the forward rotating direction of the brake disc. Install the retaining pins and tighten them slightly.

9   Install the caliper on the steering knuckle, sliding the brake disc between the pads. Install the caliper mounting bolts and tighten them to the torque listed in this Chapter's Specifications, then tighten the pad pins to the torque listed in this Chapter's Specifications.

10   Install the wheels and lower the vehicle. Tighten the wheel nuts to the torque listed in this Chapter's Specifications. Operate the right brake lever several times to seat the pads. Check the operation of the brakes carefully before riding the vehicle.

10   Front disc brakes – caliper removal, overhaul and installation

Warning: *If a caliper indicates the need of an overhaul(usually due to leaking fluid or sticky operation), all old brake fluid must be flushed from the system. Also, the dust created by the brake system may contain asbestos, which is harmful to your health. Never blow it out with compressed air and don't inhale any of it. An approved filtering mask should be worn when working on the brakes. Do not, under any circumstances, use petroleum-based solvents to clean brake parts. Use brake cleaner or denatured alcohol only!*

Removal

Refer to illustration 10.1

1   Securely support the front end of the vehicle on jackstands and remove the front wheels. **Note:** *If you're planning to disassemble the caliper, read through the overhaul procedure, paying particular attention to the steps involved in removing the piston with compressed air. If you don't have access to an air compressor, you can use the vehicle's hydraulic system to force the piston out instead. To do this, remove the pads and pump the brake lever. The hydraulic pressure will push the piston out of the bore.*

1   Remove the brake hose fitting bolt and disconnect the brake hose from the caliper **(see illustration)**. Wrap the end of the hose in a plastic bag, tightly secured with a rubber band, to prevent excess fluid loss and contamination.

2   Unscrew the caliper mounting bolts and lift it off the steering knuckle **(see illustration 9.2)**.

Overhaul

3   Remove the brake pads and anti-rattle spring from the caliper (see Section 2, if necessary). Clean the exterior of the caliper with denatured alcohol or brake system cleaner.

4   Pack a shop rag into the space that holds the brake pads. Use compressed air, directed into the caliper fluid inlet, to remove the piston. Use only enough air pressure to ease the piston out of the bore. If the piston is blown out forcefully, even with the rag in place, it may be damaged. **Warning:** *never place your fingers in front of the piston in an attempt to catch or protect it when applying compressed air, as serious injury could occur.*

5   Using a wood or plastic tool, remove the piston seals. Metal tools may cause bore damage.

6   Clean the pistons and bores with denatured alcohol, clean brake fluid or brake system cleaner and blow them dry with filtered, unlubricated compressed air.

7   Inspect the surface of the piston for nicks and burrs and loss of plating. Check the caliper bore, too. If surface defects are present, the caliper must be replaced. If the caliper is in bad shape, the master cylinder should also be checked.

8   Lubricate the piston seal with clean brake fluid and install it in its groove in the caliper bore. Make sure the seal seats completely and isn't twisted.

9   Lubricate the dust seal with brake fluid and install it in its groove, making sure it seats correctly.

10   Lubricate the piston with clean brake fluid and install it into the caliper bore. Using your thumbs, push the piston all the way in, making sure it doesn't get cocked in the bore.

Installation

11   Installation is the reverse of the removal steps, with the following additions:

a) *Space the pads apart so the disc will fit between them.*

b) *Use new sealing washers on the brake hose fitting.*

c) *Tighten the caliper mounting bolts and the brake hose union bolt to the torques listed in this Chapter's Specifications.*

12   Fill the master cylinder with the recommended brake fluid (see Chapter 1) and bleed the system (see Section 5). Check for leaks.

13   Check the operation of the brakes carefully before riding the vehicle.

11   Front brake discs - inspection, removal and installation

Inspection

1   Securely support the front of the vehicle on jackstands and remove the front wheels.

2   Visually inspect the surface of the disc for score marks and other damage. Light scratches are normal after use and won't affect brake operation, but deep grooves and heavy score marks will reduce braking efficiency and accelerate pad wear. If the discs are badly grooved they must be machined or replaced.

3   To check disc runout, mount a dial indicator to the steering knuckle, with the plunger on the indicator touching the surface of the disc about 1/2-inch from the outer edge. Slowly turn the wheel and watch the indicator needle, comparing your reading with the limit listed in this Chapter's Specifications. If the runout is greater than allowed, check the hub bearings for play (see Chapter 1). If the bearings are worn, replace them and repeat this check. If the disc runout is still excessive, the disc will have to be replaced.

4   The disc must not be machined or allowed to wear down to a thickness less than the allowable minimum listed in this Chapter's Specifications. The thickness of the disc can be checked with a micrometer. If the thickness of the disc is less than the minimum allowable, it must be replaced. The minimum thickness is normally stamped into the disc.

Removal

5   Remove the brake caliper and wheel (see Sections 10 and 13). **Caution:** *Don't lay the wheel down and allow it to rest on the disc – the disc could become warped. Set the wheel on wood blocks so the disc doesn't support the weight of the wheel.*

6   Mark the relationship of the disc to the wheel, so it can be reinstalled in the same position. Remove the bolts that retain the disc to the wheel **(see illustration 10.1)**. Loosen the bolts a little at a time, in a criss-cross pattern, to avoid distorting the disc.

7   Take note of any paper shims that may be present where the disc mates to the wheel. If there are any, mark their position and be sure to include them when reinstalling the disc.

Installation

8   Position the disc on the wheel, aligning the previously applied matchmarks (if you're reinstalling the original disc).

9   Install the bolts, tightening them a little at a time in a criss-cross pattern, to the torque listed in this Chapter's Specifications. Clean off all grease from the brake disc using acetone or brake system cleaner.

10   Install the caliper and wheel.

11   Operate the brake lever several times to bring the pads into contact with the disc. Check the operation of the brakes carefully before riding the vehicle.

6

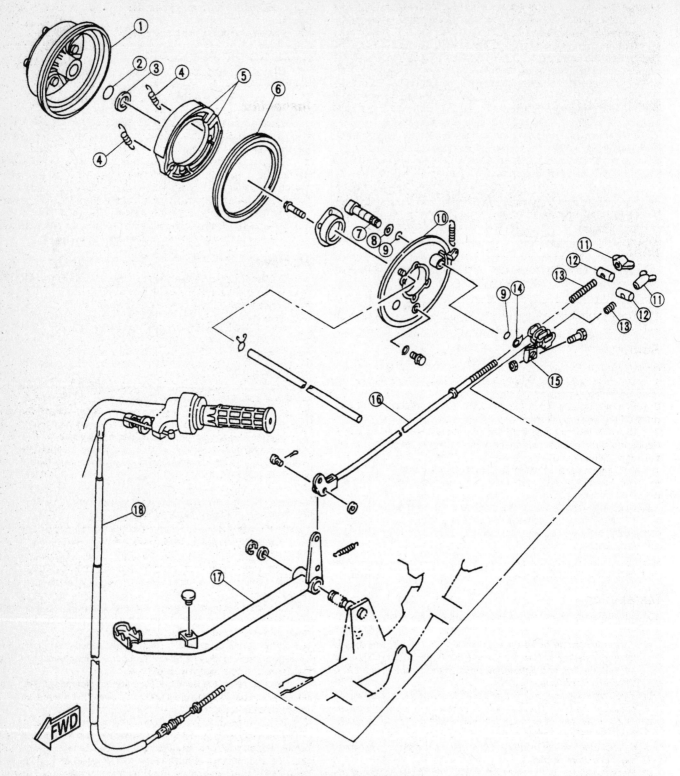

12.2 Rear drum brake – exploded view

1	Brake drum	7	Brake cam	13	Springs
2	O-ring	8	Washer	14	Wear indicator plate
3	Plain washer	9	O-ring	15	Brake camshaft lever
4	Shoe return springs	10	Brake panel	16	Brake rod
5	Brake shoes	11	Adjuster wingnuts	17	Brake pedal
6	Dust seal	12	Pins	18	Brake cable

13.7 Be sure the directional arrow points in the forward rotating direction of the tire

12 Rear drum brake – removal, inspection and installation

Removal

Refer to illustration 12.2

1   Securely support the rear end of the vehicle on jackstands and remove the right rear wheel.
2   Remove the cotter pin, hub nut and washer, then pull the brake drum off the axle **(see illustration)**.
3   Unscrew the wingnuts from the end of the brake rod and cable. Separate the rod and cable from the end pins, then take the pins out of the adjusters and remove the springs.
4   Disconnect the breather hose from the brake panel.
5   Remove the O-ring and plain washer from the axle end.
6   Fold the brake shoes into a V and remove them from the brake panel. Disengage the springs from the shoes.

Inspection

9   Inspection is the same as for YFM350ER front drum brakes, described in Section 2. The anchor pin is integral with the brake panel and can't be replaced separately.

Installation

10   Installation is the reverse of the removal steps, with the following additions:

a) *If you remove the brake panel from the hub, use silicone sealant when reinstalling it. Use non-permanent thread locking agent on the bolt threads and tighten the bolts to the torque listed in this Chapter's Specifications.*
b) *If you removed the brake cam, apply a thin coat of multipurpose grease to the shaft. Don't forget to reinstall its O-ring and washer.*
c) *Apply a thin film of high-temperature brake grease to the brake cam and the pivot areas of the anchor pin, as well as to the shoe contact areas on the brake panel. Be sure not to get any grease on the brake drum or linings.*
d) *Place the shoes on the brake panel with their flat ends against the brake cam and their rounded ends over the anchor pin.*
e) *Lubricate the drum seal with high temperature brake grease. Be sure not to get any grease on the inside of the drum; if you do, clean it off with a non-residue solvent such as brake cleaner or lacquer thinner.*
f) *Tighten the hub nut to the torque listed in this Chapter's Specifications and install a new cotter pin. If necessary, tighten the nut further to align the cotter pin hole in the axle with the slots in the nut. Don't loosen the nut.*

g) *Once the nut is tightened properly, bend the cotter pin to secure it.*
h) *Refer to Chapter 1 and adjust the brakes.*

13 Wheels - inspection, removal and installation

Inspection

1   Clean the wheels thoroughly to remove mud and dirt that may interfere with the inspection procedure or mask defects. Make a general check of the wheels and tires as described in Chapter 1.
2   The wheels should be visually inspected for cracks, flat spots on the rim and other damage. Since tubeless tires are involved, look very closely for dents in the area where the tire bead contacts the rim. Dents in this area may prevent complete sealing of the tire against the rim, which leads to deflation of the tire over a period of time.
3   If damage is evident, the wheel will have to be replaced with a new one. Never attempt to repair a damaged wheel.

Removal

4   Securely block the wheels at the opposite end of the vehicle from the wheel being removed, so it can't roll.
5   Loosen the lug nuts on the wheel being removed. Jack up one end of the vehicle and support it securely on jackstands.
6   Remove the lug nuts and pull the wheel off.

Installation

Refer to illustration 13.7

7   Position the wheel on the studs. Make sure the directional arrow on the tire points in the forward rotating direction of the wheel.
8   Install the wheel nuts with their tapered sides toward the wheel. This is necessary to locate the wheel accurately on the hub.
9   Snug the wheel nuts evenly in a criss-cross pattern.
10   Remove the jackstands, lower the vehicle and tighten the wheel nuts, again in a criss-cross pattern, to the torque listed in this Chapter's Specifications.

14 Tires - general information

1   Tubeless tires are used as standard equipment on this vehicle. Unlike motorcycle tires, they run at very low air pressures and are completely unsuited for use on pavement. Inflating ATV tires to excessive pressures will rupture them, making replacement of the tire necessary.
2   The force required to break the seal between the rim and the bead of the tire is substantial, much more than required for motorcycle tires, and is beyond the capabilities of an individual working with normal tire irons or even a normal bead breaker. A special bead breaker is required for ATV tires; it produces a great deal of force and concentrates it in a relatively small area.
3   Also, repair of the punctured tire and replacement on the wheel rim requires special tools, skills and experience that the average do-it-do-it-yourselfer lacks.
4   For these reasons, if a puncture or flat occurs with an ATV tire, the wheel should be removed from the vehicle and taken to a dealer service department or a repair shop for repair or replacement of the tire. The accompanying illustrations can be used as a guide to tire replacement in an emergency, provided the necessary bead breaker is available.

15 Wheel hubs - removal and installation

Removal

Refer to illustration 15.1

1   Front hubs on 2WD models and some 4WD models are integral

6

Deflate the tire and remove the valve core. Release the bead on the side opposite the tire valve with an ATV bead breaker, following the manufacturer's instructions. Make sure you have the correct blades for the tire size (using the wrong size blade may damage the wheel, the tire or the blade). Lubricate the bead with water before removal (don't use soap or any type of lubricant).

TIRE CHANGING SEQUENCE

Turn the tire over and release the other bead.

If one side of the wheel has a smaller flange, remove and install the tire from that side. Use two tire levers to work the bead over the edge of the rim.

Before installing, ensure the tire is suitable for the wheel. Take note of any sidewall markings such as direction of rotation arrows, then work the first bead over the rim flange.

Use tire levers to start the second bead over the rim flange.

Hold the bead while you work the last section of it over the rim flange. Install the valve core and inflate the tire, making sure not to overinflate it.

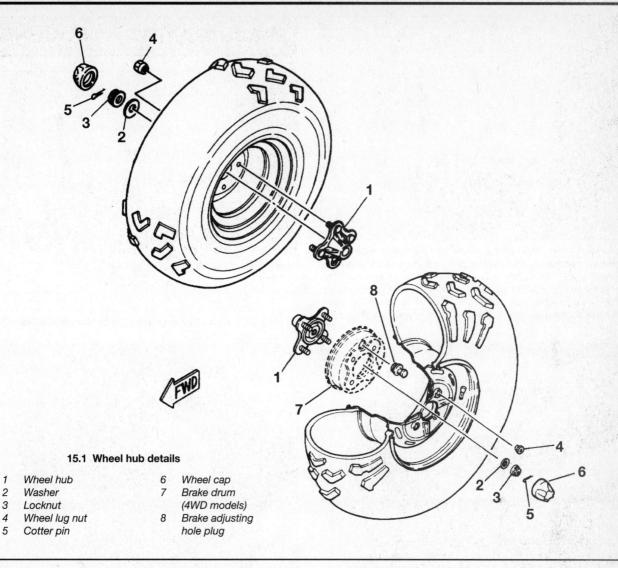

15.1 Wheel hub details

1	Wheel hub	6	Wheel cap
2	Washer	7	Brake drum
3	Locknut		(4WD models)
4	Wheel lug nut	8	Brake adjusting
5	Cotter pin		hole plug

with the brake drums. Front hubs on some 4WD models are separate from the brake drums, but can be removed together with them **(see illustration)**; refer to Section 3 for removal procedures.

2　Refer to Section 9 and remove the rear wheel(s).

3　Bend back the cotter pin and pull it out of the hub nut **(see illustration 15.1)**.

4　Unscrew the hub nut and remove the washer.

5　Pull the hub off the axle shaft.

Installation

6　Installation is the reverse of the removal steps, with the following additions:

a) *Lubricate the axle shaft and hub splines with multi-purpose grease.*

b) *Tighten the hub nut to the torque listed in this Chapter's Specifications. If necessary, tighten it an additional amount to align the cotter pin slots. Don't loosen the nut to align the slots.*

c) *Install a new cotter pin and bend it to secure the nut.*

6

Notes

Chapter 7
Bodywork and frame

Contents

1   General information

This Chapter covers the procedures necessary to remove and install the fenders and other body parts. Since many service and repair operations on these vehicles require removal of the fenders and/or other body parts, the procedures are grouped here and referred to from other Chapters.

In the case of damage to the fenders or other body parts, it is usually necessary to remove the broken component and replace it with a new (or used) one. The material that the fenders and other plastic body parts is composed of doesn't lend itself to conventional repair techniques. There are, however, some shops that specialize in "plastic welding", so it would be advantageous to check around first before throwing the damaged part away. **Note:** *When attempting to remove any body panel, first study the panel closely, noting any fasteners and associated fittings, to be sure of returning everything to its correct place on installation. In most cases, the aid of an assistant will be*

required when removing panels, to help avoid damaging the paint. Once the visible fasteners have been removed, try to lift off the panel as described but DO NOT FORCE the panel - if it will not release, check that all fasteners have been removed and try again. Where a panel engages another by means of lugs and grommets, be careful not to break the lugs or to damage the bodywork. Remember that a few moments of patience at this stage will save you a lot of money in replacing broken panels!

2   Seat - removal and installation

Refer to illustrations 2.1 and 2.2

1   Lift the seat latch **(see illustration)** and lift the back end of the seat.

2   Disengage the front end of the seat from the brackets **(see illustration)** and lift the seat off the vehicle.

3   Installation is the reverse of removal.

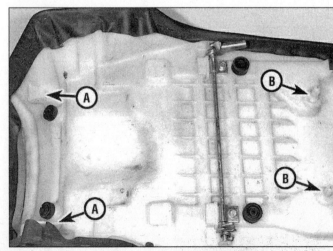

2.1 The plastic hooks (A) and posts (B) . . .

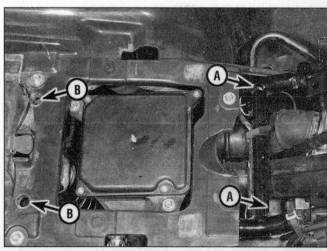

2.2 . . . engage the catches (A) and fit in the holes (B)

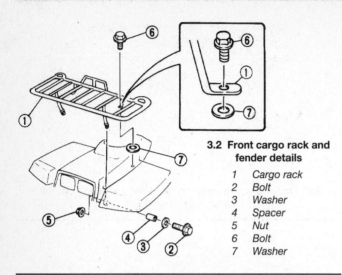

3.2 Front cargo rack and fender details

1   Cargo rack
2   Bolt
3   Washer
4   Spacer
5   Nut
6   Bolt
7   Washer

---

3   Front cargo rack and fender - removal and installation

YFM350ER and 1987 through 1996 YFM350FW

Refer to illustrations 3.2, 3.4, 3.7a, 3.7b, 3.7c, 3.7d and 3.8

1   The front fender is a one-piece unit that spans the front of the vehicle and covers both front tires. A separate flap is attached to each side of the center unit.

2   Remove the cargo rack mounting bolts and lift the cargo rack off,

3.4 The shift select lever is retained by two screws (arrows)

taking care not to scratch the plastic fender **(see illustration)**.

3   Disconnect the headlight electrical connectors, located beneath the right side of the fender.

4   Remove two screws and detach the knob from the shift select lever **(see illustration)**.

5   Remove the handlebars (see Chapter 5).

6   Remove the fuel tank cover (see Chapter 3).

7   Remove the fender mounting bolts and screws and lift the fender off the vehicle **(see illustrations)**. Have an assistant support one side if necessary, so the fender can be lifted off without scratching it. Tilt the fender forward and lift it off, taking care not to snag the fender on the

3.7a Remove the screws at the top of the fender (these screws also secure the leading edge of the fuel tank cover) . . .

3.7b . . . the upper cargo rack bolts (one on each side) . . .

3.7c . . . the lower Allen bolts (one on each side) . . .

3.7d . . . and the fender stay screws in each mudflap

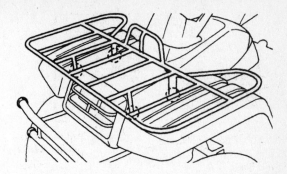

3.8 Fender flap mounting details

1	Fender flap	6	Plate
2	Stay	7	Washer
3	Bolt	8	Nut
4	Bolt	9	Washer
5	Bolt	10	Nut

odometer/speedometer.

8   To remove the fender flaps, remove the screws **(see illustration)**.

9   Installation is the reverse of removal.

1997 YFM350FW and 1996 through 1998 YFM350U

Refer to illustrations 3.10, 3.11, 3.12 and 3.13

9   Remove the seat (see Section 2). Remove the fuel tank filler cap, cover and rubber mounting damper (see Chapter 4). Reinstall the filler cap.

10   Unbolt the front cargo rack and lift it off **(see illustration)**.

11   Disconnect the headlight and main switch connectors **(see illustration)**.

12   Unbolt the fender and lift it off **(see illustration)**.

13   Unbolt the front bumper and lift it off **(see illustration)**.

14   Installation is the reverse of the removal steps.

YFM350FWB and 1999 YFM350U

Refer to illustrations 3.16, 3.17 and 3.19

15   Remove the seat (see Section 2).

16   Unbolt the front cargo rack and lift it off **(see illustration)**.

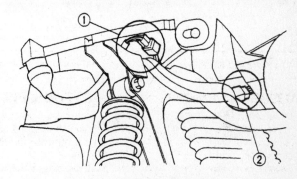

3.10 Unbolt the front cargo rack (1997 YFM350FW and 1996 through 1998 YFM350U) . . .

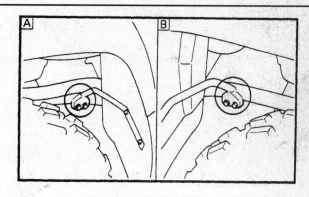

3.11 . . . disconnect the main switch connector (1) and headlight connector (2) . . .

3.12 . . . unbolt the fender from the stay on the left side (A) and right side (B) . . .

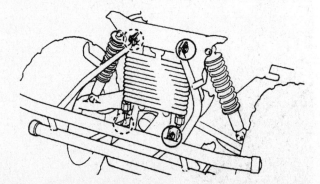

3.13 . . . and unbolt the front bumper

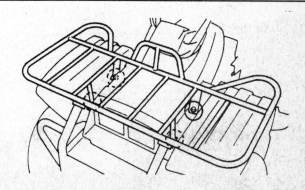

3.16 Unbolt the front cargo rack (YFM350FWB and 1999 YFM350U) . . .

7

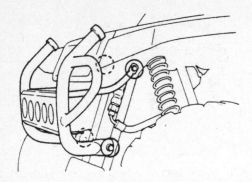

3.17 ... unbolt the front bumper ...

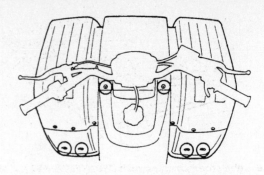

3.19 ... and unbolt the fender in the center and at the mud flaps

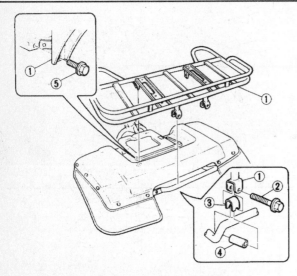

4.1 Cargo rack mounting details

1	Cargo rack	4	Sleeve
2	Bolt	5	Bolt
3	Collar		

17   Unbolt the front bumper and lift it off **(see illustration)**.
18   Disconnect the headlight connector.
19   Unbolt the fender and lift it off **(see illustration)**.

4   Rear cargo rack and fender - removal and installation

YFM350ER and 1987 through 1996 YFM350FW
Refer to illustrations 4.1, 4.2 and 4.3
1   Remove the rear cargo rack's mounting bolts and lift the cargo rack off the vehicle **(see illustration)**.
2   Remove the fender bolts, nuts and screws **(see illustration)**.
3   If necessary, remove the fender flaps **(see illustration)**.
4   Installation is the reverse of removal.

1997 YFM350FW and 1996 through 1998 YFM350U
Refer to illustrations 4.6, 4.7a, 4.7b, 4.8 and 4.9
5   Remove the seat (see Section 2) and the fuel tank (see Chapter 4).
6   Unbolt the rear cargo rack and lift it off **(see illustration)**.

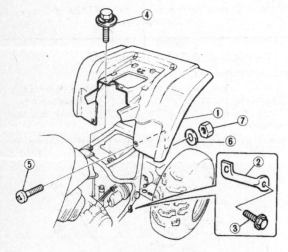

4.2 Rear fender details

1	Rear fender	5	Screw
2	Fender stay	6	Washer
3	Bolt	7	Nut
4	Bolt		

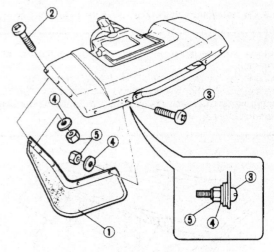

4.3 Rear fender extension details

1	Fender extension	4	Washer
2	Screw	5	Nut
3	Screw		

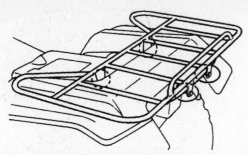

4.6 Unbolt the rear cargo rack (1997 YFM350FW and 1996 through 1998 YFM350U) . . .

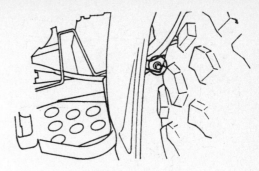

4.7a . . . and unbolt the fender at the lower front . . .

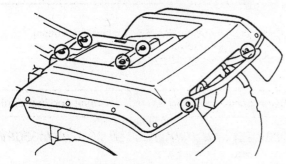

4.7b . . . the center and the rear . . .

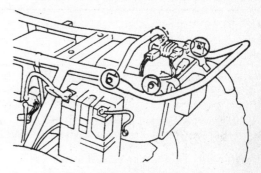

4.8 . . . unbolt the rack bar

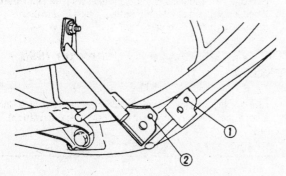

4.9 On installation, fit the post (1) in the hole in the stay (2)

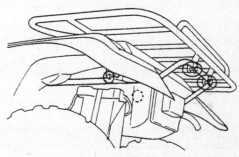

4.11 Unbolt the rear cargo rack (YFM350FWB and 1999 YFM350U) . . .

7   Unbolt the rear fender at the lower front, center and rear **(see illustrations)**.
8   Unbolt the rear rack bar and lift it off **(see illustration)**.
9   Installation is the reverse of the removal steps. Be sure the locating post on the frame fits into the hole in the fender stay **(see illustration)**.

YFM350FWB and 1999 YFM350U

Refer to illustrations 4.11, 4.12a, 4.12b and 4.13
10   Remove the seat (see Section 2) and the fuel tank (see Chapter 4).
11   Unbolt the rear cargo rack and lift it off **(see illustration)**.
12   Unbolt the rear fender at the lower front, center and rear **(see illustrations)**.

7

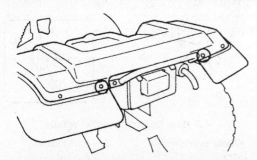

4.12a . . . and unbolt the rear fender at the rear . . .

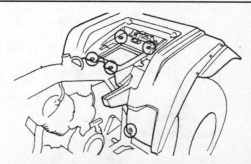

4.12b . . . center and front . . .

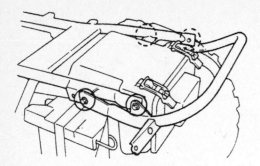

4.13 . . . unbolt the rack bar

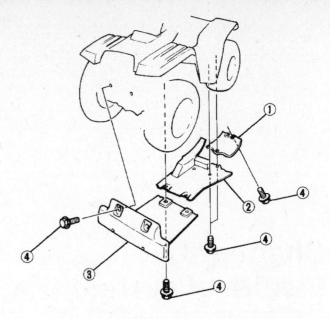

5.1 Skid plate details

1	Rear skid plate	3	Front skid plate
2	Center skid plate	4	Bolt

13   Unbolt the rear rack bar and lift it off **(see illustration)**.
14   Installation is the reverse of the removal steps.

5   Skidplates - removal and installation

Refer to illustration 5.1
1   Skidplates are secured to the underside of the vehicle by bolts **(see illustration)**. To remove a skidplate, unscrew its bolts, lower it clear and take it out.
2   Installation is the reverse of the removal steps.

6   Footrests - removal and installation

Refer to illustration 6.1
1   To remove the footrest, remove its mounting bolts **(see illustration)**.
2   Install the footrest, then install the mounting bolts and tighten them securely.

7   Trailer hitch - removal and installation

Trailer hitch removal is part of the rear final drive unit removal procedure, described in Chapter 5.

8   Frame - general information, inspection and repair

1   All models use a double-cradle frame made of cylindrical steel tubing.
2   The frame shouldn't require attention unless accident damage has occurred. In most cases, frame replacement is the only satisfactory remedy for such damage. A few frame specialists have the jigs and other equipment necessary for straightening the frame to the required standard of accuracy, but even then there is no simple way of assessing to what extent the frame may have been overstressed.
3   After the machine has accumulated a lot of miles, the frame should be examined closely for signs of cracking or splitting at the welded joints. Corrosion can also cause weakness at these joints.

6.1 The footrest mounting bolts are accessible from below (arrows); two of the four bolts are hidden behind the footrest

Loose engine mount bolts can cause ovaling or fracturing to the engine mounting points. Minor damage can often be repaired by welding, depending on the nature and extent of the damage.
4   Remember that a frame that is out of alignment will cause handling problems. If misalignment is suspected as the result of an accident, it will be necessary to strip the machine completely so the frame can be thoroughly checked.

Chapter 8
Electrical system

Contents

Specifications

Battery

Type	12V 14 Ah
Bulbs	
Headlights	25/25 watts
Tail light	7.5 watts
Indicator lights	3.4 watts

Charging system

Charging output voltage	14.0 to 15.0 volts at 5000 rpm
Charging output amperage	12 amps or more at 3000 rpm; 17 amps or less at 8000 rpm
Stator coil resistance	0.70 to 0.86 ohms at 20-degrees C (68-degrees F)

Starting system

Brush length	
Standard	12.0 mm (0.47 inch)
Minimum	8.5 mm (0.33 inch)
Commutator diameter	
Standard	28 mm (1.10 inch)
Minimum	27 mm (1.06 inch)
Mica depth	0.6 mm (0.024 inch)
Neutral and starting circuit cut-off relay resistance	72 to 88 ohms
Fuse rating	30 amps

Torque specifications

Alternator cover bolts (inner and outer)	10 Nm (84 in-lbs)
Alternator rotor bolt	50 Nm (36 ft-lbs)
Charging coil/CDI magneto screws	7 Nm (61 inch-lbs)*
Starter motor mounting bolts	10 Nm (84 in-lbs)
Starter clutch Torx bolts	30 Nm (22 ft-lbs)*

Apply non-permanent thread locking agent to the threads.

1   General information

The machines covered by this manual are equipped with a 12-volt electrical system. The components include a three-phase permanent magnet alternator and a regulator/rectifier unit. The regulator/rectifier unit maintains the charging system output within the specified range to prevent overcharging and converts the AC (alternating current) output of the alternator to DC (direct current) to power the lights and other components and to charge the battery.

An electric starter mounted to the engine case behind the cylinder is standard equipment. A recoil (pull rope) starter is optional. The starting system includes the motor, the battery, the starter relay and starting circuit cut-off relay and the various wires and switches. If the engine kill switch and the main key switch are both in the On position, the cut-off relay allows the starter motor to operate only if the transmission is in Neutral. **Note:** *Keep in mind that electrical parts, once purchased, can't be returned. To avoid unnecessary expense, make very sure the faulty component has been positively identified before buying a replacement part.*

2   Electrical troubleshooting

A typical electrical circuit consists of an electrical component, the switches, relays, etc. related to that component and the wiring and connectors that hook the component to both the battery and the frame. To aid in locating a problem in any electrical circuit, wiring diagrams are included at the end of this Chapter.

Before tackling any troublesome electrical circuit, first study the appropriate diagrams thoroughly to get a complete picture of what makes up that individual circuit. Trouble spots, for instance, can often be narrowed down by noting if other components related to that circuit are operating properly or not. If several components or circuits fail at one time, chances are the fault lies in the fuse or ground/earth connection, as several circuits often are routed through the same fuse and ground/earth connections.

Electrical problems often stem from simple causes, such as loose or corroded connections or a blown fuse. Prior to any electrical troubleshooting, always visually check the condition of the fuse, wires and connections in the problem circuit.

If testing instruments are going to be utilized, use the diagrams to plan where you will make the necessary connections in order to accurately pinpoint the trouble spot.

The basic tools needed for electrical troubleshooting include a test light or voltmeter, a continuity tester (which includes a bulb, battery and set of test leads) and a jumper wire, preferably with a circuit breaker incorporated, which can be used to bypass electrical components. Specific checks described later in this Chapter may also require an ammeter or ohmmeter.

Voltage checks should be performed if a circuit is not functioning properly. Connect one lead of a test light or voltmeter to either the negative battery terminal or a known good ground/earth. Connect the other lead to a connector in the circuit being tested, preferably nearest to the battery or fuse. If the bulb lights, voltage is reaching that point, which means the part of the circuit between that connector and the battery is problem-free. Continue checking the remainder of the circuit in the same manner. When you reach a point where no voltage is present, the problem lies between there and the last good test point. Most of the time the problem is due to a loose connection. Since these vehicles are designed for off-road use, the problem may also be water or corrosion in a connector. Keep in mind that some circuits only receive voltage when the ignition key is in the On position.

One method of finding short circuits is to remove the fuse and connect a test light or voltmeter in its place to the fuse terminals. There should be no load in the circuit. Move the wiring harness from side-to-side while watching the test light. If the bulb lights, there is a short to ground/earth somewhere in that area, probably where insulation has rubbed off a wire. The same test can be performed on other components in the circuit, including the switch.

A ground/earth check should be done to see if a component is grounded/earthed properly. Disconnect the battery and connect one lead of a self-powered test light (such as a continuity tester) to a known good ground/earth. Connect the other lead to the wire or ground/earth connection being tested. If the bulb lights, the ground/earth is good. If the bulb does not light, the ground/earth is not good.

A continuity check is performed to see if a circuit, section of circuit or individual component is capable of passing electricity through it. Disconnect the battery and connect one lead of a self-powered test light (such as a continuity tester) to one end of the circuit being tested and the other lead to the other end of the circuit. If the bulb lights, there is continuity, which means the circuit is passing electricity through it properly. Switches can be checked in the same way.

Remember that all electrical circuits are designed to conduct electricity from the battery, through the wires, switches, relays, etc. to the electrical component (light bulb, motor, etc.). From there it is directed to the frame (ground/earth) where it is passed back to the battery. Electrical problems are basically an interruption in the flow of electricity from the battery or back to it.

3   Battery - inspection and maintenance

1   Most battery damage is caused by heat, vibration, and/or low electrolyte levels, so keep the battery securely mounted, check the electrolyte level frequently and make sure the charging system is functioning properly. The battery used on these vehicles is a maintenance free (sealed) type and therefore doesn't require the addition of water. However, the following checks should still be regularly performed. **Warning:** *Always disconnect the negative cable first and connect it last to prevent sparks which could the battery to explode.*

2   Refer to Chapter 1 for electrolyte level and specific gravity checking procedures.

3   Check around the base inside of the battery for sediment, which is the result of sulfation caused by low electrolyte levels. These deposits will cause internal short circuits, which can quickly discharge the battery. Look for cracks in the case and replace the battery if either of these conditions is found.

4   Check the battery terminals and cable ends for tightness and corrosion. If corrosion is evident, disconnect the cables from the battery, disconnecting the negative (-) terminal first, and clean the terminals and cable ends with a wire brush or knife and emery paper. Reconnect the cables, connecting the negative cable last, and apply a thin coat of petroleum jelly to the cables to slow further corrosion.

5.1a The fuse holder is located inside this rubber cover . . .

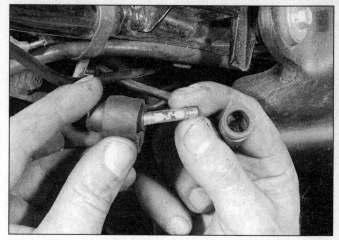

5.1b . . . pull the cover apart for access to the fuse

5   The battery case should be kept clean to prevent current leakage, which can discharge the battery over a period of time (especially when it sits unused). Wash the outside of the case with a solution of baking soda and water. Do not get any baking soda solution in the battery cells. Rinse the battery thoroughly, then dry it.

6   If acid has been spilled on the frame or battery box, neutralize it with a baking soda and water solution, then touch up any damaged paint. Make sure the battery vent tube (if equipped) is directed away from the frame and is not kinked or pinched **(see illustrations 4.13a and 4.13b in Chapter 1)**.

7   If the vehicle sits unused for long periods of time, disconnect the cables from the battery terminals. Refer to Section 4 and charge the battery approximately once every month.

4   Battery - charging

1   If the machine sits idle for extended periods or if the charging system malfunctions, the battery can be charged from an external source.

2   To properly charge the battery, you will need a charger of the correct rating, a hydrometer, a clean rag and a syringe for adding distilled water to the battery cells.

3   The maximum charging rate for any battery is 1/10th of the rated amp-hour capacity. As an example, the maximum charge rate for a 14 amp/hour battery would be 1.4 amps. If the battery is charged at a higher rate, it could overheat, causing the plates inside the battery to buckle.

4   Do not allow the battery to be subjected to a so-called quick charge (high charge rate over a short period of time) unless you are prepared to buy a new battery.

5   When charging the battery, always remove it from the machine and be sure to check the electrolyte level before hooking up the charger. Add distilled water to any cells that are low.

6   Loosen the cell caps, hook up the battery charger leads (positive lead to battery positive terminal, negative lead to battery negative terminal), cover the top of the battery with a clean rag, then, and only then, plug in the battery charger. **Warning:** *The hydrogen gas escaping from a charging battery is explosive, so keep open flames and sparks well away from the area. Also, the electrolyte is extremely corrosive and will damage anything it comes in contact with.*

7   Allow the battery to charge until the specific gravity is as specified (refer to Chapter 1 for the specific gravity checking procedure). The charger must be unplugged and disconnected from the battery when making specific gravity checks. If the battery overheats or gases excessively, the charging rate is too high. Either disconnect the charger or lower the charging rate to prevent damage to the battery.

8   If one or more of the cells do not show an increase in specific

gravity after a long slow charge, or if the battery as a whole does not seem to want to take a charge, it's time for a new battery.

9   When the battery is fully charged, unplug the charger first, then disconnect the leads from the battery. Install the cell caps and wipe any electrolyte off the outside of the battery case.

10   If the recharged battery discharges rapidly when left disconnected, it's likely that an internal short caused by physical damage or sulfation has occurred. A new battery will be required. A sound battery will tend to lose its charge at about 1-percent per day.

5   Fuse and circuit breaker - check and replacement

Fuse

YFM350ER and 1987 through 1996 YFM350FW models
Refer to illustrations 5.1a and 5.1b

1   These models use a single 30 amp fuse, located under the seat on the right side of the vehicle **(see illustration)**. The fuse is mounted in a plastic holder, which is contained in a rubber cover. A spare fuse is mounted behind the fuse holder. The fuse can be removed and checked visually. Pull open the rubber cover and pull the fuse out **(see illustration)**. A blown fuse is easily identified by a break in the element.

YFM350FWB, YFM350U and 1997 YFM350FW models
Refer to illustrations 5.2a and 5.2b

2   These models use a single 30-amp main fuse of the bayonet type, located under the seat **(see illustration)**. Some models are also equipped with an auxiliary fuse to protect the auxiliary DC circuit **(see**

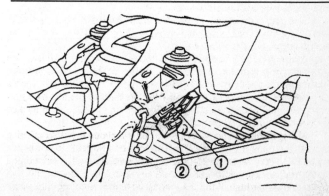

5.2a The main fuse (1) and a spare (2) are located under the seat

8

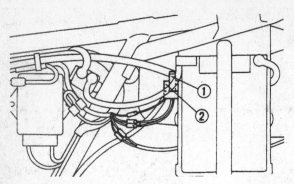

5.2b Some late models have an auxiliary fuse for the DC circuit (1) with a spare (2)

7.1a On YFM350ER and YFM350FW models, remove the screws (arrows) and take off the headlight cover . . .

illustration). The fuse can be checked visually without removing it from its holder; just look through the plastic to see if the metal element inside is broken. If so, pull the fuse out and push a new one in.

3   If the fuse blows, be sure to check the wiring harnesses very carefully for evidence of a short circuit. Look for bare wires and chafed, melted or burned insulation. If a fuse is replaced before the cause is located, the new fuse will blow immediately.

4   Never, under any circumstances, use a higher rated fuse or bridge the fuse terminals, as damage to the electrical system - or even a fire - could result.

5   Occasionally a fuse will blow or cause an open circuit for no obvious reason. Corrosion of the fuse ends and fuse holder terminals may occur and cause poor fuse contact. If this happens, remove the corrosion with a wire brush or emery paper, then spray the fuse end and terminals with electrical contact cleaner.

Circuit breaker

6   Early models use a circuit breaker to protect the auxiliary DC accessory terminal.

7   To reset the circuit breaker, switch off the main key switch and any equipment connected to the accessory terminal. Wait 30 seconds, then push in the knob on the circuit breaker (it's located next to the fuse holder).

8   Turn on the main key switch and the equipment connected to the accessory terminal. If the circuit breaker trips again, check the wiring for breaks or poor connections, referring to the Wiring diagrams at the end of the book. The circuit breaker will also trip if equipment connected to the accessory terminal draws too much current.

---

6   Lighting system - check

1   The battery provides power for operation of the headlights, tail light, brake light (if equipped) and instrument cluster lights. If none of the lights operate, always check battery voltage before proceeding. Low battery voltage indicates either a faulty battery, low battery electrolyte level or a defective charging system. Refer to Chapter 1 and Section 3 of this Chapter for battery checks and Sections 21 through 24 for charging system tests. Also, check the condition of the fuse and replace it with a new one if its blown.

Headlights

2   If both of the headlight bulbs are out with the headlight switch in Lo or Hi and the main key switch On, check the fuse (see Section 5).

3   If only one headlight is out, try installing the bulb from the working headlight. If this solves the problem, replace the defective bulb. If not, test further as described below.

4   Disconnect the electrical connector from the bulb that doesn't light. Connect the negative lead of a voltmeter to the black wire terminal in the wiring harness. Turn the main key switch On and connect the positive lead to the green wire terminal (low beam) and the

yellow wire terminal (high beam). The voltmeter should indicate 12 volts or more.

a) *If there's voltage at the terminals, the bulb is burned out or the bulb socket is corroded.*

b) *If there's no voltage, the problem lies in the wiring or one of the switches in the circuit. Refer to Sections 13 and 14 for the switch testing procedures, and also the wiring diagrams at the end of this Chapter.*

Tail light

5   If the tail light fails to work, check the bulb and the bulb terminals first.

6   If the bulb and terminals are good, disconnect the tail light electrical connector. Connect a voltmeter negative lead to the black wire in the wiring harness and the positive lead to the blue wire. With the main key switch and lighting switch On, the voltmeter should indicate 12 volts or more.

a) *If there's voltage at the terminals, the bulb is burned out or the bulb socket is corroded.*

b   *If there's no voltage, the problem lies in the wiring or one of the switches in the circuit. Refer to Sections 13 and 14 for the switch testing procedures, and also the wiring diagrams at the end of this Chapter.*

7   If no voltage is indicated, check the ground/earth wire and the wiring between the tail light and the lighting switch, then check the switch.

Brake light

8   If the machine is equipped with a brake light, see Section 10 for the brake light circuit checking procedure.

Neutral indicator light

9   If the neutral light fails to operate when the transmission is in Neutral, check the fuse and the bulb (see Section 11 for bulb removal procedures). If the bulb and fuse are in good condition, check for battery voltage at the wire attached to the neutral switch on the left side of the engine. If battery voltage is present, refer to Section 16 for the neutral switch check and replacement procedures.

10   If no voltage is indicated, check the wiring to the bulb, to the switch and between the switch and the bulb for open circuits and poor connections.

---

7   Headlight bulb - replacement

Refer to illustrations 7.1a, 7.1b, 7.2a, 7.2b and 7.3
Warning: *If the headlight has just burned out, give the bulb time to cool before changing the bulb to avoid burning your fingers.*

1   If you're working on a YFM350ER or YFM350FW model, remove

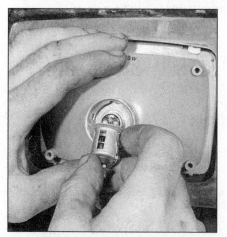

7.1b . . . on YFM350FWB and YFM350U models, remove the screws (circled) and pull out the headlight assembly . . .

7.2a . . . pull off the rubber cover . . .

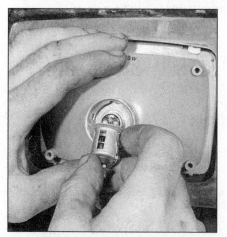

7.2b . . . turn the bulb socket counterclockwise and remove it from the case . . .

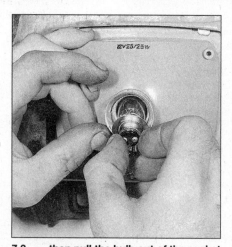

7.3 . . . then pull the bulb out of the socket without touching the glass

8.3 The headlight adjusting screw is mounted below each headlight (arrow)

the headlight cover screws and take off the cover **(see illustration)**. If you're working on a YFM350FWB or YFM350U model, remove the screws and take out the headlight assembly **(see illustration)**.

2   Pull the rubber cover off the bulb. Twist the bulb socket counter-clockwise and remove it from the headlight case **(see illustrations)**.

3   Pull the bulb out without touching the glass **(see illustration)**.

4   Installation is the reverse of the removal procedure, with the following additions:

   a) *Be sure not to touch the bulb with your fingers - oil from your skin will cause the bulb to overheat and fail prematurely. If you do touch the bulb, wipe it off with a clean rag dampened with rubbing alcohol.*

   b) *Align the tab on the metal bulb flange with the slot in the headlight case.*

   c) *Make sure the arrow mark on the headlight cover is facing up.*

8   Headlight aim - check and adjustment

Refer to illustration 8.3

1   An improperly adjusted headlight may cause problems for oncoming traffic or provide poor, unsafe illumination of the terrain ahead. Before adjusting the headlight, be sure to consult with local traffic laws and regulations. Yamaha doesn't provide specifications for headlight adjustment.

2   The headlight beam can be adjusted vertically. Before performing the adjustment, make sure the fuel tank is at least half full, and have an assistant sit on the seat.

3   Insert a Phillips screwdriver into the vertical adjuster screw **(see**

illustration), then turn the adjuster as necessary to raise or lower the beam.

9   Tail light and brake light bulbs - replacement

Tail light

Refer to illustrations 9.1 and 9.2

1   Remove the tail light lens screws and take off the lens **(see illustration)**.

9.1 Remove the lens screws and take off the lens . . .

8

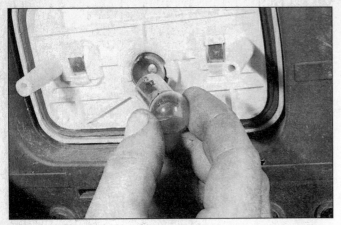

9.2 . . . press the bulb into the socket, turn it counterclockwise (anti-clockwise) and pull it out

10.8 Left handlebar switch details

A   Brake switch retaining prong   B   Switch housing screws

2   Press the bulb into its socket and turn it counterclockwise to remove **(see illustration)**.

3   Check the socket terminals for corrosion and clean them if necessary.

4   Press the bulb into its socket, turn counterclockwise (anti-clockwise) to engage the pins, then release the bulb.

5   Install the lens and tighten the screws securely, but not enough to crack the plastic.

Brake light

6   The brake light bulb on vehicles so equipped is replaced in the same way as the tail light bulb.

10   Brake switches - check and replacement

1   All models use an electrical switch at the left brake lever. The switch is part of the starting circuit. The starting system is designed so the starter won't operate unless the machine is in neutral and the drive select lever is in forward, or the left brake lever is pulled in. The purpose of the switch is to indicate to the starting system that the lever is pulled in.

2   Some models are equipped with a brake light. On these models, the light is operated by switches at the brake lever and right handlebar.

3   Before checking any electrical circuit, check the fuses (see Section 5).

4   Using a test light connected to a good ground/earth, check for voltage to the wire at the brake light switch. If there's no voltage present, check the wire between the switch and the ignition switch (see the wiring diagrams at the end of the book).

5   If voltage is available, touch the probe of the test light to the other terminal of the switch, then pull the brake lever or depress the brake pedal - if the test light doesn't light up, replace the switch.

6   If the test light does light, check the wiring between the switch and the brake lights (see the wiring diagrams at the end of the book).

Switch replacement

Brake lever switch

Refer to illustration 10.8

7   Unplug the electrical connector from the switch.

8   Press in on the prong that secures the switch to the lever **(see illustration)**. Slip the switch out and push a new one in until the prong engages with its hole.

Brake pedal switch

9   Unplug the electrical connector in the switch harness.

10   Disconnect the spring from the brake pedal switch.

11   Hold the adjuster nut from turning and rotate the switch body all the way up until it clears the nut threads, then lift it out.

12   Install the switch by reversing the removal procedure.

11   Indicator bulbs and odometer/speedometer - replacement

Indicator bulbs

Refer to illustrations 11.1, 11.2a and 11.2b

1   Pull the plastic bulb cluster clips free of the handlebar and turn it

11.1 Free the bulb housing from the handlebar and turn it over . . .

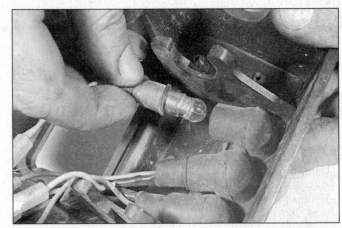

11.2a . . . pull the bulb socket out of the rubber housing . . .

11.2b . . . press the bulb into the socket and turn counterclockwise (anti-clockwise) to remove

11.5 Pull out the clips and remove the mounting dampers to free the odometer/speedometer (odometer shown)

A   Cable nut   B   Clips

over to expose the bulb sockets **(see illustration)**.

2   To replace a bulb, pull the appropriate rubber socket out of the handlebar cover **(see illustration)**. Press the bulb into its socket, turn it counterclockwise and pull the bulb out of the socket **(see illustration)**.

3   If the socket contacts are dirty or corroded, they should be scraped clean and sprayed with electrical contact cleaner before new bulbs are installed.

4   Push the new bulb into its socket, turn it clockwise and release it. Install the bulb cluster on the handlebar.

Odometer/speedometer

Cable

Refer to illustrations 11.5 and 11.6

5   Unscrew the nut and pull the upper end of the cable out of the odometer or speedometer **(see illustration)**.

6   Remove the retaining screw completely (don't just loosen it) from the clutch cover at the lower end of the cable and pull the cable out **(see illustration)**.

7   Detach the cable from any retainers or clips and remove it from the machine.

8   Installation is the reverse of the removal steps. Be sure to reinstall the retainer for the reverse lockout release cable when you install the retaining screw.

Gauge

9   Disconnect the cable from the gauge as described above.

10   Pull out the retaining clips and remove the dampers, then lift the gauge off the bracket **(see illustration 11.5)**.

11   Installation is the reverse of the removal steps.

Gears

Refer to illustrations 11.13a and 11.13b

12   Remove the clutch cover from the right side of the engine (see Chapter 2).

13   Remove the screw and retainer from the clutch cover, then remove the gears **(see illustrations)**.

14   Installation is the reverse of the removal steps.

---

12   Oil temperature warning system - check and switch replacement

---

Check

Refer to illustration 12.4

1   These vehicles are equipped with an oil temperature warning system that turns on an indicator light on the handlebars when the oil overheats. The system consists of an oil temperature switch mounted on the left side of the engine, a thermistor and a warning indicator light in the handlebar cover. The indicator light should come on for a few seconds when the engine is first started, then turn off. **Caution:** *If the light comes on while the engine is running, shut it off immediately and let it cool for at least 10 minutes. Continued operation with overheated oil can cause serious engine damage.*

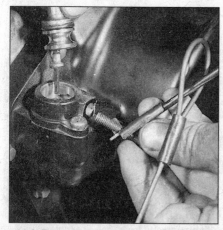

11.6 Remove the screw completely and pull the cable out of the clutch cover

11.13a Remove the screw (arrow) and retainer

11.13b The gears are accessible from inside the clutch cover

8

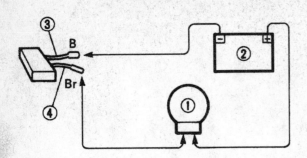

12.4 Thermistor test circuit

1	*Bulb*	3	*Thermistor black wire*
2	*Battery*	4	*Thermistor brown wire*

2   If the oil temperature warning light doesn't come on at all, check the bulb and replace it if it's burned out.

3   If the light doesn't come on (with a good bulb) or doesn't turn off, locate the thermistor. It's mounted beneath the rear end of the seat and can be identified by its two wires, one brown and one black.

4   Disconnect the thermistor electrical connector and connect the thermistor in series with the vehicle's battery and the oil temperature indicator bulb, using lengths of wire **(see illustration)**. The bulb should light, then go out. The time required varies according to temperature; it may be a minute or more.

5   If the bulb lights and goes out as described, the thermistor is good. Check the wiring in the oil warning circuit for breaks or poor connections.

6   If the wiring is good and the system still doesn't perform properly, the oil temperature switch is probably defective. Since the switch can't be returned once it's purchased, it's a good idea to have the system tested by a Yamaha dealer or substitute a known good switch before buying a new one.

Switch replacement

Refer to illustration 12.7

7   Locate the switch on the left side of the engine **(see illustration)**. Disconnect its electrical connector, unscrew the switch and remove the sealing washer.

8   Install the switch with a new sealing washer, tighten it securely and connect the electrical connector.

12.7 The oil temperature switch is located on the left side of the engine (YFM350FW shown)

13   Ignition main (key) switch - check and replacement

Check

1   Follow the wiring harness from the ignition switch to the connector and unplug the connector.

2   Using an ohmmeter, check the continuity of the terminal pairs indicated in the wiring diagrams at the end of the book. Continuity should exist between the terminals connected by a solid line when the switch is in the indicated position.

3   If the switch fails any of the tests, replace it.

Replacement

Refer to illustration 13.4

4   The ignition switch is secured to the front fender by a plastic nut **(see illustration)**.

5   If you haven't already done so, unplug the switch electrical connector. Unscrew the nut and lower the switch out of the fender.

6   Installation is the reverse of the removal procedure.

14   Handlebar switches - check

1   Generally speaking, the switches are reliable and trouble-free. Most troubles, when they do occur, are caused by dirty or corroded contacts, but wear and breakage of internal parts is a possibility that should not be overlooked. If breakage does occur, the entire switch and related wiring harness will have to be replaced with a new one, since individual parts are not usually available.

2   The switches can be checked for continuity with an ohmmeter or a continuity test light. Always disconnect the battery negative cable, which will prevent the possibility of a short circuit, before making the checks.

3   Trace the wiring harness of the switch in question and unplug the electrical connectors.

4   Using the ohmmeter or test light, check for continuity between the terminals of the switch harness with the switch in the various positions. Refer to the continuity diagrams contained in the wiring diagrams at the end of the book. Continuity should exist between the terminals connected by a solid line when the switch is in the indicated position.

5   If the continuity check indicates a problem exists, refer to Section 15, disassemble the switch and spray the switch contacts with electrical contact cleaner. If they are accessible, the contacts can be scraped clean with a knife or polished with crocus cloth. If switch components are damaged or broken, it will be obvious when the switch is disassembled.

13.4 Remove the plastic nut (arrow) to detach the ignition main (key) switch from the fender

15.1 The handlebar switches are mounted in the left handlebar housing

16.1a The neutral switch is located on the left side of the engine near the shift pedal shaft

15 Handlebar switches - removal and installation

Refer to illustration 15.1

1   The handlebar switches are composed of two halves that clamp around the bars. They are easily removed for cleaning or inspection by taking out the clamp screws and pulling the switch halves away from the handlebars **(see illustration 10.8 and the accompanying illustration)**.

2   To completely remove the switches, the electrical connectors in the wiring harness must be unplugged and the harness separated from the tie wraps and retainers.

3   When installing the switches, make sure the wiring harness is properly routed to avoid pinching or stretching the wires.

16 Gear position switches – check and replacement

YFM350ER, YFM350FW and 1996 through 1998 YFM350U models

Refer to illustrations 16.1a and 16.1b

1   Disconnect the electrical connector from the switch being tested **(see illustrations)**.

2   Connect one lead of an ohmmeter to a good ground/earth and the other lead to the terminal post on the switch being tested.

3   When the transmission is in neutral, the ohmmeter should read 0 ohms between the neutral switch and ground/earth - in any other gear, the meter should read infinite resistance.

4   When the shift select lever is in reverse, the ohmmeter should read infinite resistance between the reverse switch and ground/earth - in High or Low forward, the meter should read 0 ohms.

5   If the switch doesn't check out as described, replace it.

6   Wrap the threads of the switch with Teflon tape or apply a thin coat of RTV sealant to them. Install the switch in the case with a new sealing washer and tighten it to the torque listed in this Chapter's Specifications.

7   Reconnect the switch wires.

YFM350FWB and 1999 YFM350U models

8   These models use a single gear position switch to indicate Neutral and Reverse. It's mounted inside the right crankcase cover, behind the secondary clutch **(see illustration 17.8 in Chapter 2)**.

9   Follow the connector from the grommet at the right rear of the engine (where the right crankcase cover meets the crankcase) to its connector (brown and green wires). Disconnect the connector.

10   Connect one lead of an ohmmeter to a good ground/earth and the

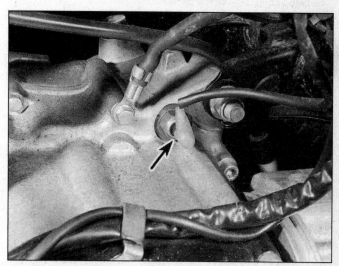

16.1b The reverse switch (arrow) is located on the left side of the engine above the middle gear case

other lead to the connector terminal of the switch being tested (the switch side of the connector, not the wiring harness side). The brown wire is for the neutral switch and the green wire is for the reverse switch.

11   Place the transmission in gear (neutral or reverse). When the shifter is in neutral, the ohmmeter should show continuity (little or no resistance) between the brown wire's terminal and ground. When the shifter is in reverse, the ohmmeter should show continuity (little or no resistance) between the green wire's terminal and ground.

12   If the switch doesn't perform as described, remove the right crankcase cover and secondary clutch and replace the switch (See Sections 16 and 17 in Chapter 2).

17 Starter circuit - check and component replacement

1   Depending on the procedure, it may be necessary to remove the seat, rear cargo rack or rear fender for access to other parts (see Chapter 7).

Starter relay

Check

Refer to illustration 17.2

Warning: *Make sure the transmission is in Neutral before performing this test.*

8

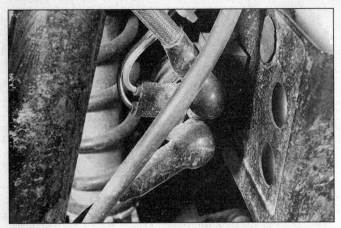

17.2 The starter relay is located forward of the battery

2   Locate the starter relay at the left rear of the vehicle near the battery **(see illustration)**.
3   Disconnect the electrical connector for the two thin wires connected to the relay.
4   Connect a length of wire from the red/white wire terminal in the connector to the battery positive terminal (the side of the connector that runs to the relay, not the harness side). Connect another length of wire from the battery negative terminal to the blue/white wire terminal in the connector. The starter should crank the engine. If it doesn't, the problem may be in the starter itself (refer to Sections 18 and 19 for removal and inspection procedures), in the electrical cables between the battery and starter relay, or in the starter relay. If the starter is good and the cables are in good condition and properly connected, the relay is probably at fault.

Replacement

5   Disconnect the negative cable from the battery.
6   Pull back the rubber covers from the terminal nuts, remove the nuts and disconnect the starter relay cables **(see illustration 17.2)**. Disconnect the remaining electrical connector from the starter relay.
7   Pull the relay's rubber mount off the metal bracket and pull the relay out of the mount.
8   Installation is the reverse of removal. Reconnect the negative battery cable after all the other electrical connections are made.

Starting circuit cut-off relay

Check

Refer to illustrations 17.9, 17.11 and 17.12

9   Locate the relay beneath the rear fender **(see illustration)**. Disconnect the connector from the relay.
10   If you're working on a YFM350ER model, connect an ohmmeter between the yellow/black and one of the red/white terminals in the side of the connector that leads to the relay. Compare the resistance

17.9 Location of the electrical components under the rear fender varies slightly according to model; they can be identified by wire colors

A   Starting circuit cut-off relay   *C   Regulator/rectifier*
B   Neutral relay   *D   Reverse relay*

reading with the value listed in this Chapter's Specifications. If it's incorrect, replace the relay.
11   On YFM350ER, YFM350FW and 1996 through 1998 YFM350U models, connect the ohmmeter between the yellow/black and one of the red/white terminals in the side of the connector that leads to the relay **(see illustration)**. Connect a 12-volt battery (the vehicle's battery will work if it's fully charged) between the blue/white terminal and the other red/white terminal. With the battery connected, the ohmmeter should indicate 0 ohms. With the battery disconnected, the ohmmeter should indicate infinite resistance. If the relay doesn't perform as described, replace it.
12   On YFM350FWB and 1999 YFM350U models, connect the ohmmeter between the yellow/black and one of the brown terminals in the side of the connector that leads to the relay **(see illustration)**. Connect a 12-volt battery (the vehicle's battery will work if it's fully charged) between the blue/white terminal and the other brown terminal. With the battery connected, the ohmmeter should indicate 0 ohms. With the battery disconnected, the ohmmeter should indicate infinite resistance. If the relay doesn't perform as described, replace it.

Replacement

13   If you haven't already done so, disconnect the relay's electrical connector. Pull the relay off its mounting bracket and push on a new one, then connect the wiring harness.

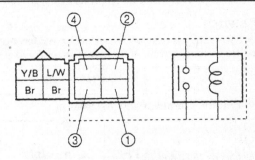

17.12 Starting circuit cut-off relay test circuit (YFM350FWB and 1999 YFM350U)

1   Brown terminal (battery positive terminal)
2   Black/yellow terminal (battery negative terminal)
3   Brown terminal (ohmmeter positive terminal)
4   Blue/white terminal (ohmmeter negative terminal)

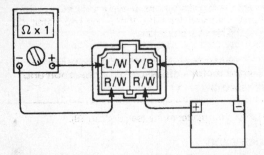

17.11 Starting circuit cut-off relay test circuit (YFM350ER, YFM350FW and 1996 through 1998 YFM350U)

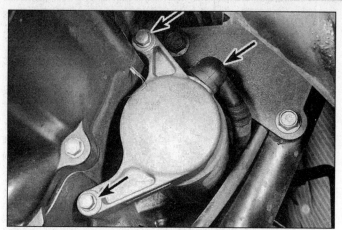

18.2a Starter motor mounting details (YFM350ER, YFM350FW and 1996 through 1998 YFM350U)

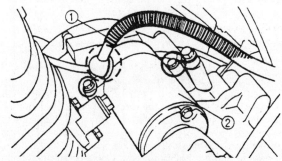

18.2b Starter motor mounting details (YFM350FWB and 1999 YFM350U)

Neutral relay (YFM350ER, YFM350FW and 1996 through 1998 YFM350U)

14   Checking and replacement for the neutral relay are the same as for the starting circuit cut-off relay described above, with the exception of different wire colors. When checking resistance on 2WD models, connect the ohmmeter negative lead to the green/yellow wire terminal and the positive lead to the brown wire terminal. When checking resistance with an ohmmeter and battery, connect as follows:

a) Ohmmeter positive lead to sky blue
b) Ohmmeter negative lead to white/black
c) Battery positive terminal to brown
d) Battery negative terminal to green/yellow.

Starter switch

15   The starter switch is part of the switch assembly on the left handlebar. Refer to Section 14 for checking and replacement procedures.

18 Starter motor - removal and installation

Removal

Refer to illustrations 18.2a and 18.2b

1   Disconnect the cable from the negative terminal of the battery.
2   Pull back the rubber boot and remove the nut retaining the starter cable to the starter **(see illustrations)**. Remove the starter mounting bolts.
3   Lift the outer end of the starter up a little bit and slide the starter out of the engine case. **Caution:** *Don't drop or strike the starter - its magnets may be demagnetized, which will ruin it.*

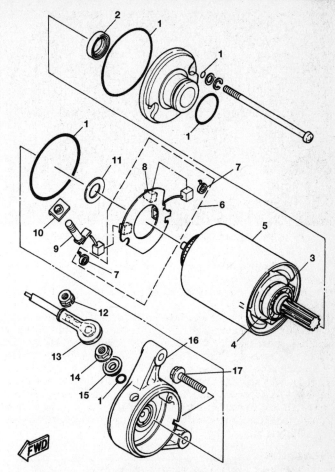

19.2a Starter (YFM350ER, YFM350FW and 1996 through 1998 YFM350U) – exploded view

1	O-rings	10	Insulator
2	Seal	11	Shim(s)
3	Bearing	12	Cable nut
4	Armature	13	Rubber cover and cable
5	Starter housing	14	Terminal nut
6	Brush set	15	Insulator
7	Brush springs	16	Bracket
8	Brush plate	17	Mounting bolt
9	Terminal bolt		

4   Check the condition of the O-ring on the end of the starter that fits into the engine and replace it if necessary

Installation

5   Remove any corrosion or dirt from the mounting lugs on the starter and the mounting points on the crankcase.
6   Apply a little engine oil to the O-ring and install the starter by reversing the removal procedure.

19 Starter motor - disassembly, inspection and reassembly

1   Remove the starter motor (see Section 18).

Disassembly

Refer to illustrations 19.2a, 19.2b, 19.2c, 19.3, 19.4 and 19.5

2   One of the through-bolts should be centered between alignment marks **(see illustrations)**. Make your own marks if they aren't visible.

8

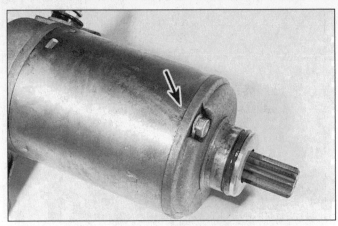

19.2c Position of the through-bolts is indicated by alignment marks (arrow)

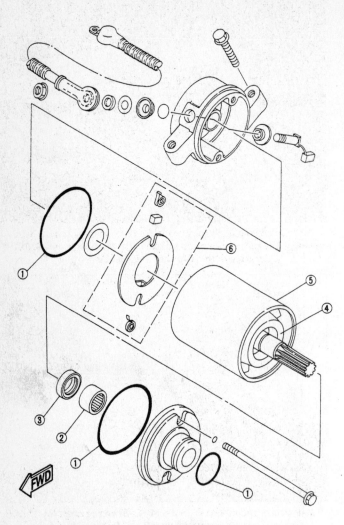

19.2b Starter motor (YFM350FWB and 1999 YFM350U) – exploded view

1	O-ring	4	Armature coil assembly
2	Bearing	5	Yoke assembly
3	Oil seal	6	Brush set

19.3 Remove the through-bolts and pull the cover off

3   Unscrew the two through-bolts, then remove the cover with its O-ring from the motor **(see illustration)**.

4   Remove the bracket with its O-ring and the brush set from the motor **(see illustration)**.

5   Slide off the insulating washer and shim(s) from the armature, noting their locations, and withdraw the armature from the housing **(see illustration)**.

19.4 Pull the bracket and brush plate off the housing; the housing tab, brush plate slot and bracket slot (arrows) must be aligned on assembly

19.5 Pull the armature out of the housing and note the location of the shims on each end

19.6 Detach the positive brush from the brush plate and lift the plate out

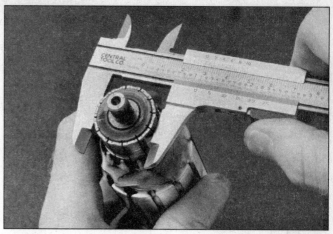

19.8 Check the commutator for cracks and discoloring, then measure the diameter and compare it with the minimum diameter listed in this Chapter's Specifications

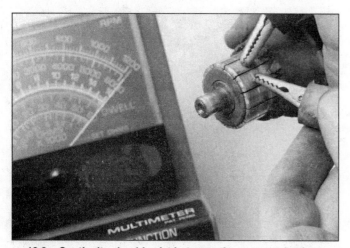

19.9a Continuity should exist between the commutator bars

19.9b There should be no continuity between each commutator bar and the armature shaft

Inspection

Refer to illustrations 19.6, 19.8, 19.9a, 19.9b, 19.10 and 19.15

Note: *Check carefully which components are available as replacements before starting overhaul procedures.*

6   Lift the brush springs and slide the brushes out of their holders **(see illustration).**

7   The parts of the starter motor that most likely will require attention are the brushes. If one brush must be replaced, replace both of them. The brushes are replaced together with the terminal bolt and the brush plate. Brushes must be replaced if they are worn excessively, cracked, chipped, or otherwise damaged. Measure the length of the brushes and compare the results to the brush length listed in this Chapter's Specifications. If either of the brushes is worn beyond the specified limits, replace them both.

8   Inspect the commutator for scoring, scratches and discoloration. The commutator can be cleaned and polished with 600-grit emery paper, but do not remove copper from the commutator. After cleaning, clean out the grooves and wipe away any residue with a cloth soaked in an electrical system cleaner or denatured alcohol. Measure the commutator diameter and compare it to the diameter listed in this Chapter's Specifications **(see illustration).** If it's less than the service limit, the motor must be replaced with a new one.

9   Using an ohmmeter or a continuity test light, check for continuity between the commutator bars **(see illustration).** Continuity should exist between each bar and all of the others. Also, check for continuity between the commutator bars and the armature shaft **(see illustration).** There should be no continuity between the commutator

and the shaft. If the checks indicate otherwise, the armature is defective.

10   Check the undercut of the mica between the commutator bars **(see illustration).** If it isn't deep enough, carefully scrape away mica with a broken-off piece of hacksaw blade until the undercut is as listed in this Chapter's Specifications.

11   Check the seal in the cover for wear or damage. Check the bearing on the armature for roughness, looseness or loss of lubricant. Check with a motorcycle shop or Yamaha dealer to see if the seal and bearing can be replaced separately; if this isn't possible, replace the starter motor.

12   Inspect the bushing in the bracket. Replace the starter motor if the bushing is worn or damaged.

13   Check the starter pinion for worn, chipped or broken teeth. If the gear is damaged or worn, replace the starter motor.

8

19.10 Measure the depth of the mica and undercut it if necessary

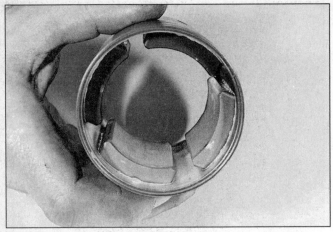

19.15　Replace the starter if the magnets inside the housing are damaged or weak

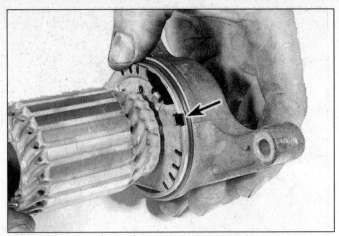

19.18　Align the brush plate and bracket notches (arrow)

20.2a　Pull off the starter wheel gear (arrow) . . .

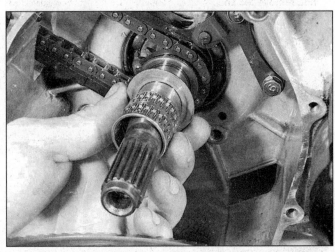

20.2b　. . . then remove the needle roller bearing and washer

14　Inspect the insulating washers and shims for signs of damage and replace if necessary.

15　Check the magnets inside the starter housing for damage or loss of magnetism **(see illustration)**. Replace the starter motor if the magnets are damaged.

Reassembly

Refer to illustration 19.18

16　Lift the brush springs and slide the brushes back into position in their holders.

17　Make sure the shim(s) are in place on the bracket end of the armature.

18　Install the brush plate in the bracket, making sure its notch is correctly aligned with the housing notch **(see illustration)**. Insert the terminal bolt through the bracket, then install the O-ring, insulator and nut on the terminal bolt.

19　Insert the armature in the housing, locating the brushes to the commutator bars **(see illustration 19.18)**. Check that each brush is securely pressed against the commutator by its spring and is free to move easily in its holder.

20　Install the large O-ring and housing on the bracket; make sure the tab on the housing aligns with the notches in the brush plate and bracket **(see illustration 19.4)**.

21　Apply a smear of grease to the cover seal lip.

22　Slide the shim(s) onto the front end of the armature shaft. Fit the large O-ring to the housing and carefully slide the front cover into

position, aligning the marks on each side of the through-bolt hole **(see illustration 19.2b)**.

23　Fit the through-bolts and tighten them securely.

20　Starter clutch and reduction gears - removal, inspection and installation

Removal

Refer to illustrations 20.2a, 20.2b and 20.3

1　Refer to Section 23 and remove the alternator cover and rotor.

YFM350ER, YFM350FW and 1996 through 1998 YFM350U models

2　Pull the starter wheel gear off the end of the crankshaft, then remove the bearing and plain washer **(see illustrations)**.

3　Support the starter idle gear and pull its shaft out of the crankcase, together with the snap-ring, washer and two needle roller bearings **(see illustration)**.

YFM350FWB and 1999 YFM350U models

4　Remove the snap-rings and slide the starter idler gears off their shafts **(see illustration)**.

5　Remove the Woodruff key, starter wheel gear, needle roller bearing and washer from the crankshaft **(see illustration)**.

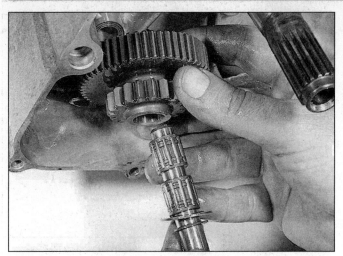

20.3 The idle gear shaft should pull out of the crankcase easily; if not, remove the snap-ring and washer, then slide the gear and two needle roller bearings off the shaft

20.8 Check the starter clutch for visible wear and damage

Inspection

Refer to illustrations 20.8 and 20.10

6   Check the gears for worn or broken teeth. Check the shafts and the friction surface on the gears for wear or damage and replace any parts that show defects.

7   Since needle roller bearing wear is difficult to see, the bearings should be replaced if there's any doubt about their condition.

8   Check the starter clutch in the back of the alternator rotor for visible wear and damage and replace it as described below if problems are found **(see illustration)**.

9   Place the alternator rotor in the starter clutch. Hold the alternator rotor with one hand so its open side is toward you and the starter wheel gear is away from you. Try to rotate the starter wheel gear with the other hand. The gear should rotate counterclockwise (anti-clockwise) smoothly, but not rotate clockwise at all.

10   If the gear rotates both ways or neither way, or if its movement is rough, remove the Torx bolts and separate the starter clutch from the alternator rotor **(see illustration)**.

11   Install the starter clutch in the alternator rotor with its arrow mark facing away from the rotor. Before you tighten the Torx bolts, place the starter wheel gear in the rotor and try to turn it both ways. It should turn counterclockwise (anti-clockwise) but not clockwise, as described in Step 7. If the gear turns the wrong way, the starter clutch is installed backwards.

12   Apply non-permanent thread locking agent to the threads of the Torx bolts and tighten them to the torque listed in this Chapter's Specifications.

Installation

13   Installation is the reverse of the removal steps, with the following addition: Lubricate the gears, bearings and shafts with clean engine oil.

21   Charging system testing - general information and precautions

1   If the performance of the charging system is suspect, the system as a whole should be checked first, followed by testing of the individual components (the alternator and the regulator/rectifier). **Note:** *Before beginning the checks, make sure the battery is fully charged and that all system connections are clean and tight.*

2   Checking the output of the charging system and the performance of the various components within the charging system requires the use of an ohmmeter; voltmeter or ammeter (depending on model); or the equivalent multimeter.

3   When making the checks, follow the procedures carefully to

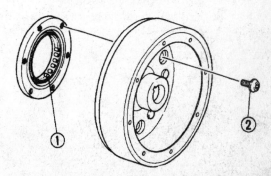

20.10 Remove the six Torx bolts, then remove the starter clutch

    1   *Starter clutch*   2   *Torx bolt*

prevent incorrect connections or short circuits, as irreparable damage to electrical system components may result if short circuits occur.

4   If the necessary test equipment is not available, it is recommended that charging system tests be left to a dealer service department or a reputable ATV repair shop.

22   Charging system - output test

1   If a charging system problem is suspected, perform the following checks. Start by checking the fuse (see Section 5) and battery (see Section 3 and Chapter 1). If necessary, charge the battery (see Section 4).

2   Start the engine and let it warm up to normal operating temperature.

1987 through 1989 YFM350ER models, all YFM350FW models

3   With the engine idling, attach the positive lead of a 0 to 20 volt voltmeter to the positive (+) battery terminal and the negative lead to the battery negative (-) terminal.

4   Slowly increase the engine speed to 5000 rpm and compare the voltmeter reading to the value listed in this Chapter's Specifications.

5   If the output is as specified, the alternator is functioning properly.

1990 and later YFM350ER models

Refer to illustration 22.6

6   Disconnect the positive cable from the battery and connect an

8

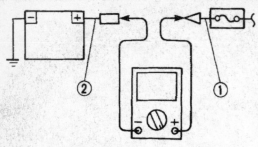

22.6 Charging system test circuit (with ammeter)

ammeter in series between the battery positive terminal and the cable **(see illustration). Caution:** *Don't connect the ammeter between the battery terminals or the ammeter will be ruined.*

7   Start the engine. Raise engine speed to 3000 rpm, then to 8000 rpm and note the ammeter reading at each point. Compare the readings with the values listed in this Chapter's Specifications.

YFM350FWB and YFM350U models

8   With the engine idling, attach the positive lead of a 0-20 volt voltmeter to the positive (+) battery terminal and the negative lead to

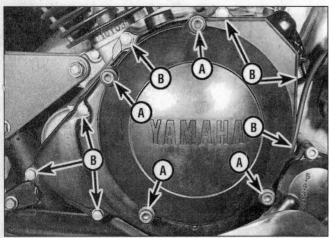

23.6a The alternator outer cover is secured by Allen bolts (A); the main cover is secured by hex bolts (B) (two rear bolts hidden) . . .

23.6b . . . the upper rear bolt secures a wiring harness retainer; the lower rear bolt has a copper washer

23.7 To remove the rotor bolt and rotor, hold the rotor with a wrench (or use a clutch holding tool if the vehicle has a recoil starter) and undo the bolt with a socket . . .

23.8 . . . then pull the rotor out

the battery negative (-) terminal.

9   Slowly increase the engine speed to 3000 rpm and compare the voltmeter reading to the value listed in this Chapter's Specifications.

10   If the output is as specified, the alternator is functioning properly.

All models

11   Low voltage or amperage may be the result of damaged windings in the alternator stator coils or wiring problems. Make sure all electrical connections are clean and tight, then refer to the following Sections to check the alternator stator coils and the regulator/rectifier.

12   On models tested for voltage, output above the specified range indicates a defective voltage regulator/rectifier. Refer to Section 24 for regulator testing and replacement procedures.

13   Disconnect the test equipment. On models tested for amperage, disconnect the negative cable from the battery. Connect the positive cable, then the negative cable.

23   Alternator charging coils and rotor - check and replacement

Charging coil check

1   Locate and disconnect the coil connector on the left side of the vehicle frame. The connector can be identified by its three white wires.

2   Connect an ohmmeter between each of the terminals in the side of the connector that runs back to the engine (connect the positive lead to one of the terminal and the negative lead to each of the two remaining terminals in turn). If the readings are outside the range listed in this Chapter's Specifications, replace the charging coils as described below.

3   Connect the ohmmeter between a good ground/earth on the vehicle and each of the connector terminals in turn. The meter should indicate infinite resistance (no continuity). If not, replace the charging coils.

Charging coil and CDI magneto replacement
YFM350ER, YFM350FW and 1996 through 1998 YFM350U models
Refer to illustrations 23.6a, 23.6b, 23.7, 23.8, 23.10 and 23.11

4   Drain the engine oil (see Chapter 1).

5   If the vehicle has a recoil starter, remove it (see Chapter 2).

6   If you're working on a machine without a recoil starter, remove the outer cover from the left crankcase cover **(see illustrations)**.

7   Remove the bolt that secures the rotor to the alternator rotor. If the vehicle has a recoil starter, hold the rotor from turning with a clutch

holding tool of the type described in Chapter 2 or a chain wrench. If it doesn't have a recoil starter, hold the rotor with a large open end or adjustable wrench **(see illustration)**.

8　Pull the rotor out of the cover **(see illustration)**.

9　Remove the cover bolts **(see illustrations 23.6a and 23.6b)**. Pull the cover off the engine. You may need to pull firmly to overcome the resistance of the rotor magnets, but don't use excessive force. If the cover seems to be stuck, check to make sure all fasteners have been removed.

10　Remove the charging coil screws and the CDI magneto screws **(see illustration)**, then remove the charging coils and CDI magneto together (they're replaced as a unit).

11　Check the seal in the cover for wear or damage. Spin the bearing inner race with a finger and check for roughness, looseness or noise. If the bearing or seal needs to be replaced, remove the Torx screws, take off the retainer, pry out the seal and remove the bearing **(see illustration 23.8 and the accompanying illustration)**.

23.10　The charging coils and CDI magneto are secured by Phillips screws (arrows)

23.11　Left side crankcase details (YFM350ER, YFM350FW and 1996 through 1998 YFM350U)

1　Intake cam chain guide
2　Plain washer
3　Bearing
4　Starter wheel gear
5　Woodruff key for alternator rotor
6　Starter idle gear shaft
7　Needle roller bearings
8　Starter idle gear
9　Plain washer
10　Snap-ring
11　Alternator cover dowels
12　Cover gasket
13　Alternator rotor
14　Charging coils
15　Timing plug
16　O-ring
17　Alternator cover
18　Bearing
19　Oil seal
20　Rotor (recoil starter type shown)
21　O-ring
22　Outer cover
23　Oil filter
24　Oil filter inner cover
25　Oil filter outer cover

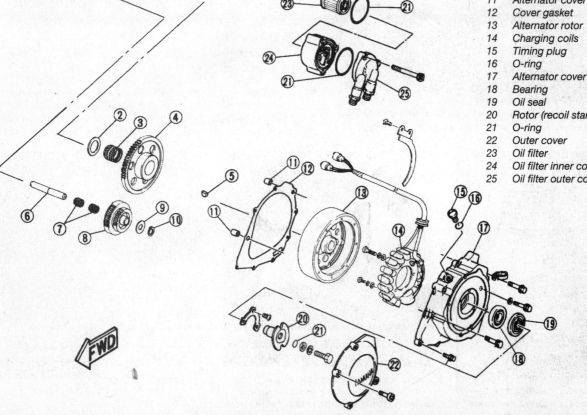

8

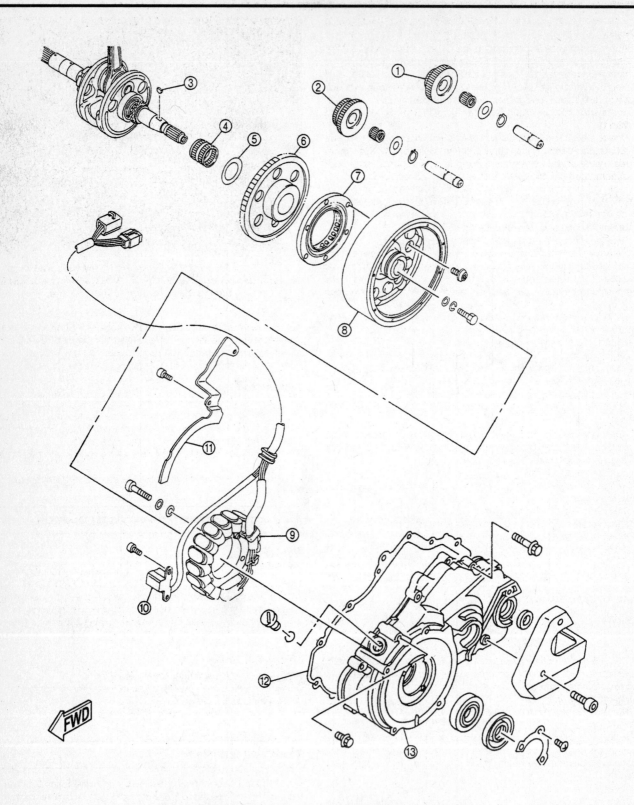

23.15 Left side crankcase details – YFM350FWB and 1999 YFM350U

1	No. 1 starter idle gear	5	Washer	8	Alternator rotor	11	Wiring harness retainer
2	No. 2 starter idle gear	6	Starter wheel gear	9	Stator coil assembly	12	Gasket
3	Woodruff key	7	Starter clutch	10	Pickup coil assembly	13	Left crankcase cover
4	Bearing					

12   Installation is the reverse of the removal steps, with the following additions:

a) *Apply non-permanent thread locking agent to the threads of the charging coil and CDI magneto screws, then tighten them to the torque listed in this Chapter's Specifications.*

b) *Remove all old gasket material from the alternator cover and crankcase. Use a new gasket on the alternator cover.*

c) *Make sure the cover dowels are in position* (**see illustration 23.11**).

d) *Use a new copper washer on the lower rear cover bolt* (**see illustration 23.6b**). *Install the wiring harness retainer on the upper rear cover bolt. Tighten the cover bolts evenly, in a criss-cross pattern, to the torque listed in this Chapter's Specifications.*

YFM350FWB and 1999 YFM350U models

Refer to illustration 23.15

13   Drain the engine oil (see Chapter 1).

14   Remove the recoil starter (see Chapter 2).

15   Remove the left crankcase cover bolts. Pull the cover off the engine (**see illustration**). You may need to pull firmly to overcome the resistance of the rotor magnets, but don't use excessive force. If the cover seems to be stuck, check to make sure all fasteners have been removed.

16   Remove the stator coil screws and pickup coil screws (**see illustration 23.15**), then remove the charging coils and CDI magneto together (they're replaced as a unit).

17   Check the seal in the cover for wear or damage. Spin the bearing inner race with a finger and check for roughness, looseness or noise. If the bearing or seal needs to be replaced, remove the screws, take out the retainer, pry out the seal and remove the bearing.

18   Installation is the reverse of the removal steps, with the following additions:

a) *Apply non-permanent thread locking agent to the threads of the stator coil and pickup coil screws, then tighten them to the torque listed in this Chapter's Specifications.*

b) *Don't forget to reinstall the wiring harness retainer in the cover.*

c) *Remove all old gasket material from the cover and crankcase. Use a new cover gasket.*

d) *Make sure the cover dowels are in position.*

e) *Slip a rod through the cover into the alternator rotor to keep them in alignment while you install the cover. Don't force the cover on or the oil seal may be damaged.*

f) *Tighten the cover bolts evenly, in a criss-cross pattern, to the torque listed in this Chapter's Specifications.*

Rotor replacement

Removal

Refer to illustration 23.21

Note: *To remove the alternator rotor, the special Yamaha puller (part no. YM-01404) or an aftermarket equivalent will be required. Don't try to remove the rotor without the proper puller, as it's almost sure to be damaged. Pullers are readily available from motorcycle dealers and aftermarket tool suppliers.*

19   Remove the alternator cover as described above for access to the rotor.

20   Hold the alternator rotor with a strap wrench. If you don't have one and the engine is in the frame, the crankshaft can be held stationary by placing the transmission in gear and holding the rear brake on.

21   Thread the outer portion of the puller onto the rotor (**see illustrations**). Hold the flats of the outer portion with a wrench and turn the bolt with another wrench to separate the rotor from the crankshaft.

22   Pull the rotor off, together with the starter clutch.

23   Check the rotor Woodruff key; if it's not secure in its slot, pull it

23.21 Thread the rotor puller onto the threaded portion of the rotor (arrow) and hold the flats (arrow) with a wrench while turning the puller bolt to free the rotor

out and set it aside for safekeeping. A convenient method is to stick the Woodruff key to the magnets inside the rotor, but be certain not to forget it's there, as serious damage to the rotor and charging coils will occur if the engine is run with anything stuck to the magnets.

Installation

24   Degrease the center of the rotor and the end of the crankshaft.

25   Make sure the Woodruff key is positioned securely in its slot.

26   Align the rotor slot with the Woodruff key. Place the rotor, together with the starter clutch, on the crankshaft.

27   Take a look to make sure there isn't anything stuck to the inside of the rotor.

28   The remainder of installation is the reverse of the removal steps.

---

24   Regulator/rectifier - check and replacement

Check

1   The regulator/rectifier is tested by process of elimination (when all other possible causes of charging system failure have been checked and eliminated, the rectifier/regulator is defective). Since it's easy to miss a problem, it's a good idea to have the charging system tested by a Yamaha dealer or substitute a known good unit before buying a new one.

Replacement

2   Remove the rear fender (see Chapter 7).

3   Disconnect the rectifier/regulator electrical connector (**see illustration 17.9**). Remove the mounting bolts and lift it off the frame.

4   Installation is the reverse of the removal steps.

---

25   Wiring diagrams

Prior to troubleshooting a circuit, check the fuses to make sure they're in good condition. Make sure the battery is fully charged and check the cable connections.

When checking a circuit, make sure all connectors are clean, with no broken or loose terminals or wires. When unplugging a connector, don't pull on the wires - pull only on the connector housings.

8

Notes

Wiring diagram color codes

B	Black	W	White
L	Blue	B/R	Black/Red
G	Green	B/W	Black/White
Y	Yellow	W/B	White/Black
R	Red	L/W	Blue/White
P	Pink	G/L	Green/Blue
O	Orange	G/Y	Green/Yellow
Br	Brown	Y/B	Yellow/Black
W/G	White/Green	R/W	Red/White
Sb	Sky blue	W/L	White/Blue

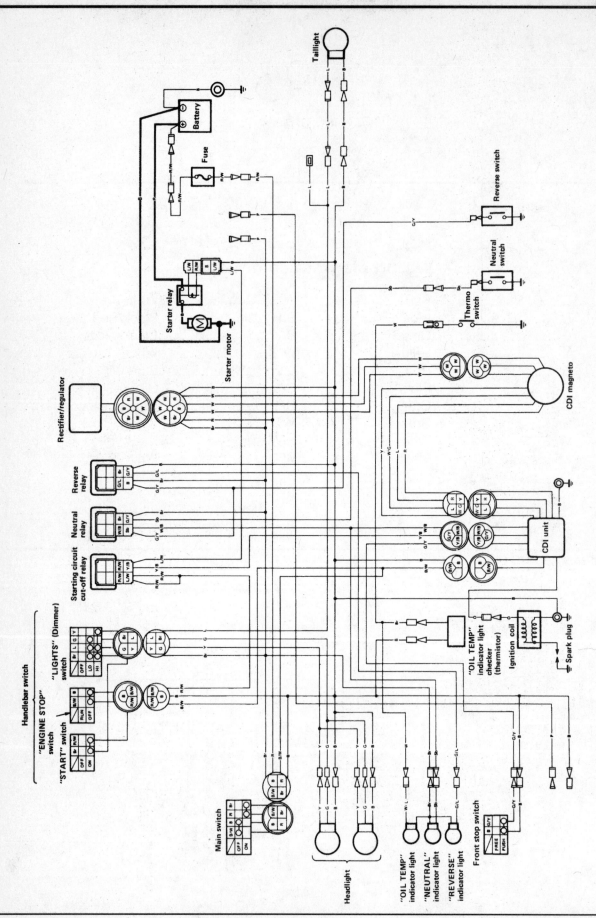

Wiring diagram - YFM350ER models

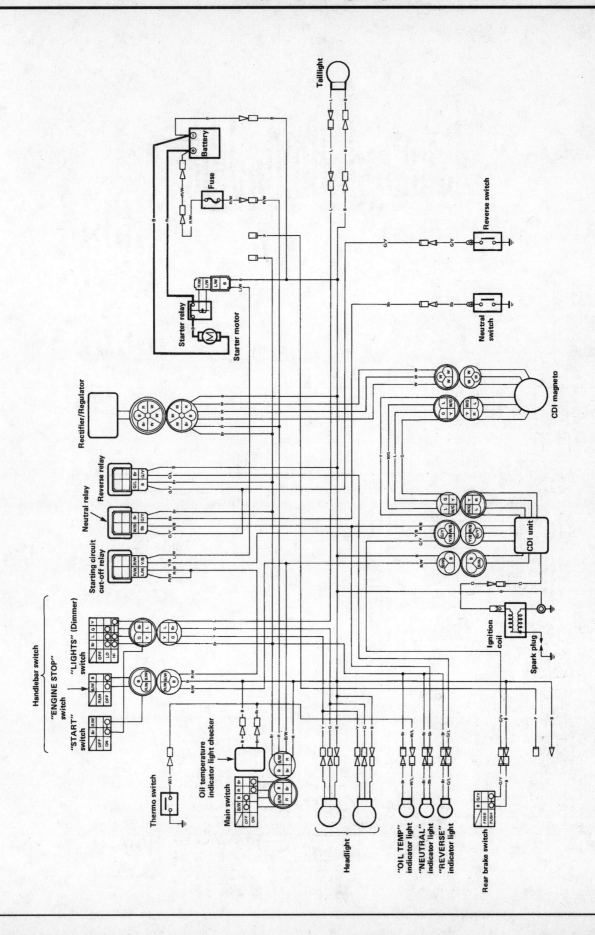

Wiring diagram - 1987 through 1996 YFM350FW models

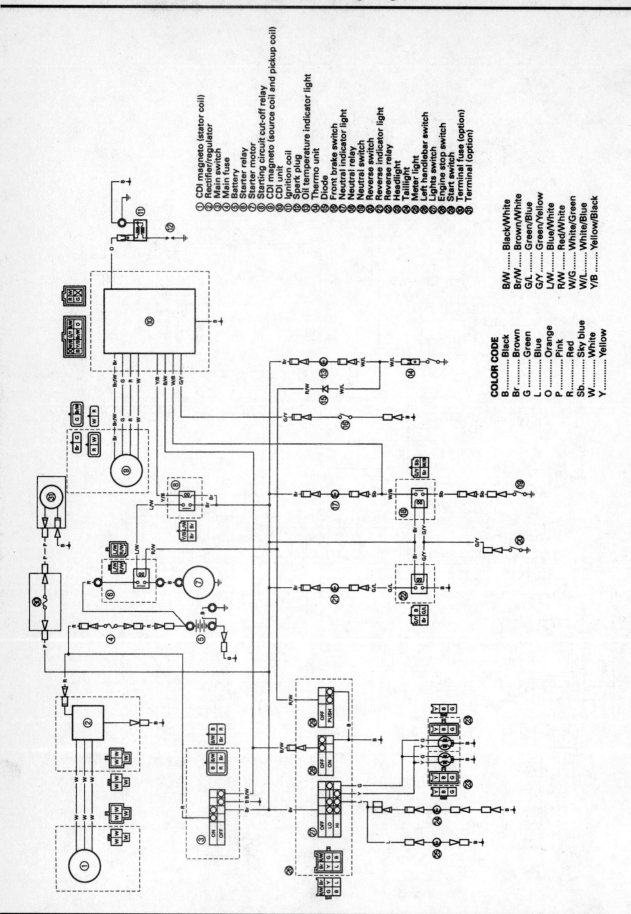

① CDI magneto (stator coil)
② Rectifier/regulator
③ Main switch
④ Main fuse
⑤ Battery
⑥ Starter relay
⑦ Starter motor
⑧ Starting circuit cut-off relay
⑨ CDI magneto (source coil and pickup coil)
⑩ CDI unit
⑪ Ignition coil
⑫ Spark plug
⑬ Oil temperature indicator light
⑭ Thermo unit
⑮ Diode
⑯ Front brake switch
⑰ Neutral indicator light
⑱ Neutral relay
⑲ Neutral switch
⑳ Reverse indicator light
㉑ Reverse switch
㉒ Reverse relay
㉓ Headlight
㉔ Taillight
㉕ Meter light
㉖ Left handlebar switch
㉗ Lights switch
㉘ Engine stop switch
㉙ Start switch
㉚ Terminal fuse (option)
㉛ Terminal (option)

COLOR CODE

B	Black
Br	Brown
G	Green
L	Blue
O	Orange
P	Pink
R	Red
Sb	Sky blue
W	White
Y	Yellow

B/W	Black/White
Br/W	Brown/White
G/L	Green/Blue
G/Y	Green/Yellow
L/W	Blue/White
R/W	Red/White
W/G	White/Green
W/L	White/Blue
Y/B	Yellow/Black

Wiring diagram – 1997 YFM350FW models

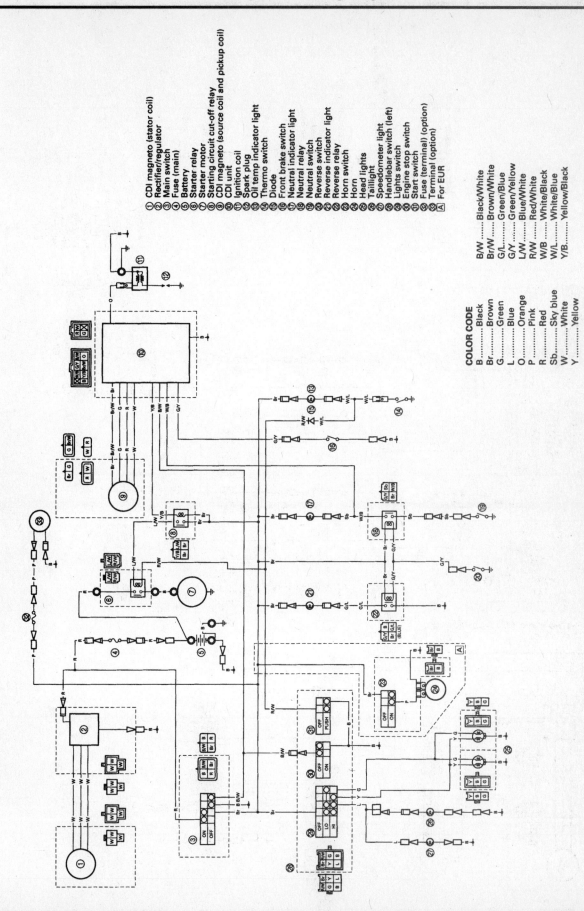

Wiring diagram – YFM350U models (except Australia)

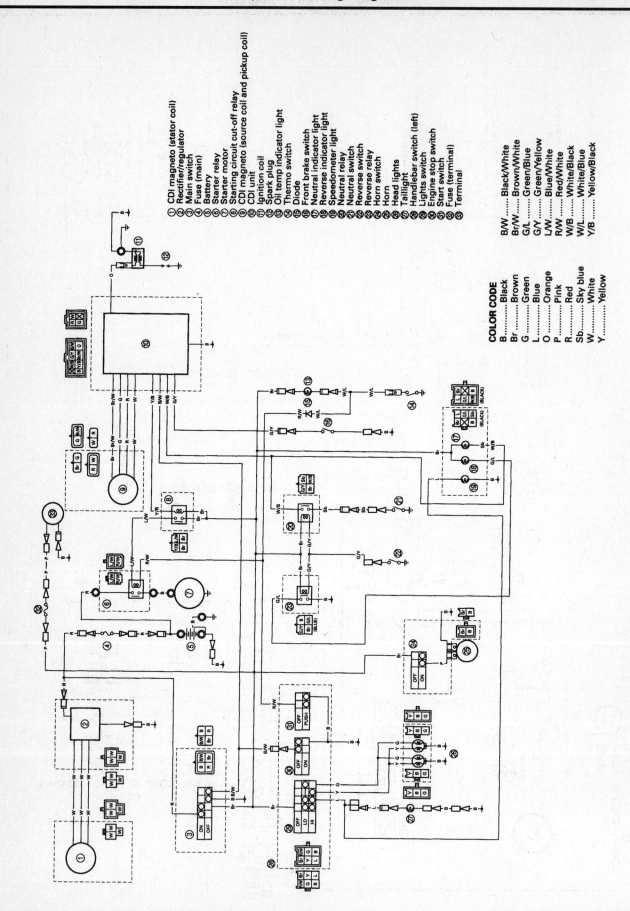

Wiring diagram – YFM350U models (Australia)

① CDI magneto (stator coil)
② Rectifier/regulator
③ Main switch
④ Fuse (main)
⑤ Battery
⑥ Starter relay
⑦ Starter motor
⑧ Starting circuit cut-off relay
⑨ CDI magneto (source coil and pickup coil)
⑩ CDI unit
⑪ Ignition coil
⑫ Spark plug
⑬ Oil temp indicator light
⑭ Thermo switch
⑮ Diode
⑯ Front brake switch
⑰ Neutral indicator light
⑱ Reverse indicator light
⑲ Speedometer light
⑳ Neutral relay
㉑ Neutral switch
㉒ Reverse switch
㉓ Reverse relay
㉔ Horn switch
㉕ Horn
㉖ Head lights
㉗ Taillight
㉘ Handlebar switch (left)
㉙ Lights switch
㉚ Engine stop switch
㉛ Start switch
㉜ Fuse (terminal)
㉝ Terminal

COLOR CODE

B .... Black
Br .... Brown
G .... Green
L .... Blue
O .... Orange
P .... Pink
R .... Red
Sb .... Sky blue
W .... White
Y .... Yellow

B/W ...... Black/White
Br/W ...... Brown/White
G/L ...... Green/Blue
G/Y ...... Green/Yellow
L/W ...... Blue/White
R/W ...... Red/White
W/B ...... White/Black
W/L ...... White/Blue
Y/B ...... Yellow/Black

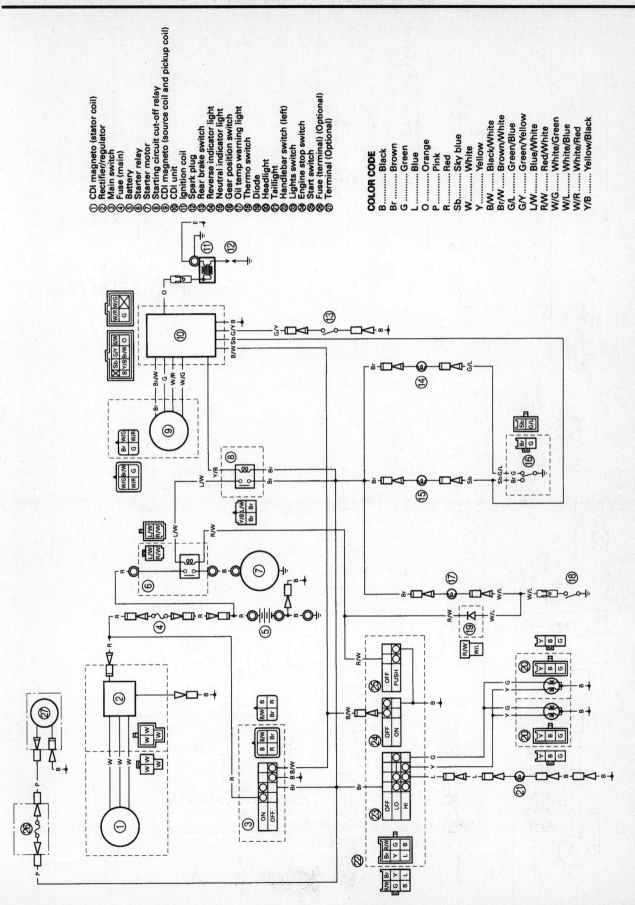

① CDI magneto (stator coil)
② Rectifier/regulator
③ Main switch
④ Fuse (main)
⑤ Battery
⑥ Starter relay
⑦ Starter motor
⑧ Starting circuit cut-off relay
⑨ CDI magneto (source coil and pickup coil)
⑩ CDI unit
⑪ Ignition coil
⑫ Spark plug
⑬ Rear brake switch
⑭ Reverse indicator light
⑮ Neutral indicator light
⑯ Gear position switch
⑰ Oil temp warning light
⑱ Thermo switch
⑲ Diode
⑳ Headlight
㉑ Taillight
㉒ Handlebar switch (left)
㉓ Lights switch
㉔ Engine stop switch
㉕ Start switch
㉖ Fuse (terminal) (Optional)
㉗ Terminal (Optional)

COLOR CODE
B........Black
Br.......Brown
G........Green
L........Blue
O........Orange
P........Pink
R........Red
Sb.......Sky blue
W........White
Y........Yellow
B/W.......Black/White
Br/W.......Brown/White
G/L.......Green/Blue
G/Y.......Green/Yellow
L/W.......Blue/White
R/W.......Red/White
W/G.......White/Green
W/L.......White/Blue
W/R.......White/Red
Y/B.......Yellow/Black

Wiring diagram – YFM350FWB models

9

Conversion factors

Length (distance)

Inches (in)	X 25.4	= Millimetres (mm)	X 0.0394	= Inches (in)
Feet (ft)	X 0.305	= Metres (m)	X 3.281	= Feet (ft)
Miles	X 1.609	= Kilometres (km)	X 0.621	= Miles

Volume (capacity)

Cubic inches (cu in; in³)	X 16.387	= Cubic centimetres (cc; cm³)	X 0.061	= Cubic inches (cu in; in³)
Imperial pints (Imp pt)	X 0.568	= Litres (l)	X 1.76	= Imperial pints (Imp pt)
Imperial quarts (Imp qt)	X 1.137	= Litres (l)	X 0.88	= Imperial quarts (Imp qt)
Imperial quarts (Imp qt)	X 1.201	= US quarts (US qt)	X 0.833	= Imperial quarts (Imp qt)
US quarts (US qt)	X 0.946	= Litres (l)	X 1.057	= US quarts (US qt)
Imperial gallons (Imp gal)	X 4.546	= Litres (l)	X 0.22	= Imperial gallons (Imp gal)
Imperial gallons (Imp gal)	X 1.201	= US gallons (US gal)	X 0.833	= Imperial gallons (Imp gal)
US gallons (US gal)	X 3.785	= Litres (l)	X 0.264	= US gallons (US gal)

Mass (weight)

Ounces (oz)	X 28.35	= Grams (g)	X 0.035	= Ounces (oz)
Pounds (lb)	X 0.454	= Kilograms (kg)	X 2.205	= Pounds (lb)

Force

Ounces-force (ozf; oz)	X 0.278	= Newtons (N)	X 3.6	= Ounces-force (ozf; oz)
Pounds-force (lbf; lb)	X 4.448	= Newtons (N)	X 0.225	= Pounds-force (lbf; lb)
Newtons (N)	X 0.1	= Kilograms-force (kgf; kg)	X 9.81	= Newtons (N)

Pressure

Pounds-force per square inch (psi; lbf/in²; lb/in²)	X 0.070	= Kilograms-force per square centimetre (kgf/cm²; kg/cm²)	X 14.223	= Pounds-force per square inch (psi; lbf/in²; lb/in²)
Pounds-force per square inch (psi; lbf/in²; lb/in²)	X 0.068	= Atmospheres (atm)	X 14.696	= Pounds-force per square inch (psi; lbf/in²; lb/in²)
Pounds-force per square inch (psi; lbf/in²; lb/in²)	X 0.069	= Bars	X 14.5	= Pounds-force per square inch (psi; lbf/in²; lb/in²)
Pounds-force per square inch (psi; lbf/in²; lb/in²)	X 6.895	= Kilopascals (kPa)	X 0.145	= Pounds-force per square inch (psi; lbf/in²; lb/in²)
Kilopascals (kPa)	X 0.01	= Kilograms-force per square centimetre (kgf/cm²; kg/cm²)	X 98.1	= Kilopascals (kPa)
Millibar (mbar)	X 100	= Pascals (Pa)	X 0.01	= Millibar (mbar)
Millibar (mbar)	X 0.0145	= Pounds-force per square inch (psi; lbf/in²; lb/in²)	X 68.947	= Millibar (mbar)
Millibar (mbar)	X 0.75	= Millimetres of mercury (mmHg)	X 1.333	= Millibar (mbar)
Millibar (mbar)	X 0.401	= Inches of water (inH₂O)	X 2.491	= Millibar (mbar)
Millimetres of mercury (mmHg)	X 0.535	= Inches of water (inH₂O)	X 1.868	= Millimetres of mercury (mmHg)
Inches of water (inH₂O)	X 0.036	= Pounds-force per square inch (psi; lbf/in²; lb/in²)	X 27.68	= Inches of water (inH₂O)

Torque (moment of force)

Pounds-force inches (lbf in; lb in)	X 1.152	= Kilograms-force centimetre (kgf cm; kg cm)	X 0.868	= Pounds-force inches (lbf in; lb in)
Pounds-force inches (lbf in; lb in)	X 0.113	= Newton metres (Nm)	X 8.85	= Pounds-force inches (lbf in; lb in)
Pounds-force inches (lbf in; lb in)	X 0.083	= Pounds-force feet (lbf ft; lb ft)	X 12	= Pounds-force inches (lbf in; lb in)
Pounds-force feet (lbf ft; lb ft)	X 0.138	= Kilograms-force metres (kgf m; kg m)	X 7.233	= Pounds-force feet (lbf ft; lb ft)
Pounds-force feet (lbf ft; lb ft)	X 1.356	= Newton metres (Nm)	X 0.738	= Pounds-force feet (lbf ft; lb ft)
Newton metres (Nm)	X 0.102	= Kilograms-force metres (kgf m; kg m)	X 9.804	= Newton metres (Nm)

Power

Horsepower (hp)	X 745.7	= Watts (W)	X 0.0013	= Horsepower (hp)

Velocity (speed)

Miles per hour (miles/hr; mph)	X 1.609	= Kilometres per hour (km/hr; kph)	X 0.621	= Miles per hour (miles/hr; mph)

Fuel consumption*

Miles per gallon, Imperial (mpg)	X 0.354	= Kilometres per litre (km/l)	X 2.825	= Miles per gallon, Imperial (mpg)
Miles per gallon, US (mpg)	X 0.425	= Kilometres per litre (km/l)	X 2.352	= Miles per gallon, US (mpg)

Temperature

Degrees Fahrenheit = (°C x 1.8) + 32   Degrees Celsius (Degrees Centigrade; °C) = (°F - 32) x 0.56

It is common practice to convert from miles per gallon (mpg) to litres/100 kilometres (l/100km), where mpg (Imperial) x l/100 km = 282 and mpg (US) x l/100 km = 235

Fraction/Decimal/Millimeter Equivalents

DECIMALS TO MILLIMETERS

Decimal	mm	Decimal	mm
0.001	0.0254	0.500	12.7000
0.002	0.0508	0.510	12.9540
0.003	0.0762	0.520	13.2080
0.004	0.1016	0.530	13.4620
0.005	0.1270	0.540	13.7160
0.006	0.1524	0.550	13.9700
0.007	0.1778	0.560	14.2240
0.008	0.2032	0.570	14.4780
0.009	0.2286	0.580	14.7320
		0.590	14.9860
0.010	0.2540		
0.020	0.5080		
0.030	0.7620		
0.040	1.0160	0.600	15.2400
0.050	1.2700	0.610	15.4940
0.060	1.5240	0.620	15.7480
0.070	1.7780	0.630	16.0020
0.080	2.0320	0.640	16.2560
0.090	2.2860	0.650	16.5100
		0.660	16.7640
0.100	2.5400	0.670	17.0180
0.110	2.7940	0.680	17.2720
0.120	3.0480	0.690	17.5260
0.130	3.3020		
0.140	3.5560		
0.150	3.8100		
0.160	4.0640	0.700	17.7800
0.170	4.3180	0.710	18.0340
0.180	4.5720	0.720	18.2880
0.190	4.8260	0.730	18.5420
		0.740	18.7960
0.200	5.0800	0.750	19.0500
0.210	5.3340	0.760	19.3040
0.220	5.5880	0.770	19.5580
0.230	5.8420	0.780	19.8120
0.240	6.0960	0.790	20.0660
0.250	6.3500		
0.260	6.6040		
0.270	6.8580	0.800	20.3200
0.280	7.1120	0.810	20.5740
0.290	7.3660	0.820	21.8280
		0.830	21.0820
0.300	7.6200	0.840	21.3360
0.310	7.8740	0.850	21.5900
0.320	8.1280	0.860	21.8440
0.330	8.3820	0.870	22.0980
0.340	8.6360	0.880	22.3520
0.350	8.8900	0.890	22.6060
0.360	9.1440		
0.370	9.3980		
0.380	9.6520		
0.390	9.9060	0.900	22.8600
0.400	10.1600	0.910	23.1140
0.410	10.4140	0.920	23.3680
0.420	10.6680	0.930	23.6220
0.430	10.9220	0.940	23.8760
0.440	11.1760	0.950	24.1300
0.450	11.4300	0.960	24.3840
0.460	11.6840	0.970	24.6380
0.470	11.9380	0.980	24.8920
0.480	12.1920	0.990	25.1460
0.490	12.4460	1.000	25.4000

FRACTIONS TO DECIMALS TO MILLIMETERS

Fraction	Decimal	mm	Fraction	Decimal	mm
1/64	0.0156	0.3969	33/64	0.5156	13.0969
1/32	0.0312	0.7938	17/32	0.5312	13.4938
3/64	0.0469	1.1906	35/64	0.5469	13.8906
1/16	0.0625	1.5875	9/16	0.5625	14.2875
5/64	0.0781	1.9844	37/64	0.5781	14.6844
3/32	0.0938	2.3812	19/32	0.5938	15.0812
7/64	0.1094	2.7781	39/64	0.6094	15.4781
1/8	0.1250	3.1750	5/8	0.6250	15.8750
9/64	0.1406	3.5719	41/64	0.6406	16.2719
5/32	0.1562	3.9688	21/32	0.6562	16.6688
11/64	0.1719	4.3656	43/64	0.6719	17.0656
3/16	0.1875	4.7625	11/16	0.6875	17.4625
13/64	0.2031	5.1594	45/64	0.7031	17.8594
7/32	0.2188	5.5562	23/32	0.7188	18.2562
15/64	0.2344	5.9531	47/64	0.7344	18.6531
1/4	0.2500	6.3500	3/4	0.7500	19.0500
17/64	0.2656	6.7469	49/64	0.7656	19.4469
9/32	0.2812	7.1438	25/32	0.7812	19.8438
19/64	0.2969	7.5406	51/64	0.7969	20.2406
5/16	0.3125	7.9375	13/16	0.8125	20.6375
21/64	0.3281	8.3344	53/64	0.8281	21.0344
11/32	0.3438	8.7312	27/32	0.8438	21.4312
23/64	0.3594	9.1281	55/64	0.8594	21.8281
3/8	0.3750	9.5250	7/8	0.8750	22.2250
25/64	0.3906	9.9219	57/64	0.8906	22.6219
13/32	0.4062	10.3188	29/32	0.9062	23.0188
27/64	0.4219	10.7156	59/64	0.9219	23.4156
7/16	0.4375	11.1125	15/16	0.9375	23.8125
29/64	0.4531	11.5094	61/64	0.9531	24.2094
15/32	0.4688	11.9062	31/32	0.9688	24.6062
31/64	0.4844	12.3031	63/64	0.9844	25.0031
1/2	0.5000	12.7000	1	1.0000	25.4000

Service record

Date	Mileage/hours	Work performed

Service record (continued)

Date	Mileage/hours	Work performed

Service record (continued)

Date	Mileage/hours	Work performed

Trail rules

Just when you're ready to have some fun out in the dirt you get slapped with more rules. But by following these rules you'll ensure everyone's enjoyment, not just your own. It's important that all off-roaders follow these rules, as it will help to keep the trails open and keep us in good standing with other trail users. Really, these rules are no more than common sense and common courtesy.

- **Don't ride where you're not supposed to.** Stay off private property and obey all signs marking areas that are off limits to motorized vehicles. Also, as much fun as it might be, don't ride in State or Federal wilderness areas.

- **Leave the land as you found it.** When you've left the area, the only thing you should leave behind are your tire tracks. Use good judgement - if the ground is muddy, don't ride; you'll make deep ruts which will eventually harden and leave a rough (and possibly hazardous) surface. Stay on the trails, too. There are plenty of trails to ride on without blazing new ones. Be sure to carry out all litter that you create (and if you want to do a good deed, pick up any litter that you come across). Be sure to leave gates as you found them, or if the gate has a sign on it, comply with whatever the sign says (some people don't close gates after passing through them. Others may close gates when the landowner actually wants to keep them open).

- **Give other trail users the right-of-way.** There has been an ongoing dispute amongst trail users as to who belongs there and who doesn't. If the off-roading community shows respect and courtesy to hikers and equestrians, we stand a far better chance of being able to enjoy our sport in the years to come, and to keep the trails open for our children. When you ride up behind hikers or horses, give them plenty of room and pass slowly so as not to startle them. When you approach an equestrian from the opposite direction, stop your machine when the horse nears you so it won't get frightened and bolt.

- **Don't scare the animals!** Whether it be horses, cattle or wild animals like deer, rabbits or coyotes, leave them alone. Remember, you're visiting their home, so treat them with respect. Besides, startling animals can be dangerous. Loud noises or your sudden appearance can trigger an animal's defensive instinct, which could mean bad news for you.

- **Don't ride "over your head."** Sometimes the trails start to resemble ski runs, with a few irresponsible riders going so fast that they're barely able to maintain control of their vehicles. They'd never be able to stop to avoid another trail user if they had to. Most collisions on the trail are caused by such individuals and the results are occasionally tragic. You should only ride fast in areas where you can clearly see a good distance ahead - never on trails with blind corners or rises high enough that prevent you from seeing what's on the other side.

- **Be prepared.** Carry everything you think you may need to make minor repairs should your machine break down. Know how to make basic repairs and keep your ATV in good mechanical condition to minimize the chances of becoming stranded. Always let someone know where you're going, and ride with a friend whenever possible.

Notes

Index